Committees and Commissions in India
1978

Concepts in Communication
Informatics & Librarianship-52

General Editor : **S.P. Agrawal**

Committees and Commissions in India 1978

Volume 16

PART A

A Concept's Project

Compiled by a team of professionals
guided by
VIRENDRA KUMAR

CONCEPT PUBLISHING COMPANY, NEW DELHI 110059

ISBN 81-7022-489-6 (Vol. 16, Part A)

First Published 1994

Published and Printed by
Ashok Kumar Mittal
Concept Publishing Company
A/15-16, Commercial Block, Mohan Garden
NEW DELHI 110059 (India)

Lasertypeset by
Printing Express
H-13, Bali Nagar
NEW DELHI 110015

GENERAL EDITOR'S INTRODUCTION

In the context of the changing world, the role of the government – be it at central, state or local level – is becoming more pervasive in the modern society. Everyday, it has to encounter new problems and face new issues which demand quite a new thinking and novel strategies to overcome them. Thus, the increasing role of the government in every sphere of people's life has broadened its functions and responsibilities tremendously and enlarged its activities to such an extent that the government machinery of its own can hardly manage its affairs. Moreover, its functions are becoming more complicated and complex requiring the assistance of outside specialists, technocrats and specialized agencies.

In view of this, the modern government has to set-up committees and commissions and working or study groups on various problems and issues from time to time. In the light of the recommendations of these committees and commissions, the government take decisions on key issues and problems. Often the government is obliged to seek the assistance of a committee to evaluate some of its schemes in operation so that on the basis of the evaluation reports of the committee, it may either continue, modify or scrap the on-going schemes. In other words, the committees or commissions, etc., exercise a great deal of pivotal force in shaping the policies and programmes of the government and for this purpose submit a large number of reports.

In these volumes of *Committees and Commissions in India*, now being published under the *Concepts in Communication Informatics and Librarianship (CICIL)* series, an attempt has been made to cover the period from 1974 onwards. The volumes include the vital data about only those reports of the committees and commissions which have been constituted by the Central Government. We have made every endeavour to include the digest of all the important reports on various vital issues of great importance and on major areas of national development.

We have also an ambitious plan to publish the digests of the important reports of the committees and commissions appointed by different state governments, the semi-government organisations and the learned bodies as also the reports published during the period of the British Government.

The publication has been brought out under the guidance of Shri Virendra Kumar, specialist in his own right with vast experience of working in Government Documents Section in the Central Secretariat Library and having the privilege of the blessings of Dr. S.R. Ranganathan – the father of Indian Library Science. I also put on record the collaborative help provided by Shri M.W.K. Sherwani.

We are sure that this compilation will prove a very useful reference tool for researchers, serious students and scholars of the public administration and political science, administrators, policy-makers, educationists and historians.

S.P. AGRAWAL

PREFACE

This volume of *Committees and Commissions in India* attempts to understand the activities of the various Committees and Commissions during the period 1974.

A 'Commission' is a governmental agency created to perform a particular function such as special investigations or on governmental regulations of business. It is appointed mainly when it is thought that a matter involves some financial questions. There are other reasons for which a Commission is appointed, e.g., in matters pertaining to welfare of the State and its citizens and/or improving the efficiency in an administration. The status of a 'Committee' is also the same as that of a 'Commission', but it does not possess as wide powers as are enjoyed by a Commission and has to limit itself to specific work assigned to it under its terms of reference. While arriving at decisions in the form of recommendations, a Commission or Committee ensures that such decisions are representative of interests of various types of people and also a safeguard against abuse of power.

A Committee or a Commission comprises a Chairman, the Members and Member Secretary (sometimes there is also an Assistant Secretary). In some cases, there are even One-man Commissions and the enquiry in such Commissions is entrusted to an Officer-on-Special Duty.

The Chairman of a Commission is a person well-versed mostly in legal matters and is often a retired judge of a High Court or the Supreme Court of India. Occasionally, a Member of Parliament is also appointed as the Chairman of a Commission. On the other hand, the Chairman of the Committee is mostly a specialist in the subject of the Committee. He can be a Leader or a Convenor also, if he heads a Panel, a Study Group or a Delegation, etc.

The Members of a Commission, Committee, Panel, Study Group etc., are specialists in their respective fields and provide valuable guidance to the Commission or the Committee in making recommendations.

The Member-Secretary or Secretary is generally nominated from among the experienced officials who have the requisite competent knowledge of the subject on which the Commission or the Committee is appointed.

Committees and Commissions in India provides in chronological order vital information about Committees and Commissions appointed by the Government from time to time. Information for each Committee or Commission is presented in a compact form in four parts, namely; Constitution; Appointment; Terms of Reference and Recommendations.

CONTENTS

PART B

1

RAILWAY ACCIDENTS ENQUIRY COMMITTEE, 1978 — REPORT[1]

Chairman Shri M.S. Sikri

Members Dr. Murli Manohar Joshi; Shri Khurshid Alam Khan; Shri Bagaram Tulpule; Shri P. Sahai; Shri C.S. Parameswaran; Shri Arya Bhushan.

Secretary Shri R.S. Soin (Replaced Shri V.K. Thapar).

Appointment

The later part of the second half of 1977 saw two serious railway accident in quick succession, involving heavy casualties and damage to railway property. The first was the collision between Howrah-Amritsar Deluxe Express and a goods train at Naini Station on Mughalsarai-Allahabad broad gauge section of Northern Railway on October 10, 1977 and the second was the derailment of Ahmedabad-Delhi Mail between Ajarka and Bawal Stations on Bandikui-Rewari metre gauge section of the Western Railway on November 11, 1977. These accidents had greatly agitated the public and deep concern was voiced in the Parliament and the Press. It was against this background that the Minister of Railways Prof. Madhu Dandavate having regard to the views expressed by the Members of Parliament and others on the recent rail accidents while making a statement in the Rajya Sabha on December 19, 1977 announced the Governments decision to constitute a Committee to go into the whole question of accidents. So the Government of India, the Ministry of Railways appointed the Railway Accidents Enquiry Committee Vide Notification No. ERBI/77/21/86 dated January 3, 1978.

1. Report, New Delhi, Government of India, Ministry of Railways, 1979, 480 p.

Terms of Reference

1. to review the position of accidents on the Indian Railways since the appointment of the Railway Accidents Inquiry Committee, 1968 and to review the implementation of their recommendations; and

2. to examine the adequacy of the existing organisation, equipment and practices for ensuring safe running of trains on the Indian Railways, and to suggest measures for prevention of accidents.

Contents

Constitution of the Committee and their terms of reference; Methodology; Review of accidents on Indian Railways; Review of Implementation of the Recommendations made by the Wanchoo Committee; Assessment of adequacy of the existing organisation, equipment and practices for ensuring safe running of trains; Brief Statistical Appreciation of Important Categories of train accidents during the period 1968-69 to 1977-78; Serious accidents during the year 1968-69 to 1977-78 — Causes and consequences; Review of the Implementation of Recommendations made by the Wanchoo Committee; Human Elements, Training of Staff, Other Staff matters, Permanent Way, Level Crossing, Signalling and interlocking, Motive Power, Goods and Coaching Stock, Miscellaneous matters and Research, Designs and Standards Organisation; Summary of Findings and Recommendations; Annexures from I to LXXII; Appendix; Graphs from 1 to 6.

Recommendations

Brief Statistical Appreciation of Important Categories of Train Accidents During the Period 1968-69 to 1977-78

1. We find that, after a steady fall in the incidence of total accidents to 10.4 per million train kilometres during 1971-72, it sharply rose to 15.2 in 1972-73 and further to 25.0 in 1974-75. This was followed by a decline for two years and then a rise again in 1977-78 when the incidence of total accidents per million train kilometres was 20.9 as compared to 18.7 in the previous year. This does not reveal a healthy trend. (Para 14)

2. There was, by and large, a fall in the incidence of important accidents per million train kilometres except for the year 1974-75 and

1975-76 during which there was an increase. After some improvement in 1976-77, the incidence of important accidents again increased in 1977-78 both on the broad and metre gauges. On the narrow gauge, after an abrupt fall during 1968-69, the incidence of important accidents for million train kilometres steadily rose to 6.10 during 1973-74. This was followed by a decline for three years to 4.10 in 1976-77. In 1977-78 there was a significant increase in the incident of important accidents to 5.84 per million train kilometres. (Paras 17 and 18)

3. On the broad gauge, after a sharp drop in the incidence of train collisions to 0.12 per million train kilometres in 1968-69 as compared to 0.16 in the previous year, it fluctuated between 0.12 and 0.15 till 1973-74 when there was a sharp increase to 0.19. This was followed by a declining trend. On the metre gauge also, there has been a general declining trend. On the narrow gauge too, the incidence of train collision has come down in recent years. (Paras 21 and 22)

4. The incidence of collisions involving passenger trains on the broad gauge fluctuated considerably during the last decade. The declining trend from 1968-69 to 1972-73 got reversed during 1973-74 and 1974-75 when the incidence increased to 0.16 per million train kilometres, thus going back to the level obtaining in 1967-68. It then declined for two years to 0.09 in 1976-77 but again rose to 0.15 in 1977-78. In the case of goods trains on the broad gauge, after a general rising trend from 1968-69 to 1973-74, during which period the incidence increased from 0.11 to 0.22 per million train kilometres, there has been a steady decline in the incidence during the last five years and was 0.08 during 1977-78. (Paras 23 and 24)

5. On the metre gauge, the incidence of collisions involving passenger trains registered a sharp decline during 1968-69, being 0.05 per million passenger train kilometres as compared to 0.15 in the previous year. During 1970-71 the incidence rose to 0.07 and has remained almost static thereafter. Collisions of goods trains on the metre gauge have shown on general declining trend except for the two intervening years 1974-75 and 1975-76 when their incidence rose sharply. (Paras 23 and 24)

6. On the broad gauge, there was a reduction in the incidence of derailments in 1968-69 as compared to the previous year, after which it has remained almost static. Taking passenger and goods trains separately, we find that while the incidence of derailments of passenger trains has not shown much change, there has been considerable decline in the incidence of goods train derailments during the 10-year

period of our study as compared to the position obtaining in the 5-year period ending 1967-68. (Paras 25 and 26)

7. On the metre gauge, the incidence of derailments of passenger trains had recorded a general decline in the quinquennium 1968-69 to 1972-73, but during the subsequent 5-year period ending 1977-78 there was considerable deterioration in the position and the incidence per million passenger train kilometres has gone back to the level obtaining prior to 1967-68. In the case of goods trains on the metre gauge, there was a sharp drop in the incidence of derailments during 1968-69 to 4.91 as compared to 7.7 in the previous year; it has remained around that level since then. (Paras 25 and 26)

8. There has been, by and large, a downward trend in the incidence of accidents at both manned and unmanned level crossings during the 10 year period ending 1977-78. Since level crossing accidents account for 45 per cent of the fatalities in all accidents, the decline in their number is a healthy sign. During the 5-year period covered by the Wanchoo Committee, the average annual number of persons killed and injured in level crossing accidents was 45 and 169 respectively. As against that, during the 10-year period ending 1977-78 the average annual number of persons killed and injured had gone up to 93 and 229 respectively. This clearly shows that the fall in the incidence of level crossing accidents does not mean a reduction in the hazard to human life and limb in these accidents. Since just less than half of the total deaths in railway accidents are accounted for by level crossing accidents, the gravity of these needs no further emphasis. (Paras 27 and 28).

9. There was a sudden drop in the incidence of fires in trains on both the broad and metre gauges during 1970-71 as compared to the previous year. This was due to the revision in classification of accidents falling in this category, consequent to implementation of recommendation 324(iii) in Part II of the report of the Wanchoo Committee, whereby fires in diesel and electric locomotives began to be treated as 'engine failures'. Thereafter, the incidence of fires in trains on the broad gauge had increased. However, since 1974-75 there has been a declining trend. On the metre gauge the incidence of fires increased during 1975-76 followed by a decline during the next two years. (Paras 29 and 30)

10. Engine failures had recorded a sharp increase in 1972-73 and the figures had more than doubled by 1975-76. The increase during 1972-73 was due to the revised classification of engine failures accord-

ing to which a diesel or electric locomotive is considered to leave failed if it causes a delay of 30 minutes or more to the train it is hauling (as against the earlier figure of 60 minutes or more). After a sharp drop in engine failures during 1976-77, their number again increased in 1977-78. (Paras 31 and 32)

11. The declining trend in the number of failures of couplings and draft gear which had set in prior to the appointment of the Wanchoo Committee, continued till 1973-74 after which there has been an upward trend. In 1976-77, the number of such failures rose sharply to 621 as compared to 382 in the previous year. Though their number dropped to 526 in 1977-78, it is still quite high as compared to the position prevailing prior to 1976-77. (Paras 31 and 33)

12. Failures of other rolling stock such as failures of tyres, axles, wheels, brake apparatus, etc., which had been steadily declining till 1973-74 had doubled during 1974-75. This was followed by a decline in such failures during 1975-76 and 1976-77. However, during 1977-78, there was an abnormal increase in their number from 300 (in the previous year) to 1267. This sudden increase is disquieting and calls for investigation and action. (Paras 31 and 34)

13. From the break-up of 1267 failures of other rolling stock during 1977-78, we find that the Central and South Eastern Railways accounted for 620 and 615 failures respectively, i.e., 97.5 per cent of the total. While surprisingly no such failure was reported on the North Eastern, Northeast Frontier and Southern Railways, only 2 such failures were reported on the Northern, 9 on the Western, 10 on the Eastern and 11 on the South Central Railways. It appears that the figures reported by most of the Railways may not be correct and the reporting of such failures and compilation of statistics in this regard need to be thoroughly looked into. (Para 34)

14. There was a sharp rise in the number of failures of permanent way during 1972-73. This was followed by a further jump in 1976-77, the rise being mainly due to increase in the number of broken rails. The incidence of broken rails per 100 kilometres of running track increased from 0.14 during 1968-69 to 1.22 during 1976-77. During 1977-78, the incidence stood at 0.91. The steep increase in the incidence during the last decade is a matter of concern and calls for corrective action. (Paras 31, 35 and 36)

15. Failures of overhead wires has sown a general decline since 1973-74. (Paras 31 and 37)

16. Compilation of separate statistics of failure of signalling ap-

paratus commenced only from 1975-76. No trend is discernible during this short period except that during 1977-78, there has been an increase in such failures as compared to the previous two years. (Paras 31 and 37)

17. The declining trend in the incidence of miscellaneous accidents, viz., trains running over obstruction, collisions involving light engines, trollies, derailment of light engines, fires at stations, etc., which had commenced prior to the appointment of the Wanchoo Committee continued till 1971-72. This was followed by an increase in the incidence of such accidents during 1972-73 and 1973-74, after which there has again been a steady decline. (Para 38)

18. There has been a general declining trend in the incidence of averted collisions, breach of block rules and disregard of signals by drivers. (Paras 39 and 40)

19. The incidence of passenger train partings per 100 million vehicle kilometres has dropped considerably during the last 10 years. During 1977-78, the incidence was 0.19 as compared to 1.36 during 1968-69. There has been a fall in the incidence of train partings on goods trains also, though not as marked as in the case of passenger trains. The incidence of goods train partings per 100 million wagon kilometres has dropped from 5.45 in 1968-69 to 3.22 in 1973-74. The incidence had gone up for 2 years during 1975-76 and 1976-77; however, during 1977-78 it dropped to 3.88 as compared to 4.62 in the previous year. (Paras 41 and 42)

20. There has been a general decline in the incidence of important accidents, miscellaneous accidents and indicative accidents during the 10-year period from 1968-69 to 1977-78 as compared to the position obtaining in the 5 year period from 1963-64 to 1967-68 which was reviewed by the Wanchoo Committee. (Para 43)

21. Failures of railway equipment, namely, locomotives, rolling stock, permanent way, etc., however, increased substantially during the period 1968-69 to 1977-78. This demands immediate attention and action. (Para 43)

22. We find that the years 1974-75 and 1975-76 stand out as two significantly bad years as far as accidents are concerned. During these years, the incidence of almost all categories of accidents increased sharply. This increase has been attributed by the Railway Board mainly to the general labour unrest which culminated in the all-India railway strike in May 1974 and its aftereffects. This clearly brings out the importance of healthy industrial relations on the Railways for safe and ef-

ficient operation of trains. (Para 43)

Serious Accidents During the Years 1968-69 to 1977-78 – Causes and Consequences

23. During the 10-year period from 1968-69 to 1977-78, there were 219 serious accidents on the Indian Railways. Out of these, in 218, statutory enquiries were held by officers of the Commission of Railway Safety and in one case enquiry was held by a Commission of Inquiry appointed under the Commissions of Inquiry Act, 1952. (Para 46)

24. While serious accidents constituted only 2.3 per cent of the total number of important accidents, these accounted for 49.1 per cent of the total fatalities, 43.7 per cent of the injuries and 20.7 per cent of the loss due to damage to railway property in all categories of important accidents. (Paras 47 and 48)

25. During the period from 1973-74 to 1977-78, there were 114 serious accidents as compared to 74, 79 and 85 serious accidents during the earlier three 5-year periods commencing from 1957-62. There was, thus, an increase in the number of serious accidents during the last 5-year period ending 1977-78. During the same period, the incidence of serious accidents per million train kilometres increased to 0.048 from 0.036 in the previous two 5-year periods. (Paras 51 to 52)

26. We find that the incidence of serious accidents which fall in the categories of important accidents when taken as a proportion of the total number of important accidents, has been continuously rising even though the number of important accidents has been falling. This *prima facie*, indicates that the consequences of important accidents are becoming more serious. (Paras 53 and 54)

27. The number of serious accidents due to failure of drivers registered an increase of 50 per cent during the periods 1968-69 to 1972-73 and 1973-74 to 1977-78 over those in the earlier two 5-year periods. (Paras 55 and 56(i))

28. Serious accidents due to failure of station staff, which decreased considerably during the period 1968-69 to 1972-73, again went up during the period 1973-74 to 1977-78 to the level obtaining prior to 1968-69. (Paras 55 and 56(ii))

29. There was a decrease in the incidence of serious accidents attributable to train wrecking during the period 1973-74 to 1977-78 as compared to the earlier 5-year period. (Paras 55 and 56(iii))

30. Accidents at level crossings due to failure of road-users increased sharply during the period 1973-74 to 1977-78 as compared to the position obtaining in the earlier three 5-year periods of our review. (Paras 55 and 56(iv))

31. The incidence of serious accidents due to failure of locomotives went up during the period 1973-74 to 1977-78. (Paras 55 and 56(v))

32. The incidence of serious accidents due to failure of rolling stock has been continuously rising since the period 1963-64 to 1967-68. This is a disturbing trend and calls for urgent corrective action. (Paras 55 and 56(vi))

33. The incidence of serious accidents due to failure of track has also increased in recent years. From 3 serious accidents during the 5-year period 1963-64 to 1967-68, their number had increased to 5 to 8 during the next two 5-year periods. (Paras 55 and 56(vii))

34. There was a substantial increase in the incidence of serious accidents due to fires in trains during the last 10 years. From 3 serious accidents during the period 1963-64 to 1967-68, their number shot up to 10 during the period 1968-69 to 1972-73 and to 12 during the period 1973-74 to 1977-78. (Paras 55 and 56(viii))

35. Miscellaneous causes, namely, faulty, securing of consignments, failure of catenary, moving train hit by objects on the platform and other causes accounted for 14 and 12 serious accidents during the two 5-year periods 1968-69 to 1972-73 and 1973-74 to 1977-78 respectively, as compared to 12 during the 5-year period 1963-64 to 1967-68 and 7 during the period 1957 to 1962. (Paras 55 and 56(ix))

36. Failure of railway staff or human element was responsible for the largest number of serious accidents. The proportion of accidents attributable to human element has remained almost static around 43 per cent during the last three 5-year periods. Failure of equipment, i.e., locomotives, rolling stock and track takes the next place after failure of railway staff and the proportion of serious accidents due to these causes has steadily increased from 7.6 to 18.4 per cent during the last three 5-year periods of our review. (Paras 57 and 58)

Review of the Implementation of Recommendations made by the Wanchoo Committee

The Human Element

37. Although the recommendations of the Wanchoo Committee

referred to in Para 63(i) and (ii) of this report were accepted in principle, it has not been possible for the Railways to implement them. The recommendation in Para 63(iii) was not accepted by the Ministry of Railways. (Paras 63 to 66)

38. While machinery exists on most of the Railways to promptly redress grievances of staff, the welfare organisation on the South Central Railway is inadequately staffed.

In a huge organisation like the Railways employing about 15 lakhs regular employees and 3 lakhs casual labour, grievances are bound to exist, especially having regard to the complicated rules and procedures. While the observance of staff welfare weeks/fortnights serves limited objectives and renders limited help, there is need for gearing up the machinery to ensure that staff representations are expeditiously attended to at all times. (Paras 67 to 72)

39. We find that some Railways are giving training to welfare inspectors while some are not. Personnel management is a specialised subject and welfare inspectors should be fully equipped for the same. We recommend that persons who are to work as welfare inspectors should be given proper training either before or within a specified period of taking up duties as welfare inspectors so that they have an idea of the background in which they have to function. (Paras 67 and 73)

40. The time taken by the Railways for finalising of accident cases exceeded in all cases the target laid down by the Railway Board. In respect of cases where minor or major penalties were imposed and also where major penalty chargesheets were issued but minor penalties were imposed, the average time taken exceeded the target by a very wide margin. Thus, the recommendation made by the Wanchoo Committee remains substantially unimplemented. We would urge the Railway Board to take steps to ensure that the causes of delay in finalising accident cases are identified and remedial measures taken to achieve the target laid down by themselves. (Paras 75 to 78)

41. In respect of the Wanchoo Committee's recommendation that senior supervisors should always be consulted in regard to promotions and transfers of staff in their charge, we find that the Railways have expressed opinions which are divergent from the views of the Railway Board. This recommendation of the Wanchoo Committee does not appear to have been fully implemented. (Paras 79 and 80)

42. In respect of the recommendation in Para 79(ii) of this report, we consider that it would be difficult to evolve scales of pay which do

not overlap at all. In any case, such as position does not ordinarily obtain in any department of the Government or any public sector undertaking. We, however, note that, to the extent the idea behind this recommendation could be accepted, action has already been taken within the framework of the recommendations of the Third Central Pay Commission. (Paras 79, 81 to 83)

43. Regarding the Wanchoo Committee's recommendation in para 79(iii) of this report in respect of upgradation of certain supervisory posts, we feel that this has been substantially implemented to the extent it was accepted by the Railway Board. (Paras 79 and 84)

44. As the figures for 1976-77 show, there is no improvement in the officer-staff ratio and the position in this regard in the major departments concerned with safety of rail travel, namely, Transportation, Civil, Mechanical, Electrical and Signal and Telecommunication Engineering has, in fact, deteriorated as compared to the position obtaining in 1962-63. The Wanchoo Committee's recommendation, therefore, remains unimplemented. We would urge the Railway Board to take urgent action to bring about an improvement in the officer-staff ratio. (Paras 85 to 90)

45. We feel that it is necessary to have a clear definition of the term 'supervisor' before determining the ratio of supervisors to staff. Having clearly identified supervisory staff, it would be necessary to take immediate steps to arrive at a rational supervisor-staff ratio and we recommend accordingly. (Paras 85, 91 to 93)

46. It has taken almost 8 years for the Railways to finalise the stages at which 'in-service' psycho-technical tests are to be administered in the case of some operating categories. No decision appears to have been taken so far for the application of psycho-technical tests at the time of conversion training of staff from steam to either diesel or electric traction. We would urge the Railway Board that the decisions now taken for 'in-service' application of psycho-technical tests to certain categories of staff should be implemented without further delay. It is also necessary that the stages for 'in-service' psycho-technical testing in the case of remaining categories of staff, directly connected with the safe running of trains are also prescribed at the earliest. (Paras 94 to 100)

47. We find that, even though the Railway Board had agreed in principle to widen the scope of activities of the Psycho-technical Cell, not much progress has been made in this direction due to inadequacy of staff. Thus, the Wanchoo Committee's recommendation for extending

the scope of labour science research on the Indian Railways remains substantially implemented. (Paras 101 to 106)

48. In the light of the views of the Ministry of Home Affairs, the Railway Board did not consider it advisable to proceed with the proposed legislation of debarring prosecution of railway staff without sanction of the competent railway authority. In some States, there are rules which provide for sanction to be obtained at an appreciably higher level in the police hierarchy before prosecution is launched. This was meant to avoid capricious prosecution of staff. Having regard to the views expressed by the Ministry of Home Affairs and the State Governments, were feel that there is no necessity to pursue this recommendation further. (Paras 107 to 111)

Training of Staff

49. We find that though the recommendation of the Wanchoo Committee for setting up centres of training for electrical signal maintainers has been substantially implemented, there are deficiencies in the facilities for training in schools/centres on some Railways, especially in respect of models of sophisticated signalling equipment. We would urge the Railway Board to ensure that the Railway Administrations provide these facilities in schools for training of signal maintainers as early as possible. (Paras 113 to 116)

50. The Wanchoo Committee's recommendation referred to in Para 117 of this report regarding recruitment training and grades of signalling staff has been substantially implemented. The Railway Board should take steps to see that their directive in this regard is implemented on the North Eastern Railway as well. (Paras 117 to 119)

51. Training facilities for panel operators are still to be developed training in some of the Railways. This recommendation has, therefore, been only partially implemented. We would urge the Railway Administrations to create the necessary facilities for training of panel operators without further delay. (Paras 120 to 123)

52. We find that though the planning for setting up a centralised training school for electric supervisory staff commenced in 1971-72, not much progress has been made in the construction of the school building; only part of the hostel accommodation has been completed and laboratory equipment models, etc., have still to be procured. Thus, the progress of setting up of this school has been extremely poor. We feel that proper training of electric supervisory staff cannot be ensured

in the absence of a centralised training school with necessary laboratory equipment, models, etc. Thus, imparting of basic training to electric supervisory staff, envisaged by the Wanchoo Committee, remains unfulfilled. The matter will not brook any further delay and we would urge the Railway Board to ensure the provision of a properly equipped centralised training school with a sense of urgency. (Paras 124 to 126)

53. The Wanchoo Committee's recommendation for setting up schools for training artisan staff employed in the maintenance of general electric and train lighting services, has been substantially implemented. Eastern and Southern Railways should take urgent steps to set up their own training centres for artisan staff for electric traction. (Paras 124, 127 and 128)

54. We find that there is no uniformity in the minimum educational qualifications prescribed for selecting staff from the steam side for conversion training in diesel and electric traction. The staff who are being given conversion training range from illiterates to matriculates. Thus, the recommendation that staff should have adequate education and technical background remains unimplemented on most Railways. We agree that the staff utilised for operating diesel and electric locomotives should possess the necessary still and aptitude and a minimum level of education for acquiring job proficiency of a reasonable standard. (Paras 129 to 136)

55. Facilities for conversion training of driving staff from steam side to diesel/electric side have been by and large, developed on all the Railways. (Paras 129 and 137)

56. The Railway Board had not accepted the recommendation regarding simulation training of drivers. The Railways have also not adopted simulation training in its accepted concept, though some form of rudimentary simulation training is in vogue on some of the Railways. (Paras 129, 138 to 140).

57. We are constrained to note that no progress has been made in the setting up of a centralised training centre for training of staff for mechanised inspection and maintenance of track, even after a lapse of 10 years, and this recommendation of the Wanchoo Committee remains unimplemented. We would urge the Railway Board to take expeditious steps for the setting up of such a centralised training school at the earliest. (Paras 141 to 144)

58. There has been a steady fall in the percentage of steam engine failures due to mismanagement by engine crew on the broad and metre

gauges. From the performance of individual Railways, however, we find that in the case of broad gauge on the North-east Frontier, South Eastern and Western Railways and metre gauge on the Central Railway, there was an increase in engine failures due to mismanagement by engine crew during 1977-78, as compared to the previous year. These Railway Administrations should take effective steps to reverse this trend. (Paras 145 to 148)

59. We find that the available training capacity is grossly underutilised. This recommendation, therefore, remains unimplemented. We feel that the factors which militate against full utilisation of the training capacity have been known for a very long time but remedial action is still wanting. Viewed against the background of heavy arrears of refresher training to be overtaken, the present position is totally indefensible. The Railway Board should take effective steps in this direction and ensure full utilisation of the training capacity. (Paras 149 to 154)

60. The Railways have attributed the backlog in refresher training to inadequacy of trainee reserve posts, failure to nominate staff for training, failure to make relief arrangements in time nominated staff reporting sick, etc. We cannot understand why the Railways are still feeling the shortage of trainee reserve posts when the Railway Board have categorically informed us that this need has already been adequately provided for. All these factors are well within the control of the Railways and should not have been put forward as an alibi. (Paras 155 to 158)

Other Staff Matters

61. We find that no clear definition of who should be treated as essential staff for the purpose of allotment of houses has so far been laid down by the Railway Board and uniformity in the criteria for so classifying the staff is still missing. (Paras 160 to 162)

62. It will be seen that the annual rate of construction of staff quarters has been falling continuously since 1965-66. As a result of this, the percentage of staff housed, which had increased to 37.81 in 1968-69 as compared to 34.81 in 1955-56, has marginally declined in recent years and stood at 37.14 in 1977-78. We feel that Parliament having approved charging of the cost of construction of staff quarters to Capital and to dividend being payable only on such Capital if the Railways have surplus after discharging all other liabilities, there

should have been an increase in the number of staff quarters constructed. We hope that necessary steps in the direction will now be taken by the Railway Board. (Paras 163 to 168)

63. We find that the Wanchoo Committee's recommendation regarding proper job analysis of the work of signal maintainers and their rostering in 8/12 hour shifts, as may be necessary, has not been implemented on all the Railways. A permanent solution to the problem of attending to failures during night has also not been possible on some Railways. We would urge the Railway Administrations to look into this for early implementation (Paras 170 to 174)

64. We are happy to note that in the case of hours of running duty of drivers grade 'A' and 'B', working mail, express and passenger trains, there has been a marked improvement and there were only stray cases of running duty exceeding 10 hours on a few Railways.

The incidence of running duty of more than 10 hours at a stretch in the case of drivers grade 'C' working goods trains is high and ranges between 14.0 per cent on the Southern Railway to 34.0 per cent on the North Eastern Railway. In comparison to the position obtaining in 1967-68, the incidence of trips with running duty exceeding 12 hours at a stretch has gone up on the Central and North Eastern Railways. The incidence of trips with more than 14 hours running duty when taken as a percentage of the total number of trips by goods train drivers were 8.8, 3.1; 7.8, 1.5, 5.8 and 1.9 on the Central, Eastern, North Eastern, Southern, South Central and Western Railways respectively. Trips of more than 20 hours running duty at a stretch accounted for 1.0, 1.1 and 0.9 per cent of the total number of trips on the Central, North Eastern and South Central Railways. We find that the recommendation made by the Wanchoo Committee and accepted by the Railway Board still remains to be implemented in the case of drivers grade 'C' working goods trains on all the Railways. It is unfortunate that in a matter which has such a direct bearing on safety the action taken so far has been tardy. (Paras 175 to 179)

65. We feel constrained to say that much remains to be done in the matter of upkeep of running rooms. In view of the introduction of new trains, changes in the pattern of train services and general improvement in the standard of living of the people, we feel that the assessment of accommodation, amenities and facilities to be provided in and maintenance of running rooms has to be a continuing process so that running staff directly connected with safety of train operation should have adequate rest in modestly furnished, clean and sanitary

rooms. (Paras 180 to 184)

66. Shortages of staff in the categories of station masters, assistant station masters, switchmen and cabinmen had increased on all the Railways in 1977-78 as compared to the position in 1967-68. In the case of most other safety categories of staff also, shortages have increased on majority of the Railways. We are unable to accept the claim made by the Railway Board that the position in respect of shortages of staff has improved to a great extent. Thus, the recommendation of the Wanchoo Committee remains unimplemented for most categories of staff on the Railways. The need to wipe out the shortages cannot be over-emphasised, and we would urge the Railway Board to take effective measures in this regard. (Paras 185 to 189)

67. From the information furnished by the Central and Western Railways, we find that the incidence of overtime working persists to a significant extent even in the case of safety categories to staff. The Railway Board should take effective steps to bring down overtime working to the minimum in the case of categories of staff connected with safety of train operations. (Paras 190 to 194)

68. The present level of leave reserves which the Railways have been permitted to operate in various categories has been found inadequate and this recommendation of the Wanchoo Committee remains unimplemented. (Paras 195 to 199)

69. There has, so far, been no reduction in the time taken for finalising the recruitment to different categories of staff; on the contrary, the time actually taken in some cases has been much in excess of the target. (Paras 200 to 206)

70. We find that guidelines for the jurisdiction of permanent way inspectors were issued before the introduction of high-speed trains on the Indian Railways. The last decade has seen considerable changes in track structure, methods of track maintenance and inspection. In view of these developments, it would be necessary to review the jurisdiction of permanent way inspectors. (Paras 207 to 209)

71. We feel that having laid down a yardstick for determining the strength of signal and telecommunication inspectors, the Railway Board must take urgent steps to implement it within the shortest possible time. (Paras 207 and 210)

72. It is necessary that the guidelines laid down for the strength of carriage and wagon inspectors are implemented without insisting on matching surrenders. (Paras 207 and 211)

73. The Railway Board felt that it was not opportune to issue a

uniform yardstick for determining the strength of loco inspector due to wide variations from railway to railway. We do not consider this as sufficient reason for not laying down a yardstick for loco inspectors. (Paras 207 and 212)

Permanent Way

74. The recommendation of the Wanchoo Committee for providing 60 kg/m rails on sections were the density of traffic may not have reached 20 gross million tonnes but may be rapidly increasing, had not been accepted by the Railway Board. Some of the Railways have informed us that even though minimum track standards for trunk routes and main lines have been laid down, there are sections carrying a large number of high-speed trains where the track structure remains below the stipulated standard. It is necessary that the track structure is brought up to the stipulated standard at the earliest. (Paras 216 to 220)

75. We are happy to note that considerable progress in the laying of long/continuous welded rails has been made on the Central and Northern Railways. On the Southern and South Central Railways, the progress in this respect has not been commensurate with their track kilometrage and would need to be accelerated. The South Eastern, North Eastern and Northeast Frontier Railways have a relatively larger proportion of fishplated track and we would urge these Railways to take effective steps for the welding of rails expeditiously. (Paras 221 to 224)

76. Railways' requirement of wooden sleepers during the 5-year period ending 1977-78 was met to the extent of only 41 and 50 per cent on the broad and metre gauges respectively. It is quite clear that the supply position of wooden sleepers has not at all been satisfactory. The forecast for their supply in the future also does not appear to be encouraging due to dwindling forest resources. Having regard to these considerations, the Railways will have to rely more and more on other types of sleepers and alternative means like axle counters for track circuiting, etc. (Paras 225 to 228)

77. We are constrained to note that the average annual progress of laying concrete sleepers during the period 1973—78 had been only 52 kilometres which was 5 per cent of the length of primary sleeper renewals done on the Railways during the said period. The supply of concrete sleepers has not built up during the last decade as was envisaged by the Wanchoo Committee and their recommendation in this regard, therefore, remains substantially unimplemented. (Paras 229 to

232)

78. The Wanchoo Committee had envisaged the use of concrete sleepers as an alternative to wooden sleepers for track circuiting. There has, however, been very little progress in the use of concrete sleepers in track circuiting. We note that due to unsatisfactory electrical resistance of the present designs of concrete sleepers, their use in track circuiting works has been permitted with reservations. Having regard to the fact that the Ministry of Railways are committed to the provision of track circuiting on a programmed basis and noting that not enough wooden sleepers would be available, we feel that unless greater efforts are made in regard to the procurement of concrete sleepers, it is unlikely that any significant progress can be made in future. For this purpose, it is also necessary to develop concrete sleepers which can be used for track circuiting without any restrictions or reservations. (Paras 233 and 234)

79. We find that recommendation of the Wanchoo Committee for providing guard rails and walkways on girder bridges has not been fully implemented on all the Railways. We hope that the Railway Board will ensure that all girder bridges, on all the Railways, are provided with guard rails and walkways, without exception, within a short period. (Paras 235 to 237)

80. We find that deficiencies still remain in the maintenance and equipment of level crossings and in the training of gatemen in safety procedures. In view of the heavy toll of life and limb that accidents at level crossings take, their proper maintenance and training of gatemen in the protection of rail and road traffic cannot be over-emphasised. It is important, therefore, that the Railway Administrations give higher priority to remedying this situation. (Paras 238 to 241)

81. With reference to Wanchoo Committee's recommendation referred to in Para 242 of this report, nothing appears to have been stipulated regarding the periodicity at which the ballast diagram should be revised. In effect, this recommendation of the Wanchoo Committee does not seem to have been accepted by the Railway Board and the earlier practice on the Railways continues. (Paras 242 and 243)

82. We are in agreement with the Railway Board that no specific percentage of clean ballast for undertaking complete reballasting need be laid down. Maintenance recoupment of ballast is a continuing process for the proper upkeep of track and such recoupment should be done on the basis of actual requirements. (Paras 244 and 245)

83. During the 5-years period ending 1977-78, the total quantity

of ballast procured by all Railways averaged 2.68 million cubic metres per annum. Some portion of the total quantity of ballast so procured must have been used on works of track renewals and increasing ballast cushion. Therefore, there is no doubt that the quantity of ballast used for recoupment has considerably fallen short of the Railway Board's own assessment of 2.8 million cubic metres per annum. We find that some Railways have shortfall while others have none. It is surprising that the information given by the Railways does not corroborate the conclusions of the Railway Board that adequate quantity of ballast is being procured for recoupment. We also do not consider as adequate the reasons given by some of the Railways for not carrying out an important work on which depends the effectiveness of track maintenance and health of the track. This recommendation of the Wanchoo Committee, therefore, has not been fully implemented. The Railway Board should take urgent steps to see that the procurement of ballast is increased to meet fully the requirements for normal recoupment. (Paras 246 to 248)

84. The Wanchoo Committee had expressed the hope that the Railways will step up the pace of track renewals and bring down the backlog. Not only has this hope been belied, but the position has deteriorated considerably and its ill-effects are becoming apparent from the rising incidence of rail breakages and imposition of speed restrictions on increasing lengths of track. We view this matter with great concern and would strongly recommend that no efforts should be spared in solving this problem in all its aspects. It is disconcerting to note that against Railway Board own estimate of requirements of funds for track renewals of Rs. 560 crores during the quinquennium 1978—83, only Rs. 350 crores are stated to have been tentatively earmarked for this purpose. We understand that this matter has also been taken up by Railway Board with the Planning Commission. We do hope that the Railway's full requirements of funds for track renewals in the coming years will be made available so that the arrears are wiped out at the earliest. (Paras 249 to 257)

85. Two branch lines which are owned by private companies and are worked by the Northeast Frontier Railways, i.e., Chaparmukh-Silighat (83.67 kilometres) and Kataghal-Lalaghat (38.10 kilometres) are being maintained with great difficulty at a restricted speed of 25 kmph and 15 kmph respectively, due to overdue track renewals, as the concerned company is not willing to share the cost of replacement. Since this is an important matter concerning the safety of train opera-

tion, we would like to impress upon the Railway Board the need to take special steps to complete track renewals on the above-mentioned lines on an urgent basis. (Para 258)

86. While the Wanchoo Committee had suggested reduction in the percentage of unserviceable sleepers to the barest minimum, we find that a significant length of track continues to have more than 20 per cent unserviceable sleepers. This recommendation has, therefore, not been implemented. (Paras 259 and 260)

87. Against 1247 bridges treated as distressed at the time of the Wanchoo Committee, the number over a period of 10 years has increased to 3553. The sharp increase in the number of distressed bridges is disquieting. A special programme designed to complete the rehabilitation of these bridges within a specified time is, therefore, called for. (Paras 261 to 264)

88. A uniform concept of what a 'distressed bridge' implies is still lacking. We consider that, for a correct appreciation of the magnitude of the problem of rehabilitation of distressed bridges, a definition of the term 'distressed bridge' is called for. (Para 265)

89. We find that the evolution of a rational formula for determining the gang strength has been considerably delayed and the Wanchoo Committee's recommendation remains unimplemented. The Railway Board should direct the Gang Strength Committee to submit its recommendations expeditiously and finalise the issue speedily. (Paras 266 to 268)

90. We find that the recommendation of the Wanchoo Committee for making available one curve corrector on each division is still to be implemented. The usefulness of the curve corrector having been proved in field trails, we consider that the Railway Board should take steps to expedite its development and make them available on each division of the Railway. (Paras 269 to 272)

91. Though annual testing of track by ultrasonic means has not been introduced on all tracks as recommended by the Wanchoo Committee, substantial progress in this direction has been made. Due to the increasing arrears in track renewals and rise in the incidence of rail breakages, we consider ultrasonic testing an essential and effective means of ensuring safety and efficiency of train operation. We hope that with the receipt of additional rail flaw detectors, not only will the periodicity of testing be increased, but increasing length of track will be covered by ultrasonic testing. (Paras 273 to 277)

92. During the 5-years period from 1973-74 to 1977-78, the num-

ber of rail fractures on running lines of Indian Railways had almost doubled, compared to those during the period 1963-64 to 1967-68. Except on the Eastern, North Eastern and Southern Railways, the number of rail fractures has increased on all the other Railways. The increase on the Northern, Northeast Frontier, South Central and South Eastern Railways is disquieting. Each rail fracture in the running lines is a potential hazard to the safety of trains. We would, therefore, urge the Railway Board and the Railway Administrations to take effective steps so that flaws in rails are detected in time and the defective rails are removed from track before these develop into fractures. (Paras 278 and 279)

93. We find that there is a wide disparity in the number of 'broken rails' as given in the accident statistics published annually by the Railway Board and the number of rail fractures on running lines as advised to us by the Railways. It would appear as if all fractures occurring on running lines on the Indian Railways are not being reported as accidents. The Railways Board and the Railway Administrations should look into this discrepancy in reporting and compilation of accident statistics and take necessary corrective action. (Para 280)

94. We note that from 18 tie-tamping machines in 1968, their number increased to 50 in 1978. Mechanised maintenance has been extended to cover 5000 kilometres of track on trunk routes and main lines of all except the North Eastern and Northeast Frontier Railways. We commend the progress so far made in mechanisation of track maintenance and hope that the same would be maintained. (Paras 281 to 283)

95. The position regarding traffic blocks for the mechanised maintenance of track leaves much to be desired and the Wanchoo Committee's recommendation has not been fully implemented. It has been admitted by the Railway Board as well as the Railway Administrations, that for various reasons, it has not been possible to give adequate traffic blocks required for working of on-track tie-tamping machines. It is inevitable that, in the circumstances, maintenance will suffer and the cumulative effects of this over a period of time will have a vital bearing on safety. The position will get further aggravated with increased use of concrete sleepers. The need for granting regular traffic blocks of sufficient duration on day-to-day basis cannot, therefore, be over-emphasised. Ways and means to arrange this must be found. (Paras 284 to 288)

96. We are happy to note that between 1970-71 to 1977-78, the

length of track monitored by track recording cars on the broad gauge had increased nearly two-fold from 39,577 to 74,748 track kilometres and on the metre gauge from 2730 to 8000 track kilometres. We hope that this progress will be maintained and increasing length of track would be brought within the scope of monitoring by track recording cars. (Paras 289 to 291)

97. We agree with the views of the RDSO and the Railway Board that no useful purpose would be served by equipping each division of the Railways with a Hallade track recorder. (Paras 292 to 295)

98. The stand now taken by the Railway Board that the custody of stores is an inseparable part of the duties of permanent ways and signal inspectors and that they cannot be divested of this responsibility is a reversal of their stand on the recommendations made by the Kunzru Committee in 1962. In view of the fact that this matter had engaged the attention of three high-level Railway Accident Enquiry Committees, i.e., the Shahnawaz Committee – 1954, the Kunzru Committee – 1962, and the Wanchoo Committee – 1968, we feel that such an important issue should not have been decided only on the basis of the views of the Pay Commission. Thus, the Wanchoo Committee's recommendation remains unimplemented. (Paras 296 to 299)

Level Crossings

99. We find that the recommendations of the Wanchoo Committee, that some norms should be fixed for deciding whether a particular unmanned level crossing should be manned and whether a manned level crossings requires upgrading, has not been implemented. The need for laying down appropriate norms for manning of unmanned level crossing and upgrading of manned level crossings cannot be over-emphasised. Considerable delay in this regard has already taken place and norms should be laid down as recommended by the Wanchoo Committee, without further delay. (Paras 306 to 310)

100. The recommendations of the Wanchoo Committee that in no case should a gate remain with only one man on duty all the 24 hours has been substantially implemented. (Paras 311 to 315)

101. The overall utilisation of the 90 per cent and 10 per cent of the Railway Safety Works Fund upto March 1979 had been only 42.6 per cent and 55.7 per cent respectively. Ninty per cent Railway Safety Works Fund of the share of West Bengal remains unutilised since 1966. In Uttar Pradesh, Madhya Pradesh and Bihar also, despite a sub-

stantial network of the railway system, the utilisation of this fund has been poor. Provision of road over-bridges and under-bridges and manning or upgrading of level crossings will undoubtedly improve the safety of rail and road traffic at level crossings. Non-utilisation of the aforesaid fund defeats the very purposes for which this fund has been set up. In our opinion there appears to be need for more persistent efforts on the part of the State Governments and the Railways to utilise the 90 per cent Railway Safety Works Fund in the shortest possible time. Utilisation of the 10 per cent Railway Safety Works Fund depends primarily on the Railways themselves. The Railway Board should ensure that each Railway plans for a sufficient number of works of manning of unmanned level crossings and upgrading of manned level crossings in their annual Works Programme for full utilisation of the 10 per cent Railway Safety Works Fund. (Paras 316 to 321)

102. The Wanchoo Committee had recommended provision of telephone communication at all mid-section manned level crossing. The Railway Board had issued instructions for provision of telephone facilities at all Special, 'A' and 'B' Class level crossings and only such of the 'C' Class manned level crossings on Rajdhani routes as are in the block section and are normally kept open to road traffic. According to the information furnished to us by the Railway Board, all Special Class level crossings have been provided with this facility. The information from the Railways, however, shows that 24 Special Class level crossing are yet to be provided with telephone communication, and a substantial number of 'A' and 'B' Class level crossings have not been provided with this facility so far. Thus, this recommendation still remains to be fully implemented. The Railway Board should complete this long outstanding work at all mid-section manned level crossings on a time-bound programme. (Paras 322 to 326)

103. Implementation of the Wanchoo Committee's recommendations regarding provision of lifting barriers at all important level crossings has necessarily to be phased. We would urge the Railway Administrations to take up this work on a time-bound basis, giving priority to important level crossings. (Paras 327 to 331)

104. The first trial with automatic half-barriers which was carried out at Unnao on the Northern Railway in September, 1972, was found to be satisfactory. No further trials could, however, be carried out due to considerable difference of opinion and reluctance on the part of the Railways. The police authorities have also not favoured such trials in metropolitan areas. (Paras 332 to 337)

105. Since 1968-69, 637 level crossings have been interlocked with signals on all the Railways. Implementation of this recommendation covering increasing number of level crossings, is necessarily a continuous process. However, we find that some level crossings on the suburban sections of the Eastern and South Eastern Railways still remain to be interlocked. On the Eastern Railway, 23 'B' Class level crossings, where the track is on a curve, also remain to be interlocked with signals. We would urge these Railway Administrations to complete the work of interlocking of gates with signals at the above noted level crossings on priority. (Paras 342 to 344)

Signalling and Interlocking

106. Good progress in the provision of colour light signalling has been made and the number of stations provided with colour light signalling has increased from 331 in 1968-69 to 1007 in 1977-78. The implementation of this recommendation is a continuous process and we hope that this progress will be maintained and even improved. (Paras 347 to 351)

107. Although the Railway Board had accepted the recommendation of the Wanchoo Committee regarding electric lighting of semaphore signals and trials on some Railways had shown satisfactory results and proven the effectiveness of this measure for improved lighting and visibility of signals, the progress made in the last eight years has been unduly slow. The Railway Board should take steps to complete this work on a time-bound basis. (Paras 352 to 357)

108. Multiple-aspect signalling still remains to be provided at 12.5 per cent of the stations on the broad and metre gauge trunk routes and 65 per cent of the stations on the main lines of both gauges. Although the implementation of the Wanchoo Committee's recommendation in this respect has necessarily to be phased, we would urge the Railway Board to take up the provision of multiple-aspect signalling at the remaining stations on trunk routes and main lines as early as possible. (Paras 358 to 362)

109. There has been no significant progress in the implementation of the Wanchoo Committee's recommendations regarding separation of warner signals in the rear of outer signals. The separation of the warner signal from the outer signal has a very important bearing on safety. The recommendation of the Wanchoo Committee having been accepted, should be implemented with a greater sense of urgency.

(Para 363)

110. We understand that there still remain considerable deficiencies in the visibility distance for the first stop signal provided in 2-aspect signalling as well as in the inter-signal distances in 2-aspect and multiple-aspect signalling and these do not conform to the emergency braking distances as determined by trials. (Paras 364 to 369)

111. We find that except for the high-speed routes, the question of resiting of signals on the basis of the results of braking distance trials on the remaining sections does not appear to have been taken up so far. Inter-signal distances have considerable bearing on safe running of trains and the need to resite signals on the basis of braking distances cannot be over emphasized. We understand that this matter along with other inter-related issues is presently under the consideration of the Railway Board, which should take a very early decision and ensure its speedy implementation. (Paras 364 to 370)

112. It is a matter of serious concern that the implementation of the Wanchoo Committee's recommendations for providing suitable reflective material, like scotchlite, on sighting boards having a direct bearing on safety of train operation has been considerably delayed on the ground of lack of foreign exchange. We feel that there has been a lack of sense of purpose and urgency when the one alternative which was being developed indigenously has been found unsatisfactory in performance. Considering that the requirement of foreign exchange for import of this material cannot be very large and that scotchlite reflective material is being used extensively by other Government departments and public sector undertakings in the country, e.g., roadways, airlines, etc., as also the relatively easier availability of foreign exchange, there is no reason why this should not be imported by the Railways also, even at this stage. (Paras 372 to 374)

113. Compared to the average of 76 stations per year provided with track circuiting during the 5-year period 1963-64 to 1967-68, 139 stations per year on an average, were track circuited during the 10-year period from 1968-69 to 1977-78. During 1977-78 track circuiting was completed at 162 stations. This progress is commendable. (Paras 375 to 378)

114. Besides 329 broad gauge and 98 metre gauge stations on the trunk routes and 'important' main lines where track circuiting work is still to be programmed, there remain another 169 broad gauge and 702 metre gauge stations on other main lines where no plans for track circuiting have been made so far. Thus, even the completion of track cir-

cuiting of run-through lines on trunk routes and main lines is not yet in sight. Early action should be taken to get this work done on a time-bound basis. (Paras 375 to 380)

115. In respect of track circuiting of all passenger lines at wayside stations, it has not been possible to make much headway due to non-availability of wooden sleepers nor are axle counters available in adequate numbers instead. There has been very little progress in use of concrete sleepers in track circuiting works. Due to the unsatisfactory supply position of wooden sleepers, it is necessary that alternatives like suitable concrete sleepers and axle counters are made available in the required numbers for completing the works of track circuiting and detection facilities at all stations where these are considered necessary. (Paras 381 to 389)

116. We find that the Railway Board are still going ahead with track circuiting between fouling marks despite the clear recommendation of the Wanchoo Committee that this should be done between the block clearance points. (Para 384 to 388)

117. Very little progress has been made in the provision of Automatic Warning and Stop System (AWS) even on the restricted scope accepted by the Railway Board. Out of 2,780 route kilometres programmed on trunk routes with speeds of 120 kmph and over and 1,128 route kilometres on suburban sections in Calcutta, Bombay and Madras areas, AWS has been provided only on 248 and 94 kilometres respectively. The poor progress in the last 15 years has been due to reluctance to import equipment and to excessive time taken for its indigenous development and manufacture of the AWS equipment. We consider that the Railway Board should take steps to fulfil atleast their diluted commitment of providing AWS on trunk routes and sub-urban sections at the earliest. In doing so, it will no doubt take full advantage of the available sources of supply in the country and undertake imports if necessary, so as to complete speedily this important safety measure. It is also necessary that a programme should be drawn up for extending AWS on all trunk routes with speeds of 100 kmph and above, covering all passenger and goods trains. (Paras 389 to 392)

118. We note that very little progress have been made in research and development in the field of cab signalling in the last decade and a half after the recommendation was first made by the Kunzru Committee. Technology in this sphere is continuously advancing and several systems are in use in foreign countries. The Indian Railways should take advantage of these developments and evolve a suitable sys-

tem for use under Indian conditions. (Paras 393 to 395)

119. As regards time blocks for maintenance of signalling equipment, the Railway Board did not accept the Wanchoo Committee's recommendation for making provision of fixed time blocks in the time table nor have they offered any solution to this vexing problem which has serious repercussions on safety. (Paras 396 to 398)

120. The strength of officers and inspectors in the signal and telecommunication department on most Railways is not commensurate with the existing workload. It is surprising that even after deficiencies in this respect had been brought out in the study undertaken by the Efficiency Bureau and accepted by the Railway Board, the Railways have been asked to rationalise the workload on the basis of the existing strength. It is disquieting that for the new equipment also, posts are not being provided as per the yardstick. Intensification of inspections apart, it would appear that even the extant schedules of inspection are not feasible due to inadequate strength of officers and inspectors. This is serious matter to which we would draw the attention of the Railway Board and urge that immediate steps should be taken to rectify the situation and ensure that meaningful inspections by officers and inspectors of the signal and telecommunication departments are carried out. We consider that any economy in this regard would be misconceived. (Paras 399 to 406)

121. We find that 65 stations on the broad and metre gauges still remain to be interlocked. We are of the opinion that even in the case of stations on river ghats or stations on sections worked under 'one engine only' system, the possibility of a derailment at the points is not precluded it the stations are interlocked. We, therefore, reiterate what the Kunzru and Wanchoo Committees had suggested, namely that rudimentary interlocking should be provided at all stations on the broad and metre gauges. (Paras 407 to 411)

122. During 1976-77 and 1977-78 there had been an increase in the incidence of failures of signal and interlocking gears related to traffic density. We would urge the Railway Board to take steps to check the rising trend and bring down the failure rate. In the case of block instruments, the incidence of failures has shown some improvement. (Paras 412 to 415)

123. The Northern Railway had the highest number of track circuit failures followed by the Western and Eastern Railways. These Railway Administrations should analyse the causes of failures and take steps to bring their down. (Paras 416 to 419)

124. The shortfall in overhaul of lever frames and block instruments and replacement of lever frames has sharply increased in recent years as compared to the position obtaining prior to 1970-71. According to the Railways, the main reason for this shortfall is non-finalisation of the yardsticks for maintenance staff and shortage of staff. This is a serious matter and if left unremedied, can only lead to further deterioration and serious repercussions. Special efforts in this regard are called for on the Eastern, Southern, South Central and South Eastern Railways where the backlog of overhaul of lever frames has increased considerably during 1977-78 as compared to the previous years. Backlog in replacement of lever frames on the Eastern and Northern Railways had increased substantially during 1977-78 as compared to the previous year and needs to be brought down.

Thus, the Wanchoo Committee's recommendations for clearing the backlog of overhauling of lever frames and block instruments and replacement of lever frames not only remain unimplemented but there has been a distinct deterioration in the situation except in the case of replacement of block instruments. We would urge the Railway Board and the Railway Administrations to take urgent steps to effect an improvement in this respect. (Paras 420 to 425)

125. Regarding the Wanchoo Committee's recommendations for laying down yardsticks for determining the strength of block, electric and mechanical signal maintainers, the Railway Board decided that it would not be practicable for a big railway system like the Indian Railways to have a uniform yardstick and the Railways were advised to evolve local yardsticks. Thus, the Wanchoo Committee's recommendation in this respect remains unimplemented. (Paras 420 and 426)

Motive Power

126. Our analysis shows that as far as engine failures are concerned, the position of steam, diesel and electric locomotives has been unsatisfactory and their performance has fallen much below the target laid down by the Railway Board. No specific reasons for this deterioration have been given either by the Railway Board or the zonal Railways nor has any indication been given of the action contemplated to improve the position. The matter calls for urgent and concerted efforts to reverse this trend, particularly when such expensive assets are involved. (Paras 430 to 437)

127. The recommendations of the Wanchoo Committee regarding

provision of speedometers/speed-recorders accepted by the Railway Board, has still not been implemented and the Railway Board's claim in this regard is not corroborated by the information supplied by the Railways. The Railway Board must ensure that speedometers/ speed-recorders are provide on all locomotives working trains and no locomotive which is to work a train leaves the shed or yard without a speedometer/speed-recorder in working order. (Paras 438 to 442)

128. We find that even after 10 years, the Railways still have no satisfactory design of a speedometer. We cannot help feeling that if a more determined effort had been made by the Railway Board, a suitable speedometer could have been developed during this period. (Paras 443 to 446)

129. While the recommendations of the Wanchoo Committee for repositioning the speedometer on the control desk of metre gauge diesel locomotive or alternatively, providing another speedometer so that the driver can refer to it conveniently, has been implemented on some Railways, it remains to be fully implemented on the Northern, Western and Southern Railways in spite of Railway Board's clear directive on the subject nine years ago. (Paras 447 to 450)

130. On the question of maintenance of speedometers, our review has shown that this is a clear case where things have been allowed to drift and although ten years have elapsed since the recommendation no appreciable headway has been made either in the manufacture of a suitable speedometer/speed-recorder or in the proper maintenance of the instruments which are presently in use. Thus, the recommendations of the Wanchoo Committee remains unimplemented. We hope that the Railway Board will now expedite the action proposed by them in this regard. (Paras 451 to 457)

131. We find that even though the provision of Drivers' Vigilance Control Device on diesel and electric locomotives had been accepted as a policy by the Railway Board, a decade has elapsed and satisfactory design of Vigilance Control Device for electric locomotives, suitable for Indian conditions, is still to be developed. While some diesel locomotives have been equipped with this safety device, none of the electric locomotives has been provided with the same. Even where this device has been provided on diesel locomotives, in many cases it is found to be not in working order. Thus, an important safety measure remains substantially unimplemented. We are concerned that it has also so far not been possible to get the drivers to accept the utility of this device, in spite of the fact that the study made by the RDSO had

shown that its operation did not generate fatigue and exhaustion in drivers to any significant extent which is likely to impair efficiency. We would urge the Railway Board to take urgent steps to equip all diesel and electric locomotives with Drivers' Vigilance Control Device at the earliest, if necessary, by resorting to imports till a successful indigenous design becomes available. It is also necessary that full cooperation of the drivers is ensured by better educational propaganda and more frequent personal contacts. (Paras 458 to 464)

132. There has been a gradual decrease in the holdings of steam locomotives due to progressive dieselisation and electrification during the last 15 years. In this background and with the steps taken by the Railway Board to give special attention to the maintenance of overaged locomotives, perhaps a reduction in the time interval between two overhauls may not be necessary. (Paras 465 to 468)

Goods and Coaching Stock

133. The recommendations made by the Kunzru and Wanchoo Committees for adoption of a uniform basis for fixing the time schedule for train examination and for determining the strength of examining gangs remain unimplemented. This is a vital affecting the safety of train operation and urge the Railway Board to take a decision expeditiously and implement the recommendations as early as possible. (Paras 471 to 475)

134. We find that it has not been possible to implement the recommendation of the Wanchoo Committee for adopting the Andal pattern of train examination due to various difficulties experienced by the Railways. (Paras 476 to 479)

135. The position of repairs to wagons in traffic yards and on trains is not entirely satisfactory. It is undesirable that wagons with rejectable defects should continue to remain in service though not permitted under the Conference Rules, Part III. We would impress upon the Railway Board to take steps and ensure that repairs to wagons on nominated lines and on trains in traffic yards are carried out satisfactorily. (Paras 480 to 485)

136. We find that whereas the Northeast Frontier Railway has indicated that machinery and tools in sicklines are provided on the basis of the Railway Board's instructions issued in 1954, all the other Railways have stated that the sicklines are being equipped as per standards recommended by the Committee appointed by the Railway Board in December, 1971. The Railways have also indicated the nonavailability

of certain types of equipment in the sicklines. We also find that ultrasonic equipment is not included in the standard lists of equipment prescribed either in 1954 or in 1971. Thus, the sicklines on the Railways are still not equipped fully with the requisite type of machinery and plant. The Railway Board should take urgent steps in this respect. (Paras 486 to 490)

137. The system of neutral control examination of wagons is in force at 59 broad gauge and 19 metre gauge sicklines where wagons are turned out after obtaining neutral control fit certificates.

From the results of checks made by the neutral control staff. We find that during 1976-77, 5.3 and 8.2 per cent of the wagons on broad gauge and metre gauge respectively, were found with rejectable defects at the time of final examination in sicklines. It is disquieting that even rejectable defects are not being fully attended to in sicklines.

We also find that wagons are being turned out of sicklines without neutral control fit certificates, thus evading neutral control examination IRCA reports have been consistently highlighting the particularly poor performance of sicklines at Rewari, Garhara, Gonda, Lumding, Katihar, Siliguri, Tinsukia, New Gauhati, Samastipur and Guntakal where the repair procedures were found generally sub-standard. Thus, even where the system of neutral control examination of wagons is in force, a substantial percentage of wagons is turned out without fit certification by the neutral control staff. This, in our opinion, is a serious matter which the Railway Board should go into and ensure that no wagon is turned out without fit certification by neutral control staff in sicklines, where examination by such staff is in force.

It is clear that the recommendations of the Wanchoo Committee have not been implemented in any substantial measure. The Railway Board should take firm steps to see that wagons are turned out after completion of all stipulated repairs. (Paras 492 to 498)

138. We are concerned that primary and secondary maintenance of some passenger carrying rakes is still carried out on lines with high level platform on one side. We strongly feel that the practice of giving primary and secondary maintenance to coaching rakes on platform lines should stop forthwith and adequate facilities should be created at the stations to undertake the statutory maintenance schedules as prescribed in the conference Rules Part IV. (Paras 499 to 502)

139. Having accepted the Wanchoo Committee's recommendations the Railway Board issued orders in 1969 that the practice of clamping and securing broken bearing springs on BOX wagons should be dis-

continued. We find that these orders are not being complied with by the Railways. (Paras 503 to 505)

140. Large-scale overloading of BOX wagons, up to the extent 8 to 10 tonnes, is a common feature at certain coal loading depots the Eastern Railway. In some cases it was as high as 18 tonnes. It appears to us that this cannot happen except with the connivance on the part of some personnel on the Railways and the loading parties. Thus, the dangerous practice of overloading of BOX wagons not only continues unabated but has aggravated in the last decade. (Paras 506 to 510)

141. It is a serious matter that in spite of strong objections by the RDSO and the Commission of Railway Safety, the practice of overloading BOX wagons as a regular measure to the extent of 2 tonnes over and above the carrying capacity has been allowed to continue. Further, higher axle loads on BOX wagons are being permitted in contravention of the Conference Rules, Part III. We are of the view that the Railway Board's directive permitting overloading beyond the carrying capacity by 2 tonnes, as a regular measure, would seriously affect safety and feel that this needs to be reviewed urgently at the highest level, in consultation with the RDSO and the Commission of Railway Safety. (Paras 511 to 518)

142. In the case of coaching stock on the broad and metre gauges, after a rise in the incidence of hot boxes during 1974-75 and 1975-76, there has been a steady fall in the last two years of our survey. During 1977-78 the all-Railways average incidence of hot boxes on coaching stock per 10 million vehicle kilometres was 0.43 broad gauge and 1.94 on metre gauge as against the Railway Board's target of 1.0 on both gauges. On the broad gauge of Northern, South Central and South Eastern Railways there has been an increase in the incidence of hot boxes on coaching stock during 1977-78 as compared to the previous year; on the metre gauge, none of the Railways were able to achieve the target of the Railway Board during 1977-78; on the other hand, the incidence of hot boxes had gone up on the Southern, South Central and Western Railways as compared to the position obtaining in the previous year. We would urge these Railways to take necessary steps so as to bring down the incidence of hot boxes. (Paras 519 to 522)

143. The overall incidence of hot boxes on goods stock per million wagon kilometres on the broad gauge has been steadily falling except during 1977-78 when there was a slight increase on some Railways as compared to the previous year, though within the target.

On the metre gauge, there has been a decline in the incidence of hot boxes on goods stock except for two intervening years 1974-75 and 1975-76 when there was an increase. Except the Southern and South Central Railways, no other Railway could keep within the target of 0.5 hot boxes per million wagon kilometres stipulated by the Railway Board. The Northern, North Eastern, Northeast Frontier and Western Railways should take effective steps to bring down the incidence of hot boxes on metre gauge goods stock within the target stipulated by the Railway Board. (Paras. 523 to 525)

144. We find that the principal causes of hot boxes on coaching and goods stock on both the broad and metre gauges continue to be the same as found by the Kunzru and Wanchoo Committees, namely dry packing badly fitted brasses, uneven loading or overloading water or dirt contaminated packing, badly metalled brass, etc. These areas of maintenance of rolling stock, therefore, call for greater attention. (Para 526)

145. We may point out that due to the increasing number of coaches and wagons fitted with roller bearings which are being put into service on the Railways, the overall incidence of hot boxes in relation to vehicle/wagon kilometres is bound to come down. We would, therefore, caution the Railways against complacency in this regard and urge that steps should continue for bringing down further the incidence of hot boxes on coaching stock and wagons on both broad and metre gauges. Also the targets may need to be appropriately revised. (Para 527)

146. Wa are sorry to note that though more than a decade has elapsed, an indigenously developed hot box detector appears nowhere in sight. With the trend towards long-distance and high-speed trains the need for detecting hot boxes in time cannot be over-emphasised. (Paras 528 and 529)

147. Checks on effective brake power by neutral control staff had shown that only 12 per cent of the originating trains and one per cent of the terminating trains had effective brake power of 85 per cent and above. We cannot escape the conclusion that most of the trains leave originating points with effective brake power much less than the prescribed minimum and position becomes worse on the run. These results belie the claims made by most of the Zonal Railways that the prescribed brake power is available on all goods trains. The Railway Board's own directive in this regard is, thus, not being followed and the recommendations of the Wanchoo Committee remains unimplemented. The safety of a train is endangered when its brake power is

poor and it must be ensured that trains leave the originating points with atleast the minimum stipulated effective brake power. (Paras 530 to 536)

148. In a number of cases the trains were started without recording on the certificate the vacuum available in the engine or the brake van. In some cases fictitious readings of vacuum in the brake van were recorded. We consider absence of vacuum gauges in the rear brake vans and incorrect preparation of brake power certificates to be highly disconcerting features. We would stress that effective measures should be taken to ensure that vacuum gauges are invariably fixed in the rear brake vans and that they are in working order and the brake power certificates are correctly prepared. (Paras 538 to 540)

149. In respect of the Wanchoo Committee's recommendations that a satisfactory solution should be evolved to overcome the difficulty of stopping diesel-hauled goods trains the Railway Board had stated that detailed tests have shown that no modification was required in the brake circuitry of the diesel locomotives. The Railway Board, therefore, felt that this recommendation did not call for any further action. (Paras 541 to 548)

150. The Wanchoo Committee's recommendations to give identifying marks on all anti-telescopic coaches has been fully implemented. In the course of our examination, it has also come out that even the extant instructions of the Railway Board of marshalling passenger trains are not always followed. The Railway Board should ensure that passenger trains are fun with the stipulated marshalling order of coaches. (Paras 549 to 552)

151. We find that all 4-wheeler brake vans on broad and metre gauges have not, so far, been equipped with modified spring arrangements although the instructions to do this were issued more than 8 years ago. (Paras 553 and 554)

152. The backlog of POH of coaching vehicles on the broad gauge was comparatively higher on the Eastern, Northern, Southern, South Central and South Eastern Railways. On the metre gauge, the backlog of POH of coaching vehicles on the Northern. Southern and South Central Railways was considerably higher than the all-Railways average. (Paras 555 to 559)

153. On the broad gauge, the percentage of wagons overdue POH on the Central, Northern and Western Railways were higher than the all-Railways average. On the metre gauge, the percentage of the wagons overdue POH on the Northern and South Central Railways was

considerably higher than the all-Railways average. These Railway Administrations should take steps to bring down the arrears in POH of wagons. (Paras 560 to 563)

154. In the face of continuing arrears in POH of wagons on almost all the Railways, the Railway Board have surprisingly issued instructions to the Railway Administrations to temporarily advance POH of wagons by six months so as to enable adequate supply of wagons to workshops for POH to avoid under-utilisation of the available POH capacity. In our opinion such a step can be justified only after POH arrears have been fully liquidated on all the Railways. If spare POH capacity is available on some Railways, it should first be utilised for clearing the arrears on other Railways to the extent possible. (Para 565)

155. We find that during 1977 the rate of failures of spherical roller bearings on ICF broad and metre gauge coaches increased to 3.25 per cent and of cylindrical roller bearings on BEML broad gauge coaches the rate of failures was 0.531 per cent. The incidence of failures of roller bearings on BOX wagons had also gone up to 0.75 and 1.06 per cent during 1976 and 1977 respectively as compared to 0.05 per cent during the period 1966-67 to 1968-69.

We feel that the maintenance of roller bearings has not received the attention that it deserves thereby resulting in increase in the rate of failure of roller bearings and deterioration in position since the appointment of the Wanchoo Committee. The Railway Board should take effective steps in this matter. (Paras 566 to 576)

156. Dust-proof rooms for overhauling of roller bearing still remain to be provided in workshops on some Railways. The Railway Board should ensure that these facilities are provided without delay. (Paras 577 and 578)

157. The Railway Board had not accepted the suggestion of the Wanchoo Committee for adopting a system similar to that on the Japanese National Railways for attention to roller bearings in workshop. Considering that there has been an appreciable increase in the rate of failures of roller bearings on the Indian Railways during the last decade, an in-depth study of the extant maintenance practices is called for. (Para 579)

158. We find that hot box detector is still under development. In the wake of increasing use of roller bearings and the introduction of more and more fast non-stop trains, it would be desirable to develop a hot box detector device at the earliest. (Paras 580 to 582)

159. Neutral control examination of coaches after POH in

workshops is in force only at 17 out of total of 31 workshops where repairs to coaching stock are undertaken.

The results of checks made by neutral control staff during 1978 show that the percentage of coaches detained due to non-completion of repairs at the time of outgoing inspection was still high in the case of some workshops. As compared to the position in 1978, there has been some deterioration in the case of certain broad gauge workshops. The Wanchoo Committee's recommendations, thus, remain unimplemented. The Railways must take effective steps to improve the quality of workmanship in the workshops and bring down the rejections at the stage of final examination by neutral control staff. (Paras 583 to 586)

160. The percentage of coaches sent out of workshops without obtaining neutral control fit certificates was quite high in some workshops. It is disquieting that in the case of broad gauge workshops at Matunga on the Central Railway, Kharagpur on the South Eastern Railway and metre gauge workshops at Gorakhpur on the North Eastern Railway, New Bongaigaon on the Northeast Frontier Railway, the number of coaches passed locally without obtaining neutral control fit certificates had increased during 1978 as compared to 1970. (Paras 587 and 588)

161. We also find that in some workshops where the percentage of coaches detained by neutral control staff due to non-completion of repairs was high, the percentage of coaches passed without-obtaining neutral control fit certificates was also high. The workshops at Matunga (CR), Alambagh, Lallaguda, Kharagpur on the broad gauge and Gorakhpur and New Bongaigaon on the metre gauge stand out glaringly in this respect. The Railway Board should look into this and take urgent corrective action. (Para 589)

162. The maintenance of rolling stock has shown signs of deterioration in recent years. In the interest of safety of train operation, it is necessary that every effort should be made to improve the condition of rolling stock. Extension of the neutral control examination would appear to be an effective means to ensure this. The Railway Board are already seized of this matter and we would stress the need for an expeditious decision. (Paras 590 to 594)

163. The performance reckoned in terms of the percentage of wagon units with unattended rejectable defects by which the Railway Board indicated an improvement in 1967-68, has slipped back to the level obtaining in 1963-64. It is also clear that the high percentage of wagons found with rejectable defects has been persisting over these

years on all the Railways. (Paras 595 to 598)

164. Spot checks conducted by neutral control flying squads during the period 1974-75 to 1976-77 show that a large number of wagons with 'rejectable defects having a direct bearing on safety', were left unattended on the broad and metre gauges. It is a matter of concern that even after the wagons have been attended to by railway staff, a very high percentage of these remained with such defects. The spot checks, though limited in nature, show that a large number of wagons are running with such defects. This reveals a serious state of affairs and calls for urgent corrective action. (Paras 599 and 600)

165. The figures in respect of overaged coaches and wagons show that there has been reduction in their number on both the broad and metre gauges.

From the age-wise information of the overaged coaches furnished by the Railways, we find that a substantial percentage of the overaged coaches has exceeded the codal life by as much as 20 years on the broad and metre gauges. We hope that priority would be given to replacing these overaged coaches. (Paras 602 to 606)

Miscellaneous Matters and Research, Designs and Standards Organisation

166. We find that double ended sidings for stabling of medical vans have not been provided at 12 stations on the Railways. The question of providing such sidings has been with the Railways for more than 15 years. We find no justification for the failure to implement this accepted recommendations. (Paras 607 to 610)

167. Narrow gauge lines are still being worked with increasing preponderance of overaged locomotives and rolling stock; there are also heavy arrears of track renewals. We consider that to continue to work them under these conditions is hazardous. They must, therefore, either be closed down or-fully rehabilitated. The Government should take an early decision in the matter. (Paras 611 to 615)

168. We note that at present only a skeleton documentation section is functioning in the RDSO and expansion of the scheme has been deferred due to financial stringency. Thus, the recommendation of the Wanchoo Committee remains unimplemented. We feel strongly that the absence of a well-equipped and modern documentation section is a severe handicap to any research organisation, more so to the only such institution in the Railways. Economy in this can only hamper the effec-

tiveness of the research organisation and hence prove to be self-defeating. (Paras 616 to 619)

169. Operations research has not, so far, been employed by the Railways to improve the standard of safety as was envisaged by the Wanchoo Committee. This recommendation, therefore, remains unimplemented. We feel that operations research will be a useful tool to improve the standard of safety in train operation and urge the Railway Board to take effective steps in this direction. The setting up of Operations Research Cells on the Railways will be a step in the right direction and should be expedited. (Paras 620 to 626)

170. In our view the setting up of a vehicle dynamics test-rig and the laying of a test-track are essential to evaluate the performance of various design concepts to the limits of their operating capabilities under controlled and simulated conditions. We would impress upon the Railway Board the need to give priority to the setting up of these facilities at the earliest.

2

WORKING GROUP ON TRIBAL DEVELOPMENT DURING MEDIUM TERM PLAN 1978-83 — REPORT
February 3, 1978[1]

Chairman Shri Dhanik Lal Mandal

Members The Secretary, Department of Agriculture, New Delhi; The Secretary, Department of Irrigation, New Delhi; The Secretary, Department of Industrial Development, New Delhi; The Secretary, Department of Cooperation, New Delhi; The Secretary, Department of Education, New Delhi; The Secretary, Department of Health, New Delhi; The Additional Secretary, Department of Transport (Roads Dev.), New Delhi; The Secretary, Department of Social Welfare, New Delhi; The Secretary, Ministry of Commerce; The Secretary, Ministry of Communictions, New Delhi; The Secretary, Ministry of Works and Housing, New Delhi; The Secretary of Labour, New Delhi; The Secretary, Planning Commission, New Delhi; The Secretary, Ministry of Home Affairs, New Delhi; The Additional Secretary, Ministry of Home Affairs, New Delhi; The Inspector General of Forests, Department of Agriculture, New Delhi; The Director, Anthropological Survey of India, Calcutta; The Regional Development Commissioner, Chhotanagpur and Santhal Parganas, Ranchi; The Secretary, Department of Tribal Areas and Welfare of Backward Classes, Government of Assam, Dispur, Gauhati; The Secretary-Cum-Commissioner, Labour, Social Welfare and Tribal Development, Government of Gujarat, Gandhinagar; The Tribal Development Commissioner and Secretary,

1. Government of India, Ministry of Home Affairs, 1978, 114 p.

Tribal Welfare Department, Government of Madhya Pradesh, Bhopal; The Tribal Development Commissioner and Secretary, Sports and Social Welfare Department, Government of Maharashtra, Bombay; The Secretary-Cum-Commissioner Tribal and Rural Welfare Department, Government of Orissa, Bhubaneshwar; Shri T. Mahadeva Menon; Shri S.L. Kalia; Shri D.R. Pratap; The Managing Director, Girijan Co-operative Development Corporation Ltd., Visakhapatnam; Dr. S.C. Dube; Prof. Moonis Raza; Dr. Sachchidananda; Dr. Surajit Chandra Sinha; Dr. B.K. Roy Burman; Prof. L. P. Vidyarthi; Shri R.K. Deshpande; Dr. S. Narasimhan; Shri Mohan Singh Mehta; Shri L.M. Shrikant; Shri Raja Ram Singh; Shri Subodh Chandra Hansda.

Special Invitees Dr. Ram K. Vepa; Shri K.A.P. Menon; Shri P.R. Dubashi and Shri Shishir Kumar.

M. Secy. Dr. B.D. Sharma

Appointment

In the Fifth plan, a new approach for the development of tribal areas and tribal communities was adopted and in the first phase, sub-plans were prepared for areas of tribal concentration. These sub-plans were conceived as integrated area development plans with focus on the development of tribal communities. Projects have been prepared for each area adopting problem solving, family oriented approach. There were some inherent limitations arising from deficiency in the formation base as also from the fact that the new tribal development programme was taken up only after the State and Central plans were practically finalised. Nevertheless, a clearer focus on tribal development in the State plans is now emerging. It has also been decided recently that the Central Ministries will set apart specific outlays for tribal areas beginning with 1978-79 and prepare suitable supporting programmes for their speedy development. The various Central Ministries/Departments and State Governments are also now reviewing their general programmes and working out the strategy of development and programmes for the next medium-term plan beginning from 1978-79. It is, therefore, necessary that the tribal scene is comprehensively reviewed and it is ensured that the various elements in the Central and

State Plans, so far as they relate to tribal areas and tribal communities, are so worked out that they make for a viable and balanced thrust for their faster development and effective protection. It has, therefore, decided to constitute a Working Group on Tribal Development during the next medium-term plan beginning with 1978-79. The Ministry of Home Affairs, Government of India vide its O.M. No. 17014/1/78-TD dated February 3, 1978 Constitute the Working Group.

Terms of Reference

(a) To review the measures planned for the protection and elimination of exploitation of tribals and their implementation by various States;

(b) To review the programmes for tribal development taken up by the States and Central Ministries;

(c) To advise on the approach, strategy and priorities in respect of protection and development programmes in the next five years;

(d) To formulate concrete proposals and suggest the phasing of tribal development programmes indicating financial and other requirements; and

(e) To review the administrative arrangements for implementation of the programme in the States in the Centre and suggest measure for improvement.

Contents

Abstract; Introduction; Review of the First Sub-Plan; Implementation, Planning and Quality of administration; Financial Investment and its Consolidation; Basic needs of Tribal Communities; Protective measures; Agriculture and Allied Sectors; Credit and Marketing; Industries and Allied Sectors; Social Services; Infrastructural Development; Primitive Groups; Dispersed Tribals; Appendix I; Annexure I & II.

Recommendations

Implementation, Planning and Quality of Administration

State Level

There should be a Project Committee at the Project-level comprising representatives of the people, local leaders, social scientists and voluntary workers. This Committee should be responsible for planning and review of implementation of developmental programmes in this area. In particular, it should approve the draft annual plan of the project before it is submitted to the State Government for being incorporated in the draft annual sub-plan of the State. This Committee should review the progress of implementation of programmes regularly. Implementation, however, must be unequivocally the function of the Project Authority;

The Project Authority should be made responsible without any further delay, for implementation of total development programmes within its area of jurisdiction;

The State Governments should place the total outlay meant for the project area at the disposal of the Concerned Project Authority; and

The Project Authorities should be delegated adequate administrative and financial powers for sanction of schemes and their implementation.

The block administration should have a clear linkage with the administration at the project level forming an integral part of the chain of command between the State and the village;

There should be horizontal integration of administration at the block level also, as was the case earlier, on the same lines as is now envisaged at the Project-level;

The block Committees should be responsible for planning and review of implementation while implementation should be responsibility of the administration under the guidance of the Project Authority.

The personnel working in the tribal area may be suitably compensated financially according to a graded scale, the quantum depending on inaccessibility, lack of social services and other factors such as unhealthiness of place of posting.

Adequate physical facilities should be provided for personnel working in these areas.

Adequate financial provisions should be made as envisaged in the First Proviso to Article 275(1) of the Constitution, by the State and the Central Government jointly for meeting the cost of schemes as above taking into account the devolution for that purpose, if any, by the Finance Commission and specific provisions made by the Planning Commission.

A system should be evolved to ensure longer tenures and greater continuity in the higher and middle levels of administration in States having sizeable tribal areas. Sub-cadres of personnel, with the liability to serve for a longer tenure in the tribal areas, may be constituted in important cadres of States having sizeable tribal population.

Preference should be given to candidates from local areas in regional and district level cadres. Minimum qualifications may be reduced for local tribal candidates in those areas where level of education is not high. Special measures may be taken to induct local personnel in departments like Revenue, Police, Forest and Education. They may be put through suitable training programmes.

A system of review should be introduced at the project, regional and State levels so that those unsuitable for working in these areas may be weeded out.

Placement policies for these areas should ensure that persons of right quality are posted and knowledge of tribals dialects must be made essential or desirable in suitable cases.

Implementation of personnel policy in the tribal areas may be specially reviewed periodically at the State and the national level for which Standing Committees may be set-up.

Unconventional methods may be adopted for attracting experienced persons in various fields to work in modest positions in the tribal areas protecting their emoluments and giving recognition for their work. The service rules may be suitably changed for this purpose.

The professional institutions may be directly approached to attract young graduates for working in the tribal areas.

A qualitative change should be brought about in the administrative structure at the contact point with the people so that a relationship of confidence and mutual respect can develop.

The village panchayat or the head man may be formally recognised as a point of reference for grievances of people in all their dealings with the administration in this area. The senior officer, while on tour, should have a dialogue with them and settle outstanding issues on the spot.

The village panchayats may be given the responsibility for overseeing all developmental activities in the village and implementation of selected programmes.

A new concept of extension work may be introduced with selection of one tribal cultivator in each village to be intensively trained with reference to programmes and problems of the village. The number of higher technical personnel may be increased and that of lower functionaries reduced. The selected cultivators may be paid moderate allowance for meeting the incidental expenses connected with the new responsibility. A similar approach may be adopted in other fields of extension, as well.

There should be greater association and involvement of social scientists in planning and implementation. Knowledge of local dialects should be compulsory for all and in suitable cases, an essential condition for recruitment.

The voluntary organisations and local tribal institutions should be assigned an important place in the scheme of development of the tribal areas particularly in relation to creation of new awareness and building up inner strength in the community. They may be assigned specific tasks according to local situations.

Central Level

In each Ministry a senior officer may be appointed for exclusively attending to the work relating to tribal areas without any further loss of time. Whenever necessary, he may be given suitable staff support.

Officers dealing with tribal development work in the Central Ministries should have the background of working in tribal areas and they should visit these areas frequently.

Inter-ministerial teams should have a schedule of visit to the projects so as to cover each project at least once in a Five Year Plan Period.

A panel of representatives of voluntary organisations and those working in the tribal areas may be prepared in each State. Persons from these panels may be associated with the visiting teams to the projects.

The departmental procedures and rules may be critically reviewed and suitably modified in relation to matters concerning tribal areas and tribal development.

A convention should be developed that matters relating to tribal development will get top priority. They should be treated as a separate category and their processing and disposal should be specially reviewed by the Chief Secretary.

Training

A comprehensive orientation programme may be drawn up for-(a) personnel at policy formulation level, (b) executive officers at the project and district level, and (c) personnel in the field at grass-root level. The content, structure and intensity of the programme may be worked out specifically for each of these groups.

Development of backward classes, including tribal development, should be a full subject in all entry-training programmes of State, Central and All India Services. In the case of a Forest Officers and all services in States having sizeable tribal population, tribal development should be a full subject covering one or two papers.

The Training Division in the Department of Personnel should have Tribal Development as a speciality in Development Administration. The Tribal Research and Training Institute, Madhya Pradesh, may be developed as a national centre providing leadership and support in development of curriculum and reading material to other Institutions in the country.

The training of tribal leaders may be interspersed with the training of personnel at various levels.

Member-training of Co-operatives may become the starting point of the movement for creating awareness amongst the people about the various problems of transition and development. The National Co-operative Union of India may assume the responsibility for coordinating and guiding this programme in its wider form.

A special unit may be seated in the N.U.C.I. for this purpose. They should draw upon the findings of researches being conducted in various institutions in the country developing training programmes relevant to the local situation and re-orienting the trainers suitably. The N.U.C.I. should be make use of all the existing institutions concerned with extension located in the sub-plan area for imparting this training.

Planning Support and Monitoring

A planning cell may be seated for each group of 5-6 ITDPs for taking up micro-level project planning on a continuing basis.

At the State level, the Tribal Research Institutes may be strengthened to build up expertise in planning, rural economics and statistics.

A monitoring cell should be established in the various departments and a strong cell may be created to support the Tribal Commissioner at the State Level.

Block Level Planning

With the finalisation of ITDPs planning at the block level may now be initiated within the overall ITDP frame. A phased programme for block level planning to cover all the blocks in the current plan may be prepared.

Areas with high proportion of landless tribals and such other problems may be taken up in the first phase.

Rationalisation of Blocks

The Community Development Blocks included under the sub-plan may be reorganised into smaller block units adopting norm similar to those for the T.D. Blocks.

Regional Plans

A long-term perspective for the development of tribal areas keeping in view their resource potential socio-economic constraint and compulsions of national economy may be urgently prepared with a view to enable the tribal community becoming a partner in the developmental process. The medium-term plans should be suitably dovetailed in this long-term perspective.

Regional plans for three tribal regions in the middle India may be prepared, which may, *inter alia* (a) work out a long-term perspective for their development, (b) provide a frame for big individual investments which at present are almost autonomous, (c) work out an action programme for next medium-term plan keeping in view the resources available from the State plans, and (d) suggest methods to supplement them for implementing a minimum programme. A suitable group may be set-up for this purpose by the Planning Commission.

Problem of Uneven Growth

The Government of India may examine the problems arising from differential rate of development-educational and economic—of different tribal communities in the country and adopt measures so that the lesser advanced communities are protected and they can also partake in the benefits reserved for the tribal communities as a whole. This question may be remitted to a inter disciplinary group for detailed study.

Administration of Scheduled Areas

The fifth Schedule Areas should be rationalised in the remaining three States as early as possible.

The provisions of the Fifth Schedule, as complementary to the sub-plan mechanism, may be fully utilised for toning up the administration of these areas and for effective implementation.

The Union Government should assume a positive role in relation to the administration of these regions.

A Central legislation may be enacted for providing a broad frame for good administration of these regions.

A Cabinet sub-committee may be constituted which may oversee the pace of development of scheduled areas and communities on the continuing basis.

Governor's Report and Tribes Advisory Councils

The Governor's Report to the President regarding administration of the Scheduled Areas should be comprehensive and deal specially with the action taken by the State Government for the peace and good, government of the Scheduled Areas as also raising the level of administration of these areas during the period covered by the report.

The scope of the Governor's report may be expanded to cover tribal development programmes in general even outside the Scheduled Areas. Suitable amendments may be made in clause (iii) of the Fifth Schedule for this purpose the Governor's Report thereafter may be obtained from all States having tribal population.

Tribes Advisory Councils may be set-up in all States having Scheduled Tribe population for which the President may consider giving suitable directions under clause (iv) of the Fifth Schedule.

Annual Report by Central Ministries

Each Central Ministry should prepare forth with a position paper on the tribal areas based on available information in relation to their respective sectors. An independent chapter in their Annual Reports should, deal with the efforts made by them for tribal development. The Ministry of Home Affairs should provide a comprehensive annual review of the administration of scheduled areas and tribal development which may be an independent but companion volume of their annual report.

Special Regulation

Regulations under the Fifth Schedule, or where necessary a central law, may be made for providing effective protection to the tribal in all his new relationships with the modern economy and administration. In particular (a) matters relating to land, (b) credit and marketing, (c) employment and working conditions, and (d) conduct of civil servants should be specially covered. Suitable provision may also be made for promotion and protection of tribals interests in new economic activities.

Administration of Justice

The administration of Justice relating to smaller matters may be simplified in the tribal areas.

Certain offences like ordinary disputes, petty thefts including cattle thefts, matrimonial offences, etc., and offences against the local community like insult of women, may be taken out of the purview of the ordinary courts.

Special speedy trial courts may be consisting with jury from the local community who may sit in notified Central villages. Their procedure should be summary and no pleaders should be allowed.

The fees chargeable by the pleaders in all cases should be regulated with a penal provision for overcharging.

A Standing Council for Tribals may be appointed in each district having a sizeable tribal population with the status of an Additional Government Pleader.

Review of Laws

The existing laws should be reviewed by the concerned State in relation to their extension, or otherwise, to the scheduled areas as earlier recommended by the Scheduled Areas and Tribes Commission. This review may be completed within one year.

Panchayati Raj

The predominantly tribal area in a district, comprising Integrated Tribal Development Projects, should be treated as a distinct tier in the Panchayati Raj institutional set-up.

The project level body should have full powers in relation to the matters in that area. The district authority may have discretion to refer back some matters, but the decision of the project level body after reconsideration should be final.

The representation of the tribals in these bodies should not be less than their proportion in the population. The positions of chairman and other important office-bearers should be reserved in their favour.

The implementation should be the undivided responsibility of the administration. The Project Committees, however, should have full powers in relation to planning and overseeing of implementation.

The traditional tribal Panchayats at the village level may be recognised as a part of the system. They should have under their jurisdiction all matters of the village including the new development functions. They may be allowed to evolve their own methods of working.

In the *gram panchayats,* covering a group of villages half the members may be inducted from traditional village panchayats, the remaining half being elected. The functions of *gram panchayats* in the tribal areas may be wider and cover some of the functions of traditional *panchayats* as well.

Financial Investment and its Consolidation

The total outlays for tribal sub-plans may be worked out in the first instance keeping in view the area, population and level of their development.

Inter-sectoral priorities for tribal sub-plans may be determine with reference to their specific problems.

Contribution of Central Ministries

Sectoral Working Groups may review broadly the situation in the tribal areas and identify certain major schemes which would require substantial supplementation by the Central Government.

The Central Ministries may determine the possible supplementation which could reasonably be expected from their plans for the key programmes. The Ministry of Home Affairs and Planning Commission may take a view about further supplementation of concerned sectors through special Central Assistance.

The Central Ministries may also identify schemes which may have to be taken up as Centrally-sponsored or as joint programmes in these areas.

In particulars shifting cultivation programme, horticulture, minor and medium irrigation, soil conservation, pasture and cattle development, social forestry, elementary and adult education, improving the quality of higher education, even geographical distribution of health services, drinking water rural road and rural electrification should be specially considered by the concerned Ministries for special supplementation.

The staff requirements for various schemes supported by the Central Ministries or State Plans should not be worked out separately. They should be assessed for the entire programme in an ITDP. Wherever, necessary the Special Central Assistance may be provided for meeting the cost of the staff component by the Ministry of Home Affairs.

A large number of projects should be prepared for tribal areas which may be economically viable and capable of being supported by institutional finance.

A suitable scheme may also be prepared to attract institutional finance for starting socially useful construction and other building infrastructure.

Financial Outlay for 1978-83

The minimum investment in the tribal areas during the medium plan years 1978-83 should be of the order of Rs. 3,000 crores comprising about Rs. 1,850 crores from State Plans and Rs. 500 crores from Central Ministries Plans, Rs. 300 crores from the Institutional finance and Rs. 350 crores special Central Assistance.

The bulk of investment for agriculture and allied sectors programmes should be provided from the sectoral plan in the State and the Centre reducing their dependence on special Central Assistance to the minimum. Education should get the highest priority in resource allocation out of special Central Assistance.

The classification of sub-plan outlays may be closely reviewed so as to evolve a uniform practice in all states making the figures of investment comparable.

Consolidation of Investments

Consolidation of assets and full utilisation of the organisational capacity already, created in the tribal areas should be the first priority in any scheme of development in these areas.

The Government of India, in consultation with the State Governments, may take up a review of level of administration of the tribal areas and suitable schemes may be prepared for upgrading it within a reasonable time frame. This review should be taken up annually and adequate out lays for items not cover otherwise, under the plan for devolution by the Finance Commission, should be provided under the First Proviso to Article 275(1).

A suitable mechanism for ensuring non-divertibility of plan outlays for tribal areas may be worked out.

The outlays for tribal sub-plans should be Treated as non-lapsable during a Five Year Plan span. A convention may by accepted to allow additional budget allocation in the first supplementary of the following year equivalent to the shortfall in the previous year. Alternatively, the practice adopted in Maharashtra of converting the unspent balance into securities to be utilised in the following years may be adopted.

A practice may be started that all programmes in each project in a year may be shown at one place in a supplement to the State budget and, as far as possible, all sub-plan schemes get incorporated in the State Budget fully scrutinised.

A suitable procedure may be worked out by the Government of India, for consolidating the total State effort at the project level, both plan and non-plan, so that investments from all yield sources optimum results in terms of the basic objectives of our national effort.

Basic Needs of Tribal Communities

In view of the destabilising factors operating in the tribal areas, a concept of basic needs should be accepted for these regions which, besides existing minimum needs programme, should include food and housing.

The areas with depleted resources and in inadequate food supply should be identified in which a massive sustained programme should be taken up which creates tangible assets, augments the local food supply and generate adequate income to enable the tribal to attain a reasonable level of consumption.

The requirement of local community including housing material should be the first consideration in forestry and associated programme. The working plans, *nistar* schemes, plantation programmes, social forestry schemes, etc., should be suitably reviewed so that these needs become a first charge on them and adequate potential is created for the sustained supply of necessary materials to satisfy local demand.

In those areas where natural resources are still plentiful, but new intrusion has begun, effective protective measures should be taken so that there is no encroachment on the tribals command over resources.

The general norms for minimum needs programme may be relaxed for the tribal areas keeping in view the sparseness of population and difficult terrain. In particular, the following norms may be adopted for different programmes:

(a) There should be 100 per cent coverage of children in the age group 6–14. There should be a built-in provisions for higher non-teacher cost, establishment of Ashram Schools in sparsely populated areas, provision of hostel, adequate scholarship and stipend, mid-day meals, etc., in the educational programme to make the coverage real;

(b) All adults in the age group 15–35 may be covered in the next 10 years. The tribal communities with less than 5 per cent literacy rate, tribal communities with less than half the general literacy level of the tribals in the State and those communities which have shown a decline in literacy rate during 1961-71 may be taken first in that order;

(c) There should be one Primary Health Centre for every 20,000 population with distribution of medical personnel in such a manner that a qualified doctor is available within a radius of 15 km., one sub-centre for 3000 population and one community health worker in each village or a group of hamlets within a radius of 5 km.;

(d) Existing drinking water sources may be improved so as to make them fit for general use and provision of a drinking water source within one km. of each hamlet;

(e) Improvement of traditionally used communication network (bridle path, etc.) with provision of crossings on a priority basis and linking up of market places should be taken up in the first phase. All groups of village with population of 1,000 or more may be linked with all weather jeepable roads;

(f) Rural electrification programme should support irrigation projects, agricultural programmes, household industries and market centres. The Central Government may give suitable grants to make these schemes viable;

(g) Housing assistance should include making available local housing material to the tribals; and

(h) Mid-day meal should be provided to all the children in the age groups of 6 to 11 and supplementary feeding programmes for all under-nourished in the age group 0-6, pregnant women and nursing mothers.

Protective Measures

Excise Policy

Excise policy for tribal areas as evolved by the Government of India, should be implemented immediately abolishing vending of liquor in tribal region within this year.

A strict watch may be kept on those connected with liquor trade in the recent past so that they may not indulge in illegal activities.

Sustained social work should be undertaken with the help of voluntary organisations to wean the tribals away from the habit of drinking.

Land Alienation

The existing laws regulating the transfer of lands belonging to Scheduled Tribes should be reviewed urgently and all loopholes should be plugged to make them effective.

The State should become a party in the case of trespass or illegal alienation of tribal lands and summary procedures should be adopted for their restoration.

The areas of high incidence of land alienation in each State should be listed. Identification of alienated land and its restoration in these high incidence areas should be taken upon a campaign basis to be completed within a period of six months to a year.

In areas where the task of land restoration in sizeable and cannot be adequately handled by the normal revenue machinery, special machinery may be created for a limited period.

The progress of restoration of land should be reviewed regularly at the state level and also the national level.

The traditional concept of communal ownership with limited individual rights on land, wherever it is still in practice may be recognised.

A quick survey may be undertaken to ascertain their local practice in each area, in consultation with representatives of the people.

Suitable regulation may be made in the concerned States recognising communal ownership in the concerned areas.

Credit facility should be extended to tribals having rights in land under communal ownership, or limited ownership rights on land assigned to them for specific purpose, on the same terms as to other with full proprietorship rights. Suitable changes may be made in the existing instructions on the subject to the co-operatives as also to other financing institutions.

Credit facilities should be extended to tribals with limited ownership rights on the same term as to others with full proprietorship rights for which suitable institutional forms may be devised.

Agriculture and Allied Sectors

Special agricultural development programmes should be prepared for each agro-climatic tribal region under the overall guidance of the Ministry of Agriculture keeping in view their resource potential and present agronomical practices of the tribals.

A few selected items may be taken up in each region for intensive extension, adaptive research and extensive field trials in compact areas.

Dry farming practices and development of minor millets and other special crops of tribal areas should be taken up on a large scale.

Research support in agriculture and agro-forestry should be provided as a long-term programmes in various tribal regions. The Indian Council of Agricultural Research should have a cell for these areas which may also help in exchange of experience and dissemination of information. Similar role may be assumed by the Forest Research Institute, Dehradun, for Agro-forestry Programme.

Shifting Cultivation

A perspective may be prepared for resettlement of shifting cultivators in all those states having the problem of shifting cultivation within a maximum period of ten years.

A comprehensive programme of re-settlement should be prepared for each specific area for which inter-disciplinary teams may be constituted to work on a continuing basis.

A specific part of the outlay on agriculture and allied sectors should be set apart for development of shifting cultivators besides which a nucleus amount, as gap-filler, may also be provided for this purpose.

The outlay may be kept at the disposal of the concerned Integrated Tribal Development Project Authorities for implementation of approved comprehensive development programme.

A high level Expert Committee may be set-up in each of these States and at the Centre, which may provide technical support as also constantly review the programmes of shifting cultivation.

Irrigation

A master plan of irrigation development in the tribal areas including flow irrigation (major, medium and minor) lift irrigation and ground water development should be prepared within the next one year.

Investigation of all minor irrigation projects and lift irrigation schemes may be completed within the next year or two in all the States.

A clear time schedule should be prepared for development of this potential through execution of various schemes.

All the existing irrigation works should be put to use by improving them within the next one year. The renovation of existing tanks should be given the highest priority in allocation of resources. Their regular maintenance may be taken up by the Irrigation departments where other satisfactory arrangement do not exist.

The Department of Irrigation may coordinate and guide the entire package of irrigation programmes in the tribal areas at the centre.

While preparing master plan for irrigation areas with growing pressure of population and limited agricultural land should be identified for taking up irrigation on a priority basis.

In each project priority should be fixed, *inter se* for each type of irrigation projects, flow irrigation getting a higher priority, followed by lift irrigation on open water sources and groundwater development.

Small irrigation wells should be taken up in a big way where there is a good chance of having groundwater.

There should be no limit about the size of holding for taking up small irrigation wells. This facility should be extended to all, who are willing to construct a well.

The rules and conditions of the co-operatives and other institutions should be suitably modified.

The risk involved in unsuccessful well should be fully covered by the State.

The displaced tribals should be rehabilitated not as individuals but as a community, as far as possible. Advance planning by sensitive officers specially charged with this task should be done. Additional financial, expenditure may also be provided wherever necessary.

The displaced persons should be given alternative land in the command of irrigation projects by acquiring and redistributing adequate land from potential beneficieries. Suitable legal measures may be taken for this purpose.

About 20 per cent of the water in a river basin may be reserved for minor irrigation and lift irrigation schemes in the upper reaches of the catchment area to be developed in the due course.

Development of the land and field channels should be a part of irrigation projects.

Water should be provided free for the first 3-years without agreement and the water rates should be gradually increased to reach the normal level in a period of another three years.

Intensive extension support should be provided for new irrigated land in the tribal areas.

The irrigation rates in the tribal areas from all sources should not be more than the normal flow irrigation rates in the State. The structure of the irrigation rates in the tribal areas may be reviewed urgently and revised in accordance with this principle.

The repayment liability of the tribal in irrigation schemes should start only after irrigation begins. The risk liability for any failures should be borne by the Project Authority or the cooperative for which a suitable scheme may be prepared.

Areas with good pastures resources should be identified around which substantial cattle development and dairy programme should be developed.

Broad perspective should be prepared for dairy, piggery, poultry, goatry, pisciculture, keeping in view the local resources potential of different tribal areas. Selected programmes may be taken up in each project on a substantial scale.

That in the animal husbandry programme may be specifically tailored to the landless labourers and marginal farmers who may be provided land for growing fodder trees as has been done in the scheme of Bhartiya Agro-Industries Foundation.

The animal husbandry programmes should be so planned that they are within the management capacity of an average tribal. They should aim at augmenting the local diet and should be linked to the local nutritional programme so that production marketing circuit is complete within a village or in a small number of village around.

Fisheries Development

Fisheries programme should be taken up extensively in the tribal areas control of formal institutions in the new programme should be confined to bigger water sources only. The Government may help the village community, both financially and technically, in improving their tanks, adopting new pisciculture practices and maintaining the assets according to their traditional customs with the objective of augmenting the dietary status of the community.

Forestry

Comprehensive plans may be prepared for all integrated tribal development projects with sizeable forest area in which tribal development and forestry development should be two co-equal goals. In forest-rich regions, forestry-oriented tribal development programmes may be prepared in which agriculture could occupy a secondary position. The reformulation of developmental and forestry schemes in all ITDPs may be taken up urgently and completed within the next one year so that the new policy can be reflected in the medium-term project plans for 1978-83.

The basic needs of the tribal economy should be provided on a priority basis as part one in all forestry plans whether conventional intensive or commercial. The second part of these plans could be decided on the basis of other relevant considerations in each case.

The Commercial Forestry Programmes should be taken up only after fully considering their implications to the local tribal economy. There may be preparatory stage in all programmes for the more backward areas. The development of the tribals in the zone of influence of intensive economic programmes should be a part of the project. All existing forestry projects and special projects should be reviewed within a year and suitably adopted so that necessary supplemental investments are provided in the medium plans for 1978-83.

A programme of large scale plantation should be taken up with the help of tribals giving them right on the trees planted by them in assigned areas and their usufruct.

In all future departmental plantation programmes there should be an adequate mix of fruit trees and others spices useful to the local tribal economy.

The tribal should have full rights on minor forest produce and remunerative prices should be fixed for their collection without charging any royalty. The purchase of minor forest produce should be organised through cooperatives eliminating the middle-man within one year.

All forestry operations should be executed through the cooperatives of forest labourers which should be encouraged by the forest department and organised by the Tribal Welfare Department. The cooperatives should be given a share in the profits accruing to the State from those operations. A phased programme should be prepared so as to complete this switchover within two to three years.

Minimum wages should be fixed for all operations undertaken by the forest department, directly or through the contractors, which should not be lower than the minimum agricultural wages.

The Tribal living in the forest villages should be given inheritable but inalienable rights over the land which they cultivate without any further loss of time in those State where this is not already done. All social and economic developmental programme should be extended to these villages on the some lines as for residents in other villages.

Horticulture

Horticulture should be taken up as a major programme in the tribal areas.

Food for Work

Selected economic programmes for the weakest sections of the community, through addressed to the individual, should quality for assistance under the schemes like food for work on the same term as community schemes.

Consolidational of Institutions

The institutional support for agricultural and allied activities in the tribal areas should be multi-purpose in character.

The working of existing institutions should be reviewed immediately by Project Committees and they should be put to maximum use by providing missing inputs and adding supplementary specialisations, if necessary.

These institutions should also be responsible for extension in surrounding villages so that there can be useful mutual interaction.

The institutional network in agriculture and allied sectors may be planned at State level keeping in view the programme profiles for the next medium-term plan for each areas.

Orientation and Adaptation

A conscious effort may be made to understand the local practices and functioning of the kinship and community power structure in the tribal areas and technical personnel should be suitably reoriented.

Only those programmes may be taken up in the tribal areas which are within the management and risk-taking capacity of tribals. All programmes should be suitably reformulated.

Training of beneficiaries should be an integral part of every programme requiring higher skills for maintenance or management.

Women should also be drawn into the training programmes. One young couple per village may be intensively trained and the entire sub-plan area should be covered in five years. Suitable institutions for this purpose may be developed which may grow into referal point for the concerned area in agriculture and allied subjects.

Integration of Programmes at ITDP Level

All special programmes taken up in the sub-plan area should be interwoven within the Integrated Tribal Development frame.

Wherever necessary, specific conditions may be prescribed for utilisation of outlays in keeping with the objective of concerned sectoral programme. The sponsoring authority should be satisfied if the envisaged level of investment in relevant programmes and/or for specified target-group is ensured in the concerned ITDP.

The Project Authorities should have a strong accounting cell, which may monitor the flow of funds from a variety of sources for different purposes and advise the Project Authorities on financial matters.

Credit and Marketing

The establishment of large size multi-purpose societies should be completed on a high priority basis where this has not been done so far.

There should be no duplication of structure with the establishment of the LAMPS. The service points already established in the remote areas should not be discontinued with the establishment of the LAMPS and they should be maintained by suitable institutional arrangement within the new societies.

There should be one credit institution at the secondary level in the tribal areas catering to short-term, medium-term, long-term, as well as consumption credit requirements. So long as there are more than one institution, the large sized multi-purpose societies should at act the local branch of all institutions in the transitional period. All large size multi-purpose societies in an ITDP area should be linked to one financing institution only.

The large size multi-purpose societies should form a federation like the Tribal Development Corporation which should gradually provide full support to these institutions for all their non-credit functions other State level organisations should operate in the tribal areas through this federation providing the benefit of their organisational support and expertise in their respective fields. The Tribal Cooperation Federation may have a branch at the project or the district level according to the need of each area so as to cater to the requirements of the federating units in that region.

The NAFED should provide support to State level tribal cooperative federations in marketing of all agricultural and minor forest produce. There should be a unit in the NAFED for attending exclusively to the marketing problems of the tribal areas.

The Reserve Bank of India may refinance consumption credit advances to the tribals by the Central Financing Agencies.

There should be special regulations for weekly markets in the tribal areas so as to give effective control of the management of these markets to the community in its catchment.

The weekly markets should not be auctioned and there should be no levy of any kind, whatsoever, on the tribals bringing small commodities for sale.

The trading in the tribal areas, outside the towns, may be subject to a licence by the competent authority. A regular system of inspection may be introduced to bring their activities under administrative control.

The tribal cooperative societies may be provided adequate credit for marketing finance by the Central Co-operative Banks and Reserve Bank of India at a concessional rate of interest.

All Block headquarters in the tribal areas should be treated as rail heads.

The transportation cost beyond these points may be pooled so that uniform prices prevail at all the outlets. This cost could also be suitably subsidised for more inaccessible regions by the government.

For certain important commodities the purchase and sale prices should be fixed for a period. Except for wide fluctuations, minor variation in prices may be absorbed by cooperative structure. The maximum price of some commodities like salt should be fixed for the entire tribal area in each State.

There should be no separate co-operative for special purpose like marketing of a specific commodity or consumer co-operative which should be covered by the LAMPS. The national scheme for the special co-operative may be suitably amended in which the LAMPS may be deemed to perform those functions and may be eligible for assistance for that sector of their activity under the scheme.

The separate co-operatives may be constituted where the specific activity is big in size or so specialised that it cannot be handled by the normal primary co-operative system. The processing cooperatives may be linked to the primary cooperatives as their ancillary activity so that the benefit of processing can be passed on to the primary producer.

The National Co-operative Development Cooperation should provide guidance to the co-operative movement in the tribal areas in all its aspects. The National Cooperative Development Cooperation should become the nodal point at the national level coordinating functions relateable to all other organisations at the national level.

Debt Redemption

All individual cases of overdues may be reviewed urgently and credit channel be opened, in favour of those individuals who claim no overdues.

Action may be taken to write off the overdues in case their claims get established.

A committee may be constituted at the project level which should oversee this review and complete it within a year.

Differential Rate of Interest

The benefit of the differential rate of interest scheme should be extended to the tribals through the network of reorganised cooperatives.

A certain amount under the DRI scheme may be earmarked for the tribal areas.

Certain selected priority production programmes may be eligible for being funded under differential rate of interest scheme.

The Reserve Bank of India may extend credit to the co-operative system at a concessional rate of interest of about one to two per cent so that the entire agricultural credit in the tribal areas can be advanced to the tribals at four per cent interest.

Industries and Allied Sectors

The traditional craftsmen and artisans in the tribal areas should be identified urgently and specific family based programmes should be prepared for these groups. The programmes should aim at building up their existing expertise.

There should be a linkage with national and international market for the tribal products through existing established institutions.

A provision should also be made for earmarking certain percentage of the total cost of new buildings, etc., in the tribal areas to be used for purchase of local arts and crafts.

Those village and household industries programmes, which have got a good potential in the tribal areas, should be identified. Perspective should be prepared for each of those programmes. The programmes should be taken up jointly by the national organisations and the projects, the former being responsible for overall direction, technical and marketing support, while the latter should be responsible for programme competent at the ground level.

Tusser development should be a major programme in Central Indian tribal regions and a long-term perspective for its development with clear targets for the medium term plan should be prepared urgently under the guidance of the Central Silk Board.

First processing of all minor forest produce should be done within the tribal areas and, as far as possible, through the co-operatives of primary producers.

A plan for establishing necessary processing capacity for important items should be prepared immediately. The programme should be spread over a period of two to three years for which adequate financial support should be provided on a priority basis.

Modern Industry

Comprehensive planning of zone of influence of industrial and mining complexes, both existing and the new ones, should be taken up on a priority basis immediately.

The Bureau of Public Enterprises may assume the leadership role in this regard and in the first instance take stock of the existing units, both in the public and private sectors, in these areas as also the likely new units to be set up in the next 10-15 years.

The Government of India may take necessary legal power for prior consultation before a big industry or other intensive economic scheme is cleared for the tribal areas.

The development of the zones of influence of industrial and mining complexes should be a joint responsibility of the project and the local government both of them assuming a positive role in this common endeavour. Suitable supplementation may be provided by the Government of India. A scheme of financing those programmes may be decided in each case depending on the local situation.

A Standing Committee may be set-up in the Government of India comprising the representatives of the Home Ministry, Bureau of Public Enterprises, Planning Commission, Ministry of Labour and Ministry of Industrial Development for overseeing the planning of these regions and guiding their harmonious development. This committee may be serviced by the Bureau of Public Enterprises.

An aggressive programme for inducting tribals at higher skilled level should be taken up in areas having industrial enterprises. A scheme may be prepared in which part of the cost of employment of tribals at skilled level may be met by the Government.

Industrially Backward Areas

All the scheduled areas, excluding the industrially advanced pockets, should be declared as industrially backward areas and all concessions and facilities admissible to industrially backward districts should be extended to them.

Industrial Training Institute

The Ministry of Labour may review the existing training arrangements in the ITIs in the tribal areas in association with the Bureau of Public Enterprises and the concerned State Governments.

Arrangements may be made for active participation of industrial undertakings in guiding the training in the ITIs functioning in their regions.

ITI courses may be suitably adapted to meet the requirements of the industrial undertakings. They may also start special course, wherever necessary.

Entrepreneurial Training

A big enough programme of entrepreneurial development should be taken up independently or, as a part of technical training programmes according to the local conditions.

Scheme should be prepared to help the trainees to establish a small traders, repair establishment owners and independent artisans for which financial support, directly or through financial institutions, marketing link-up both for raw materials and final products, etc., should be worked out.

Migrant Labour

Those areas which contribute to a large seasonal migrant labour may be identified in the States.

A programme of providing a modest advance and guidance during the period of migration, ensuring a reasonable wage for the work done, should be taken up for all these groups on a a priority basis under the Integrated Tribal Development Projects.

Social Services

The welfare needs of the tribal communities, particularly in the area of influences which are having alienating or disintegrating effect on their society should be assessed by the States as early as possible. This aspect should be given special attention in the tribal sub-plans and Integrated Tribal Development Projects, 1978-83.

Education

Education in tribal areas should be given the highest priority.

The entire package of services for education at the elementary level should be provided as a part of the educational plan.

Certain innovative institutional forms may be adopted in the special areas like sub-schools, pre-primary-cum-primary institutions, elementary school complexes and residential schools in the sparsely populated areas.

The schools timings, as also vacations, should be fixed in the tribal areas with reference to the local conditions which may be at variance with the timings and vacations in the State or in the region.

Non-formal and adult education should be planned as complementary to formal education. Citizen education should be assigned a special place in the educational scheme in the tribal areas.

The structural imbalance at the middle and higher secondary school levels should be removed expeditiously.

Improving the quality of education should new claim special attention in the areas where the institutional network is well spared.

The administration of education in the tribal areas should be rationalised and the responsibility should rest with the Education Department.

Sports should be an important part of educational curriculum in the tribal areas. Hand picked boys should be groomed for national and international events in selected fields.

In the States having substantial tribal population there should be a separate resource unit for attending to the educational problems of the tribal areas on a continuing basis. There should be a strong unit in the NCERT at the Centre for this purpose.

Peace-setting colleges may be set-up in compact tribal regions with the help of the UGC and collaboration of other universities.

Some girls schools with teachers training wing may be set-up in selected areas.

Priority should be given to low literacy pockets in establishing new schools and providing special incentives to children in case there is constraint of resources.

Special educational plans may be prepared for areas with intensive economic activity like hinterland of industrial and mining complexes.

Health Services

A strong unit in the AIIMS may be set-up for tackling the problems of primitive tribal groups in the country. All necessary support should be provided by them for this essential humane programme.

The identification of special health problem in the tribal areas should be taken up under the guidance of the Ministry of Health and completed in one year. Effective programmes for meeting these problems should be incorporated in the current plan.

The post of more than one doctor with a PHC should be optimally utilised by posting one doctor each at the HQ and selected sub-centres. The para-medical staff may be re-allocated wherever necessary housing at the sub-centre should be provided on a priority basis.

Adequate provision should be made for medicines so as to provide them free to all tribal patients. There should be a visitor's shed attached to all PHC's for the relatives of in-door patients.

Family Planning

In the tribal areas family welfare approach should be adopted instead of family planning approach. The programme for each area should be specifically worked out keeping in view the demographic structure of that area. The targets, if any, for the tribal areas should be fixed separately after taking into account all the relevant factors specifying the sub-targets for each regions.

Nutrition

A nutritional survey of tribal areas may be taken up urgently to assess their present nutrition standards and identify the areas of high deficiency.

The first concern in all the production programmes in the tribal areas should be to upgrade the nutritional status the individual. The various production programmes should suitably be adapted in these areas.

The high cost of the delivery system of nutritional services should be reduced by entrusting the implementation of programmes to the local community who may be allowed to evolve their own methods of working.

Important elements of integrated child care service programmes should be incorporated in the Integrated Tribal Development Projects so that these can be a quicker and wider coverage of nutritional services in the tribal areas.

Social Security

Special aggressive welfare programmes may be taken up around industrial and mining complexes and growing urban centres in the tribal areas.

Drinking Water

The unit of planning for drinking water supply for the tribal areas may be a hamlet. A source of drinking water should be provided to all hamlets in the next five years.

Town Planning

A special programmes may be taken up for planning emerging towns and growth centres in the tribal areas.

A provision should be made under an appropriate scheme for inducing settlement of tribals from the surrounding areas by providing some facilities to them in these centres.

Infra-structural Development

The basic road network in the tribal areas should be established after identifying the missing links and crossings which should be taken up on a high priority basis in the concerned Central or State level programmes.

All administrative headquarters up to the block level should be connected on a priority basis in the next couple of years.

Crossings of various types on road of different description, from foot-path and mule-track on the one extreme to district and state roads on the other, should be given highest priority for improving a accessibility throughout the year in the tribal areas.

All weather road links, with appropriate specifications and phasing, should be established with headquarters of a large size multi-purpose societies or weekly markets, so that they become accessible throughout the year within the next two years at the most.

The above network may be further extended to reach the subhealth centres making the accessible throughout the year in the course of next three to four years.

The road plan should fix a time frame for all-weather accessibility to the administrative headquarters, weekly markets and sub-centres according to which construction plan of the roads should be phased out.

The State Governments may work out the financial outlays necessary for executing the road plan of the tribal areas according to the stipulated time schedule.

Telecommunication

A separate plan for telecommunication development should be prepared for the tribal areas.

All administrative centres up to block level and headquarters of large size multi-purpose societies may be provided telecommunication links on a priority basis.

Those villages, which are centres of new industrial activity like a cluster of village industries or which provide a service point for an intensive agricultural development programme may be next in the order of priority.

The telecommunication network may be so planned that no village is beyond 10 to 40 kms. from the nearest point depending on the density of population in that area.

Railways

All the existing railway lines in the tribal areas should be opened to passenger traffic.

A perspective plan for development of railways in the tribal areas should be prepared. The financial norms in these cases may be suitably relaxed, waving the requirements of return on the capital investment on new lines in these areas.

Rural Electrification

The viability norms of rural electrification schemes in the tribal areas may be suitably modified. The Government of India may provide a part of the investment by the Electricity Boards in the more backward areas as subsidy so that the electrification may reach the far off points as well.

The schemes of rural electrification involving subsidy by the Central Government should be cleared on project by project basis ensuring appropriate linkage between rural electrification and economic activity.

All the tribal areas in the country should qualify for special treatment by the Central Government for extension of rural electrification irrespective of the level of development of the rural electrification in the concerned state.

Primitive Groups

High priority should be given to the programme of primitive groups in the current plan. Voluntary organisations should be associated in an increasing measure in these programmes.

Adequate flexibility should be built into these programmes by adopting society models where not already done.

Selected persons, if necessary on negotiated special terms may be posted for working amongst the primitive tribes. Senior officers willing to serve in modest positions amongst these groups may also be allowed to work by giving special terms.

Special regulations may be urgently framed for ensuring continued traditional command on their resources of the primitive tribal communities like Abujmarias, Bondo Parajas, Onges and Jarwas, and for protecting them from encroachment by the stronger groups.

Dispersed Tribals

The tribal development programmes for dispersed tribals outside the sub-plan area should be built on the general rural development programme in the concerned block.

In each block the total investment in favour of tribal communities should be earmarked on the basis of their proportion in the population with some weightage.

The tribal development programme may be wider in coverage and may include education, health, nutrition, etc., as also protective measures. The package of economic programmes for the tribals may be worked out keeping in view their economic base, adapting the general programmes and preparing special programmes, wherever necessary, particularly for tribal artisans.

A separate chapter may deal with tribal development in the block-level integrated rural development project. The Project Officer may be assisted by a Tribal Development Associate in planning and coordinating these programmes.

The supplementation for meeting the additional cost of relaxed norms and special programmes may be provided out of the provisions of the welfare of Backward Classes Sector.

The total outlays for tribal development under the welfare of Backward Classes sector in the State Plan may be utilised for dispersed tribals outside the sub-plan. The ongoing tribal development schemes in the current plan may be taken over by the general sector w.e.f. 1-4-79 after committing the relevant portion to the non-plan side.

3

COMMITTEE ON CONTROLS AND SUBSIDIES, 1978 — REPORT[1]
February 15, 1978 — May 14, 1979

Chairman Shri Vadilal Dagli

Members Shri Era Sezhiyan; Shri Bagaram Tulpule; Shri L.C. Jain; Shri Sanjoy Sen;

M. Secy. Dr. A.K. Ghosh

Appointment

The Government have decided to set-up a Committee to evaluate and review the system of controls on prices, production, distribution, licences and imports and to examine the manner in which they have been actually operated and whether or not the objectives sought to be achieved have actually been achieved. So the Government of India, Ministry of Finance (Department of Economic Affiars) constituted as Committee on Control and Subsidies Vide Resolution No. F.23011/2/78-Admn. I dated February 15, 1978.

Terms of Reference

(i) Has the system of controls on prices, production, distribution, licences and imports been an effective instrument for national planning and guidance of the national economy?

(ii) What has been the experience in the past of the operation and management of all types of controls and have the pre-determined objectives actually been realised?

(iii) In which areas of the economy have the controls been successful and hence deserve continuance with or without modification?

1. Department of Economic Affairs, Ministry of Finance, Government of India, New Delhi, May, 1979, 2 parts.

(iv) In which areas have the controls been ineffective or have since become irrelevant and hence deserve to be removed?

(v) In what manner is the system of controls connected to the system of subsidisation in the national economy? Are such subsidies justifiable and will it be possible to moderate or eliminate the system of subsidisation by suitable modifications in the system of controls?

Contents

Summary of Findings and Recommendations; Framework of Study; General Controls and Subsidies; Controls and Subsidies Pertaining to Specific Commodities/Sectors; General Issues and Alternatives; vol. II Annexures from 1.1 to 25.3; vol. III Appendices from 1 to 10.

Recommendations

1. **History of Controls and Subsidies** (Chapter 2)

Findings on Controls

(a) Many war-time controls which were devised to meet an emergency were gradually absorbed into a system devised to meet the needs of long term planning.
(b) At times the authorities instituting controls did not pay adequate attention to the machinery for the implementation of controls.
(c) There has been a multiplicity of controls to meet a multiplicity of objectives, and there have been instances when one set of controls has negated another set of controls, both separately conceived to achieve disparate objectives of policy.
(d) There have been occasions when the authorities imposing a control have just forgotten all about it, and the control has remained long after the need for it had been over.
(e) There has been of late an increase in "administrative" controls in lieu of clear-cut overt controls.

Findings on Subsidies

(a) Subsidies have grown substantially in magnitude as well as diversity lately.
(b) Nonetheless, many subsidies so designated are not of the nature

of subsidies at all.

(c) On the other hand, many new types of policy have led to the increase of covert subsidies.

(d) There have been three types of subsidies; direct subsidies given from the budget; cross subsidies without any budgetary implication where one set of consumers has subsidised others; and covert subsidies where the cost of a subsidy has been borne by the budget but not shown as such.

2. **Statutory Sanction** (Chapter 3)

Findings

(a) There is a lot of economic legislation on the statute book which today is *prima facie* out of date.

(b) The totality of economic controls in the economy encompasses, first, controls directly exercised under legislation; secondly, specific control orders issued thereunder; and finally, control notification is issued from time to time under enabling control orders or legislation.

(c) Over a period, there has been a plethora of notifications and amendments thereto, modifying the control system from time to time, but they have hardly even been consolidated and brought out in one comprehensive notification or updated control order.

(d) Apart from the legal jargon in which control orders are generally couched, the absence of any comprehensive updated version of the control system as it exists gives occasion for harassment and graft.

(e) The control system today has become so complex that even the executive authorities responsible for implementing the controls are unaware at senior levels of the exact control system which they have to implement.

(f) The Committee has been able to make only a beginning in the matter of the study of the extant controls in the Indian economy, as it has been able to example only a sample of the existing controls, and that this study cannot be deemed to be fully comprehensive or complete.

Recommendations

(1) All economic Ministries should examine all extant economic

legislation, to decide which of them are totally out of date and redundant and can therefore be removed from the statute books (Para 3.1.4).

(2) It should be a statutory requirement to update all controls at least on an annual basis, which could then be placed before Parliament for information (Para 3.2.7).

(3) In order to simplify the control system, where there is a multiplicity of control orders on the same item, unless there are strong reasons to do the contrary, the control orders should be consolidated and brought out under one comprehensive control order; it would, *inter alia*, remove the internal contradictions which may exist between divergent orders, and the control law would be made fully known to the people (Para 3.3.1).

(4) An attempt should also be made to consolidate and simplify all extant control orders (Para 3.2.2).

(5) Purely as a matter of convenience, all control notifications should be presented in a designated part of the Government Gazette, so that those who are concerned can easily study this document and get to know the control system as it exists (Para 3.2.1).

3. **Approach of the Committee** (Chapter 4)

Findings

(a) Over the years there have emerged two types of controls — promotional and corrective — to subserve long-term objectives and short-term exigencies respectively; and that controls initially imposed to meet short-term exigencies of the War have been continued thereafter in order to subserve the objectives of planning.

(b) There has also emerged a multiplicity of controls and control organisations to meet multiple objectives of policy, some controls tending to neutralise each other.

(c) As a result there has emerged a highly complex system of controls such that even the executive authorities are not always familiar with all the control orders and notifications, some of which have not been updated or brought together even for the last 30 years.

(d) In many areas, administrative controls as also informal controls have taken the place of formal or statutory controls.

(e) There has been an in-built tendency for the perpetuation of both controls and subsidies and to the proliferation of controls.

(f) Most of these controls have vested considerable discretionary powers on the control authorities.

(g) The system has as a result given scope for corruption in the administration of controls, the policy objectives being defeated owing to defective implementation.

(h) Controls have also led to considerable delays.

(i) Nonetheless both controls and subsidies have helped to promote a number of policy objectives.

(j) That in the context of the present inequal distribution of income and wealth and the imperfections of the market system in India, controls and subsidies are necessary in order to encourage or discourage certain types and forms of production and to provide support to certain categories of producers, and the consumption of certain sections of the population.

Recommendations

(1) All controls should be directed to meet the following objectives of policy:

 (a) That scarce national resources get directed to priority sectors as per national Plans and public policy;
 (b) that the basic consumption needs of the people are met, and in particular, the needs of the weaker sections of the society are provided at prices within their reach;
 (c) that disparities in income and wealth are reduced and undesirable concentration of power prevented;
 (d) that employment and income for large masses of people are protected by promoting the growth of the decentralised sector; and
 (e) that self-reliance is pursued by promoting technological capability, import substitution and exports in tune with the resource endowment of the country (Para 4.2.1).

(2) All controls and regulations should have a limited period of validity. Certain economic laws, even where these are enacted to direct the development of the economy in accord with the spirit of the Directive Principles of State Policy, need to be evaluated periodically, say, once every 5 years, and amended if necessary (Para 4.2.8).

(3) The second category of controls designed to meet temporary imbalances of one kind or the other should have a validity period of only 3 years at the most, at the end of which they should automatically lapse unless specifically extended (Para 4.2.9).

(4) All subsidies should similarly have a validity of no more than 3 years, and before any subsidy is extended beyond its stipulated life, a review of the cost and benefits of the subsidy should be placed before Parliament by the concerned Department administering the subsidy (Para 4.5.3).

(5) The target groups likely to benefit from any subsidy should be clearly identified, and the fact should be adequately publicised to ensure that the subsidies do reach the target group (Para 4.5.2).

(6) The subsidies should be overt, so that the costs and benefits thereof can be identified (Para 4.5.8).

(7) There should be a monitoring and reviewing system as part of any control mechanism (Para 4.2.10).

(8) Each control should be designed to assist or to protect, or to restrain or to discourage clearly defined target groups or specified areas of activity (Para 4.3.1).

(9) The control system should be simple and the points of control as few as possible (Para 4.3..2).

(10) Even where control is necessary as for instance for setting up industrial capacity, the final powers of approval should be vested with one authority so that different authorities do not have veto powers in regard to any proposal (Para 4.3.3).

(11) Controls should be as non-discretionary as possible and should leave the minimum of discretion to the authorities administering them (Para 4.3.5).

(12) This involves consideration of an appropriate policy-mix calculated to increase availability, like steps taken to increase output, to increase supply through imports, to regulate supplies through buffer stock operations, and to regulate demand through fiscal policy adjustments (Para 4.3.6).

(13) Price controls by themselves are of no value unless accompanied by an effective distribution system, and control of Government over an adequate share of the supply of the controlled item for public distribution (Para 4.3.9).

(14) In fixing control over prices over distribution, prior consideration should be given to the implementability of the control and the effectiveness of the control machinery (Para 4.3.9).

(15) The controlled price should not be such as to discourage the production of the controlled item (Para 4.3.9).

(16) In any case, control over prices should be limited to articles which go into the consumption basket of the common man, or to intermediate goods which are either basic or are necessary for the manufacture of consumption goods required by the common man, or are essential inputs for the decentralised sector affecting large employment (Para 4.3.10).

(17) In the matter of agricultural prices, the focus of attention should be on relative prices of competing crops so that the optimum use of land may result from the announcement of support prices (Para 4.4.2).

(18) An adequate buffer stock should be build up, to help in the management of supply of all items the output or supply of which is subject to large fluctuations (Para 4.4.2).

(19) There should be no informal or administrative controls in lieu of formal and statutory controls (Para 4.3.12).

(20) By the same token, administrative control over public sector undertakings should relate to overall performance and not in terms of day-to-day management, both in regard to pricing policy and to operational matters (Para 4.3.13).

(21) Export controls have to be devised so as to ensure adequate availability for domestic use of mass consumption goods or raw materials in short supply, but that a long-term export strategy should also be evolved to increase the output of exportable products so that a stable export market can be built up (Para 4.3.14).

(22) The consumer movement should be purposefully developed with Government aid and the actions and decisions of the authorities should be known widely and made accessible to citizens at large (Para 4.3.15).

(23) A beginning should be made by legislation calculated to make the chambers of trade, commerce and industry responsible for voluntary regulation of their members' activities and to enforce a minimum code of business conduct (Para 4.3.17).

4. **Industrial Approvals** (Chapter 5)

Findings

(a) The simplification of procedures instituted in regard to industrial licensing through the institution of the Secretariat for Industrial Approvals (SIA) has doubtless resulted in a reduction of pendencies and in delays, but that this has been achieved essentially with the administrative expediency of delicensing of all investments upto Rs. 3 crores.

(b) This permits all manner of non-priority industries to be set-up, making for a draft on scarce resources.

(c) Though there is a substantial number of industries and products reserved for future development by small scale industries, the same emphasis has not so far been given in regard to spelling out areas of production to be reserved for cottage and village industries.

(d) The type of integration between industrial licensing and overall planning which had been achieved during the Third Plan with the issue of "Programmes of Industrial Development" by the Planning Commission has not been followed lately, and that the "Guidelines for Industries" issued by the Ministry of Industry do not have the same organic link between the Plan and licensing policy.

(e) The industrial licensing system has not in consequence ensured the development of industries according to Plan priorities; has failed to prevent the growth of capacity in non-essential industries; has not also been effective in securing proper regional dispersal of industries; and has not succeed in containing monopolies and the concentration of economic power.

(f) The liberalisation of import licensing of capital goods in 1978-79 has reportedly affected some indigenous capital goods industries adversely.

(g) The new procedure evolved for licensing of capital goods import for 14 important industries is unnecessarily cumbersome and vests large discretionary powers to the administrative authorities.

(h) Import of technology has not followed any definite plan, no systematic effort being made to import technology which is vital for the pursuit of accepted policy objectives and growth strategy.

(i) There has been significant simplification and liberalisation of procedures in regard to capital issues control.

(j) As of today, notwithstanding the institution of the SIA, there is a multiplicity of authorities each of whom can successfully block applications for the creation of industrial capacity, each applying its own separate point of view or criteria, leading to delays and giving scope for lobbying.

Recommendations

(1) In regard to industrial licensing, the following approach should be adopted:

(a) a list of totally banned industries should be announced from time to time, such industries being denied all facilities including provision of land, water, power, etc.;

(b) among other industries, some should be reserved only for village and cottage industries in the interest of employment;

(c) some others should be open only to small scale industries with an investment limit on plant and equipment of Rs. 10 lakhs;

(d) the list of industries reserved for public sector should continue;

(e) there should be an "open" list in which no industrial licence would be required, creation of capacity being freely permitted subject to clearance under the MRTP Act and FERA where relevant; and

(f) residual industries should be subject to licensing, for all medium and large scale industries. The present exemption of Rs. 3 crores would continue for this category except for MRTP and FERA companies (Para 5.2.14).

(2) In order to minimise the discretionary element in approval of the last category of applications, wide publicity should be given in regard to applications accepted or rejected by the Licensing Committee, with dates of application of each (Para 5.2.15).

(3) Where there are exemptions from licensing, registration of new capacity should be made a truly statistical matter, the registration being the responsibility of the District Industries Centres, a copy of the information being merely endorsed to the DGTD for statistical purposes (Para 5.2.18).

(4) The final power to approve or veto any proposal for industrial approval should vest with one single authority (Para 5.2.17).

(5) Penalties should be considered for both under-utilisation of capacity as well as pre-emption of capacity without implementation of the capacity licensed (Para 5.2.19).

(6) Reliance in regard to capital goods imports should be placed on the tariff mechanism rather than detailed scrutiny of the type now envisaged for 14 key industries (Para 5.3.6).

(7) Scrutiny by the DGTD should be limited to the "indigenous availability" angle and not to the "essentiality" angle which is no longer relevant (Para 5.3.4).

(8) In the import of technology to be permitted, care should be taken to avoid capital intensive technology which may reduce employment, or technology in regard to products which may not be relevant from the point of view of planning goals (Para 5.4.7).

(9) With the selectivity of the type indicated earlier, updating of technology and its adaptation to Indian conditions should be encouraged (Para 5.4.7).

(10) Insofar as capital issues control is concerned, there should be further simplification of this system by the issue of guidelines in respect of bonus issues. Having done that, the Office of the Controller of Capital Issues should be abolished as capital issues control has outlived its utility. Control in regard to capital issues, insofar as FERA companies are concerned, should be exercised by the Department of Economic Affairs and in regard to the residual matters by the Department of Company Affairs (Para 5.5.7).

5. **Mining Activity** (Chapter 6)

Findings

(a) There is a lot of delay in the grant of mining leases particularly where consultation between the Centre and the State concerned involves a lot of correspondence.

(b) There is confusion and delay in regard to deemed rejection cases.

(c) Powers regarding termination of leases are somewhat wide and not clearly defined.

(d) The list of minerals in First Schedule where the State Governments need to consult the Centre, is out of date.

(e) There is no uniformity of definition in respect of "foreigners"" for mining lease purposes and for purposes of industrial licensing as per FERA.

(f) The Act requires production of an income tax clearance certificate before a prospecting licence or mining lease is granted, a requirement insisted upon earlier in respect of import licences also which has since been dispensed with in respect of the latter.

(g) There is no minimum period indicated in MMRD Act for the grant of mining leases.

(h) The State Governments have powers to reserve areas for exploitation by the Government which leads to large tracts of land unexplored and unexploited.

(i) There is a tendency on the part of State Governments to stipulate several extraneous conditions in prospecting/mining leases.

(j) There is lack of coordinated action in the grant of mining leases and industrial licences based on the use of minerals.

(k) There arise problems in regard to surface rights and mining rights particularly where surface mining is concerned.

(l) There is today no check in regard to the ravaging of the environment.

Recommendations

(1) The list of minerals in First Schedule should be updated once very five years; in this connection, the Committee has, in the body of the report, made certain suggestions in regard to the immediate possibility of certain adjustments as of now (Para 6.5.3).

(2) There should be no need for taking out 'certificates of approval' before a party can apply for a prospecting or a mining lease and this requirement should be done away with (Para 6.3.1).

(3) Some minor definitional changes are called for in the MMRD Act as for instance the definition of "foreigners" which should be made consistent with FERA, and the extension of the coverage of the MMRD Act to minerals in the ocean-bed of the continentlal shelf around India (Para 6.3.1).

(4) The time permitted today for taking a decision on lease applications by State Governments — stipulated at 12 months — is too long and should be reduced to 180 days (Para 6.5.2).

(5) There should be a stipulation in regard to the time taken by the Centre, in respect of minerals listed in First Schedule, which should be limited to 90 days (Para 6.5.2).

(6) In case of failure of either the Centre or the State Government to take a decision on the case, there should be a tribunal to finally pass orders on the case within 180 days (Para 6.5.2).

(7) For non-scheduled minerals, the procedure of "deemed rejection" and of revision petitions may be dispensed with, and the State

Governments may be authorised to take a final decision (Para 6.5.3).

(8) There should be legal provision for applicants for mining leases for non-scheduled minerals to seek recourse to the courts of law if no orders are passed within 12 months from the date of application (Para 6.5.3).

(9) The circumstances for cancellation of leases before termination should be defined more sharply, and apart from cancellation for major violations of lease conditions, cancellations should not normally be resorted to, and even where necessary, lease holders should be given some time to adjust so that loss of capital can be avoided or at least minimised (Para 6.3.2).

(10) The requirement of production of income tax clearance certificate for grant of prospecting or mining lease should be done away with and procedure of submission of an affidavit by the applicant — as accepted for import trade control — should be adopted for the issue of mining leases (Para 6.3.1).

(11) The minimum period for which leases should be granted should be laid down by Central notification under the MMRD Act, for different minerals (Para 6.3.2).

(12) No areas should be kept reserved for exploitation by the public sector for more than five years and any such areas so reserved should be explored and exploitation commenced within a period of five years failing which the areas should be dereserved (Para 6.3.2).

(13) Strict rules ought to be laid down in regard to the ravaging of environment and there should be a system of periodic inspection to ensure that no undue damage is done, the lessee being required to restore the environment at the end of surface mining operations (Para 6.3.2).

(14) While changes in royalty rates should continue to be determined by the Centre in the larger national interest, periodic review should be provided so that the States get their due share of the income arising from the exploitation of minerals (Para 6.5.4).

6. **Essential Commodities** (Chapter 7)

Findings

(a) The Indian economy is subject to temporary imbalances between supply and demand of both essential consumer goods and key industrial raw materials, so that the Essential Commodities Act is a necessary piece of legislation in the area of commodity regulation.

(b) In the past, the powers conferred under the Essential Commodities Act have been used somewhat indiscriminately, as a convenient umbrella for all manner of controls.

(c) As a result, a large number of items have been added to the list of items deemed as essential under the Act, some of which are not essential in any meaning of the terms, while some others are not suitable for detailed control of the type that can be exercised under the Act.

(d) In the issue of control orders under the Act, there has frequently not been any proper homework either about the feasibility of implementation of the control or of the machinery of control.

(e) Over a period, the control orders have become extremely complex, amendments having been issue from time to time, without the finally updated version of the control ever being brought out in one document.

(f) As a consequence the control system has become avoidably complex and difficult to understand.

(g) Even the concerned executive branch of Government is sometimes not fully aware of all the extant orders on a controlled items, some unimportant control orders remaining on the Statute Book, forgotten and ignored.

(h) The orders and notifications are frequently couched in such legalistic jargon that it is impossible for the common man to comprehend the law.

(i) As far as retail trade is concerned, there are far too many orders for different items; different licences required from different licensing authorities; and too many registers required to be maintained and too many returns to be filed, which make the task of the retailer avoidably cumbersome and expensive.

(j) This provides an opportunity for harassment and graft, particularly because the powers conferred upon the executive authority under the Essential Commodities Act are sweeping, and in fact draconian in many ways.

(k) Sometimes there is no adequate consultation between the Centre and the States, and orders are issued by State Governments without consultation which creates problems for other States.

Recommendations

(1) The Essential Commodities Act should remain on the Statute Book (Para 7.5.2).

(2) Any order issued under the Essential Commodities Act should have a limited life of not more than three years and should automatically lapse after the stipulated period; even the statutes should be reviewed every five year (Para 7.5.9).

(3) Before an item is declared an essential, there should be proper homework to consider whether it is necessary to regulate the production, supply and distribution of the item concerned through the Essential Commodities Act; the feasibility of implementing the proposed control order; and the machinery for implementation of the control (Para 7.4.4).

(4) The list of items that have been declared as essential as of now should be drastically pruned, some specific suggestions in this regard having been made in Annexure 7.2 (Para 7.5.17).

(5) Only such commodities as meet one or more of the following criteria should be regulated through the Essential Commodities Act:

 (a) that it is a mass consumption item which people cannot do without; or that it is an important raw material or component going into the production of such a mass consumption items; or

 (b) that it is a universal intermediate which goes into the production of wide range of products (Para 7.5.5).

(6) All controls under the Essential Commodities Act, which are concerned essentially with the management of demand for scarce items, should be accompanied by simultaneous measures to augment supplies (Para 7.4.8).

(7) Items declared as essential should be clearly identifiable and not covered under broad generic heads or commodity groups so as to avoid giving the executive authority sweeping powers in regard to all items included under the generic category (Para 7.5.8).

(8) There should be adequate consultation and coordination not only to ensure reasonable management of the available supplies but also for consultation between the Centre and all concerned State Governments (Para 7.5.16).

7. **Export and Import** (Chapter 8)

Findings

(a) Import and export trade control policy since 1977-78 has been re-oriented so as to enable the economy to take advantage of the structural changes that have taken place in the economy during the last few years.

(b) Although a genuine effort has been made towards doing away with import restrictions and simplifying procedures, there is still room for further improvement and in particular, there continues to be a tendency to change import policy quite frequently, even though annual policy announcements are made.

(c) Such frequent changes — particularly major policy changes such as have been introduced during the last year (namely, 1978-79) — introduce an element of uncertainty in the import/export trade.

(d) The present procedure for selection of items to be classified for import purposes as banned, restricted or freely importable, is somewhat arbitrary, and also based on short term considerations and pressures rather than on the basis of a scientific analysis of the needs of the economy.

(e) The approach to the grant of cash compensatory support has also been *ad hoc* and not based on a detailed study of the incidence of indirect taxes borne by the export product, in earlier stages of production.

(f) The aggregate duty drawback granted on the export of manufactured articles works out to around 8 per cent of the f.o.b. value of exports of such manufactured articles while even in terms of macro aggregates, indirect taxes constitute around 12 and half per cent of the national income at market price, indicating a very much larger incidence of duty on manufactures — especially since there are little or no indirect imposts on agricultural items — which does not get fully compensated by way of duty drawback at the final stage of manufacture.

(g) Among the various categories of assistance given to exporters by Government, one item popularly treated as an export subsidy, namely import replenishment, does not any longer contain any element of subsidy partly because of liberal import policy for actual users and partly because of the replenishment percentage being strictly in tune with requirements of export production.

(h) Despite the categorisation of some of these payments to exporters as export subsidies — also designated here as such — some of the payments do not necessarily constitute a "subsidy" on exports in the truly economic sense.

Recommendations

(1) Import/export policies should have a validity of three years to permit suitable adjustments in the production structure (Para 8.3.4).
(2) Swings in policy arising from pressures should be avoided by making the formulation and planning of policy a matter of study and evaluation by an import/export policy board, which should be set up in the Ministry of Commerce (Para 8.3.5.).
(3) The Board should keep under review the lists should identify each item specifically and not by generic name or category (Para 8.3.11).
(4) While short term policy adjustments are not ruled out according to changing circumstances as may be necessary, too many and too frequent changes in policy should be avoided between two policy periods (Para 8.3.7).
(5) Export plans should be drawn up in consonance with an dovetailed into overall production plans (Para 8.5.4).
(6) The actual user condition on imports under the OGL should be removed (Para 8.3.10).
(7) The list of items canalised for export and import through public sector canalising agencies should be carefully reviewed, criteria for canalisation laid down, and items not suitable for bulk imports de-canalised (Para 8.4.6).
(8) For certain items, canalisation facilities should be extended to State Government agencies, so that they can meet the needs of small scale units by bulking their import requirements (Para 8.4.5).
(9) All cash assistance rates should be reviewed and such assistance should be limited to a refund of the indirect tax element in the process of production of an export item (Para 8.6.17).
(10) The interest subsidy on export packing credit is justified and should continue (Para 8.6.18).
(11) To the extent possible, the scheme for advance licensing of imports of raw materials and components for export production

should be extended to more items; the delay in disbursement of duty drawback should be reduced; and a way found to avoid the cost to the exporter of delays in inter-bank remittances (Paras 8.6.9 and 8.5.5).

(12) No substantive part of import policy should be formulated in the G.L.I. (Para 8.3.7).

(13) Where export inspection involves the charging of a fee by export inspection agencies, these agencies should be made to bear any liability arising out of disputes as to quality (Para 8.5.2).

(14) Import policy should be modified from time to time to make it responsive to the needs of the economy; and procedure should be revised to minimise difficulties and to reduce delays (Para 8.3.1).

(15) Protection to the domestic industry should be afforded through the tariff mechanism (Para 8.3.12).

(16) Tax subsidy for market development should be given only to specified products and should be restricted to 3 years at the maximum (Para 8.6.21).

8. **Exchange Control** (Chapter 9)

Findings

(a) Exchange control purporting to check the receipt of payments for the export of goods is today cumbersome and in any case not designed to meet future requirements arising from the increasing number of export transactions likely to arise as our exports increase.

(b) The present system is in any case not able to check the under-invoicing of exports; and is also not able to plug the loophole arising from the possibility of GR duplicate and triplicate forms not entering into the RBI net.

(c) There is considerable physical movement of GR forms leading to delays; and there is also possibility of loss of GR forms over the postal system.

(d) In any case, the exchange control system is not able to ensure realisation through banking channels, of inward remittances of Indians working abroad, which are increasingly becoming an important part of total foreign exchange receipts.

(e) There is today inadequate check in regard to inward remittances of profits and dividends from the substantial investments made by

Indian firms abroad.

(f) The present rules in regard to foreign travel are complex, and different rules apply to different categories of citizens even though the total foreign exchange expenditure on this account is only of the order of one per cent of the total receipts of foreign exchange on current account.

(g) While almost all countries regulate capital transactions, the present control over repatriation of non-residents' assets arising from the dilution of foreign capital under the Foreign Exchange Regulation Act is more restrictive than warranted by the present foreign exchange position of the country.

(h) The present baggage rules as well as rules for tourists are avoidably harsh particularly in respect of Indians returning for a holiday from jobs abroad, as well as for tourists wishing to take away Indian goods including Indian jewellery, purchased at Indian prices.

Recommendations

(1) The procedure for ensuring that export receipts are realised should be simplified, the Reserve Bank responsibility being primarily directed to verification on GR originals with GR duplicates (Para 9.2.5).

(2) The task of verification of GR triplicates with GR duplicates should be undertaken by the nationalised banks who are in any case responsible for realising the export proceeds on behalf of the exporters, the responsibility of the Reserve Bank being limited to sample checking (Para 9.2.6.).

(3) The present policy of managing exchanges by having a realistic exchange rate should be continued as a guarantee of realisation not only of export receipts but also of remittances from Indians abroad (Para 9.2.8.).

(4) The rules regarding foreign travel should be simplified and suitable guidelines issued for automatic grant of exchange to intending travellers by authorised dealers in foreign exchange by entering the exchange allowed on passports, so that scrutiny of individual applications by the Reserve Bank can be dispensed with (Paras 9.3.7, 9.3.8. and 9.3.10).

(5) The rules regarding import of baggage by Indians returning from abroad as well as for tourists wishing to take away Indian goods

at Indian prices should be simplified and rationalised (Para 9.4.4).

(6) While control over capital transactions must continue, the repatriation of non-residents' assets arising from dilution of foreign capital – under the Foreign Exchange Regulation Act – may be liberalised; at the same time, the functioning of Indian joint ventures abroad should be looked into and the need and justification thereof in future re-examined in the light of data pertaining to the net gain therefrom to the economy; these data should also be presented to Parliament on an annual basis (Para 9.3.9).

(7) The focus of the exchange control system should change, and instead of undue harassment of small people with small transactions, attention should be devoted to checking transactions of companies with links abroad, particularly inward remittances of profits and dividends from the substantial investments made abroad by Indian firms (Para 9.4.6.).

9. **Housing and Construction Activity** (Chapter 10)

Findings

(a) The justification of rent control arises from the fact that there are many instances of low income group people occupying premises on controlled rental, who would be hard hit if they had to suddenly pay market rents for the accommodation occupied by them.

(b) However, rent control has also led to great hardship for retired people, widows and others who had invested their life's savings for house construction, since their income has been eroded through inflation.

(c) There are, in fact, many tenants who are more affluent than the owners of the houses occupied by them, and that even some prosperous business houses enjoy a subsidy through rent control on commercial premises occupied by them.

(d) There has developed a flourishing black market by way of a *pugree*, the benefit of such gains going frequently to the tenant rather to the house-owner.

(e) Rend control helps only those who are in occupation of rent controlled houses and not new job seekers in new areas.

(f) As far as the Urban Land (Ceiling and Regulation) Act is concerned, it has not so far given and cannot really give a boost to the construction of new dwelling units.

(g) The Urban Land (Ceiling and Regulation) Act has in fact not even been properly implemented so far.

(h) Nonetheless, it cannot be disbanded since the objectives of the Act are in line with the goals of policy.

(i) As a result of a combination of rent control and the Urban Land (Ceiling and Regulation) Act, new house construction – other than self-constructed houses – has been limited to the construction luxury residential buildings in a few urban centres making a disproportionate demand on scarce materials like steel and cement.

(j) Low income housing has not been constructed at all except by the Government, with the result that slums and shanty towns have grown up in almost all urban areas.

(k) The Municipal laws and the house building standards set by modern architects have ruled out innovative construction of houses by the poor to meet their own requirements.

(l) Municipal laws have also led to corruption and delay in approval of building plans for house construction.

Recommendations

(1) There should be no rent control of commercial and office premises. In particular, buildings occupied by corporate organisations should be freed from rent control (Para 10.3.9).

(2) For all other buildings, increases in the rent of old buildings should be allowed periodically, by gradual steps, over a period of, say, five to ten years, to bring the rental to a rational level (Para 10.3.9).

(3) In addition to the above, existing tenants should be allowed to buy up houses occupied by them at multiples of the capitalised value of the existing rent (Para 10.3.9).

(4) The L.I.C. and other house financing corporations should be authorised to give loans for purchase of existing property by tenants on the above basis. This principle should apply to Governments loans also. (Para 10.3.9).

(5) Rent control should not be maintained in respect of houses occupied by tenants who own house property in the same town which they may have let out at high rental (Para 10.3.9).

(6) As a result, where owners wish to occupy their own houses, one house of their choice owned by them should be allowed to be va-

cated in their favour, by they should not be allowed to let out the house for a minimum period of three years thereafter (Para 10.3.9).

(7) When a building is divided into apartments, maintenance of the building should be entrusted to a co-operative which all residents must be compelled to form, and the residents must share the cost of maintenance of the building (Para 10.3.9).

(8) In the interest of proper town planning, the Urban Land (Ceiling and Regulation) Act should be modified and extended to permit acquisition of all properties in entire blocks, where most houses deserve to be pulled down, so that entire areas can be re-developed into housing colonies for the less affluent (Para 10.4.13).

(9) Prior to doing so, the concerned authorities should give a minimum notice of five to ten years so that no new construction is started in the designated area (Para 10.4.13).

(10) To achieve the social purpose a penal tax may also be levied on urban property in excess of the ceiling which may compel people to gradually change their life style (Para 10.4.13).

(11) In order to encourage the poor in urban areas to build houses suited to their own requirements as well as their capacity, designated areas can be developed where "sites and services" should be provided on a subsidised basis to the poor, who would then be permitted to build houses within the areas allotted to them in accordance with their own requirements and with material improvised by them (Para 10.6.5).

(12) The present legislation providing for concessions for employers for building houses for workers should be amended to allow such concessions for construction of houses for employees drawing upto Rs. 1000 per month in metropolitan areas (Para 10.4.14).

(13) In order to encourage cheaper construction use of ordinary lime mortar in place of cement and steel should be encouraged and architectural standards for urban areas modified suitably to conform to housing constructed with such conventional raw material (Para 10.4.14).

(14) Standard designs evolved by public authorities may be widely publicised and any building conforming to any of the plans should be automatically approved by the municipal authorities, to avoid delay, who should be given a definite time limit to approve of any other plan and in the event of a plan being rejected, indi-

cate clearly a basis for accepting the building plan. (Para 10.6.5.).

(15) Cheap, standardised construction materials should also be made available by the authorities, particularly to help the poor to build their own houses economically (Para 10.6.6).

10. **Subsidies** (Chapter 11)

Findings

(a) Subsidies have grown to a sizeable figure during the seventies and are now becoming a very important part of the Central budget.

(b) Central Government subsidies – including losses of Central Government undertakings arising from pricing policies adopted by Government – are around Rs. 2000 crores per annum; losses of undertakings and services operated by State Governments are around Rs. 1000 crores per annum.

(c) Subsidies have a tendency to snowball and to become sticky so that they begin to generate inefficiency and complacency.

(d) There are a number of payments in the budget which are not really of the nature of subsidies, and on the other hand numerous subsidies which are not shown as such but hidden under various other types of budgetary outlays, which makes it difficult to make out all payments having the character of a subsidy.

(e) Only three subsidies, on food, fertilizers and exports (amounting to Rs. 1343 crores), now constitute 70 per cent of the total budgetary subsidies of Rs. 1712 crores now given by the Centre.

(f) The patterns of budgeting and manner of payment of subsidies hides the inefficiency of operation of some sectors, as for example, in the distribution of imported fertilisers.

Recommendations

(1) The costs and recipients of benefits of all subsidies should be reviewed periodically, say, once every three years (Para 11.1.2).

(2) Subsidies should in general be given only to sustain tiny unit decentralised production or to support the consumption of the weaker sections of the population (Paras 11.1.5 and 11.3.2).

(3) Where necessary, clear-cut overt subsidies should be given, in lieu of indirect subsidies, e.g., losses of public sector undertak-

ings arising out of a deliberate policy decision of Government to keep prices below the cost of production in the interest of keeping down the general price level (Paras 11.4.7 and 11.5.3).

(4) The existing subsidies from the Central Government budget should be restructured in terms of the above criteria (Para 11.2.4).

(5) The subsidy on foodgrains which arises partly for buffer stock maintenance and partly owing to distribution costs, should be broken up into these two elements, the cost of buffer stock maintenance being justified as a subsidy, the cost of distribution being fit for subsidy only to the extent that the beneficiaries comprise the people below the poverty line (Para 11.3.2).

(6) Fertiliser subsidies should be phased out in three years and a new subsidy given for promotion of organic fertilisers; increased subsidy for the use of fertilisers should be given to smaller and weaker farmers under various promotional programmes within the ambit of the Integrated Rural Development Scheme (Paras 11.3.3 and 11.3.4).

(7) Export subsidies should be restructured and granted to meet only the cumulative burden of indirect taxes in the cost of production (Para 11.3.5).

(8) In the textile sector there is justification only for subsidy on production in the decentralised sector namely handloom and khadi, and in the interim period, on production of controlled cloth in the mill sector but with necessary arrangements for distribution of the controlled cloth to the vulnerable sections of the population (Para 11.3.6).

(9) The interest subsidy should also be restructured, and losses of public sector undertakings arising from unrealistic pricing of products should be subsidised directly in full so that the nature extent of the subsidy is known and realised, and attention is focussed on such subsidies which are granted in order to keep down the price of a product below its cost of production or because the concerned undertaking is sick (Para 11.5.3).

(10) Entries designated as subsidies in the Budget, which do not merit being treated as such – as for instance the so-called subsidy to the BGML – should be removed from the list of subsidies by changing the accounting procedure (Para 11.4.11).

(11) There is a case for increased transport subsidy in favour of hilly and far-flung regions, so as to make all essential commodities available to people in those areas at reasonable prices (Paras

11.4.14 and 11.4.15).

(12) The backward area subsidy should be on a sliding scale and increased in respect of really backward areas, but given on the criterion of employment generated instead of capital invested (Para 11.4.14).

(13) There should be an increased budgetary allocation as subsidy in favour of areas hit by natural calamities to compensate the population for the capital loss; and for this purpose an allocation of one per cent of Central and State Government budgetary outlays should be made on a regular basis (Paras 11.3.7 and 11.3.8).

(14) There is a case for increasing the subsidy for housing intended for the low income people (Para 11.4.20).

(15) The subsidy to vulnerable sections of the population through schemes like the Integrated Rural Development Scheme should be increased (Para 11.3.7).

11. **Foodgrains** (Chapter 12)

Findings

(a) Despite the recent increase in food output, the supply of foodgrains in India is still very much a gamble on the monsoon.

(b) A very substantial proportion of agricultural holdings in India is of sub-marginal size, which is not adequate to grow enough food even for the cultivating family.

(c) The management of the food problem since independence until the mid-seventies has been a problem of demand/supply management in the context of perennial shortages in supplies; from the mid-seventies, the problem has become almost wholly one of supply management in the background of a generally comfortable supply situation.

(d) While the latter has been due to sustained effort to provide various inputs required for increased production, the fixation of reasonable "support" prices has also helped materially.

(e) Support prices have also let to the build up of a buffer stock.

(f) The focus of policy has therefore, shifted from the control aspect to the supply management aspect of food policy, leading to the abolition of food zones, dismantling restrictions on food movement, and various other types of controls on food.

(g) Nonetheless, the problem of reaching foodgrains at a reasonable price throughout the year to the vulnerable sections of the population in different parts of the country – some far-flung and remote and some hilly and inaccessible – remains.

(h) The present claims in regard to the extent and coverage of the public distribution system are highly misleadings; however, in the areas covered by the public distribution system, foodgrains are available at uniform prices throughout the country all through the year.

(i) The cost of public distribution in India has been higher than the cost of private retail distribution, nonetheless the former has been instrumental in exercising a moderating influence on the private trade, particularly in remote areas.

(j) The assurance of the supply has been the biggest factor in the generally smooth functioning of the distribution system in the matter of foodgrains.

(k) Over the past few years, all controls and restrictions on foodgrains have generally been lifted except for a few areas – like Calcutta and Durgapur – Asansol industrial belt – and also except for control over roller flour milling of wheat, machine hulling and milling of rice, and storage of pulses.

Recommendations

(1) The focus of attention in regard to food policy should continue to be on reasonable support prices – in line with reasonable parities, *inter se*, as between different crops – and on buffer stock operations (Para 12.3.3).

(2) The cost of buffer stock maintenance should be a legitimate charge on revenues, for achieving food security (Para 12.6.10).

(3) The subsidy required to meet the cost of distribution should not, however, be a charge on revenues except to the extent required to meet the consumption needs of people near or below the poverty line (Paras 12.6.19 and 12.6.22).

(4) The subsidisation of food should therefore be limited either to the items consumed by the target group – e.g., millets – or by issue of special ration cards to people below a certain income level (Paras 12.6.19 and 12.6.20).

(5) The latter should be systematically attempted so that subsidies reach only the deserving sections of the population (Para 12.6.21).

(6) Private distribution channels should be harnessed for the public distribution system, with a proper code of conduct laid down for the private traders, and adequate monitoring not only by Government but by consumer committees, so that these shops function in the public interest (Para 12.4.11).

(7) The cost of public distribution not only by the above means but also by increasing the turnover from the retail shops, for which specific recommendations are made in the Chapter on Distribution Control (Para 12.6.17).

(8) Input subsidies for agriculture – e.g., irrigation water, power fertilisers and seeds – should also be subsidised only for the smaller and weaker farmers, through larger subsidies under the Integrated Rural Development Scheme (Para 12.6.17).

(9) Subsidies would also be justified for the construction of godowns and storage facilities in far-flung, inaccessible and hilly areas which frequently remain cut off from the rest of the country over part of the year (Para 12.4.16).

(10) Insofar as control over roller flour mills is concerned, the expansion of capacity should be allowed to achieve better regional balance in flour milling capacity, but roller flour mills should be required to continue to obtain their wheat supplies from the FCI so that the buffer stocks can be rolled over, and the mills also do not create sudden large demands in certain markets (Para 12.5.4).

(11) Insofar as rice milling is concerned, there should be controlled, selective increase in rice milling capacity, and modernisation of old hullers of mills with rubber rolls, so that the requirements of the public distribution system can be met cheaply, and at the same time, the handpounding of rice can be encouraged so as to to provide employment (Para 12.5.7).

(12) In line with the reduction in licensing and other restrictions, there should be a reduction in the number of licences to be taken out, and the number of registers to be maintained by fair price shops, so as to reduce harassment, and make the distribution system more efficient (Para 12.4.12).

12. **Edible Oils and Vanaspati** (Chapter 13)

Findings

(a) The control over edible oils and vanaspati has in practice focussed mainly on control over vanaspati, the control affecting all facets of the industry. The industry has not been allowed to expand capacity. The input-mix of the industry has been strictly laid down, and a very substantial part of the input supplied through canalised import of cheap oils. There has been control over the production, quality, price, distribution and stocking of vanaspati. Nonetheless, the market price of vanaspati has frequently been considerably higher than the controlled price.

(b) There have been a number of other controls relative to this sector. The extant controls pertain to the manufacture, sale and movement of solvent extracted oil, deoiled meal and edible flour; the processing of refined imported palm oil, the quality of vegetable oil products; the storage of edible oilseeds and edible oils beyond certain limits; and a ban on forward trading and limitation of delivery period in respect of Non-Transferable Specific Delivery contracts for oilseeds and vegetable oils. There is also, as of now, canalisation of all imports of vegetable oils.

(c) There has not only been a wide gap between the demand for edible oils and its indigenous production, but the gap is likely to continue, the estimate for supply and demand by the end of the Sixth Plan making for a deficit in vegetable oil supply of approximately 11.50 lakh tonnes by 1982-83.

(d) The main thrust of the control system in the past has been to keep down the price of vanaspati by supply of cheap imported oils as the input for vanaspati manufacture, and thereby to keep down price of edible oils by diverting the demand from the vanaspati industry away from indigenous oils to imported oils. In the result, prices of edible oil within the country, used for direct consumption, have frequently been higher than the controlled price of vanaspati, which has had the benefit of having cheap imported oil as the input.

Recommendations

(1) In view of the gap between demand and supply which is likely to continue, cheaper edible oil should continue to be imported, but apart from providing an input for the vanaspati industry, it should also be made available for direct consumption by the masses of people, through fair price shops (Para 13.6.4).

(2) The control over the input-mix of the vanaspati industry should continue, so that indigenous groundnut oil is available for direct

consumption as an edible oil (Para 13.4.5).

(3) The STC should be asked to go in for long-term supply contracts and arrange for the requisite qualities of vegetable oil import (Para 13.6.4).

(4) Adequate storage capacity for oils should be built around the country, particularly in deficit areas, with a view to both buffer stocking of oils and to preventing sharp increases in prices during the off-season (Para 13.6.4).

(5) Realistic support prices for edible oils should also be announced to encourage the increased cultivation of edible oilseeds, and the import of cheaper oil should not be allowed to depress the internal market (Para 13.6.4).

(6) For this purpose, both the canalisation of import of vegetable oils and the fiscal system by way of import duty adjustments should be used to ensure that prices of edible oilseeds and oils do not get out of hand (Para 13.6.4).

(7) Among the other controls on the edible oils and vanaspati sector, there is need for continuance of the storage control order in the background of the general deficit in oil supply, and of the ban on forward trading, with selective relaxation of the time allowed for NTSD contracts (Para 13.6.5).

(8) The Solvent Extracted Oil, De-oiled Meal and Edible Flour (Control) Order does not appear to have any relevance today and should be withdrawn (Para 13.6.5).

(9) There is a case for selective relaxation of control over the licensing of capacity in the vanaspati industry, the relatively uneconomic units being permitted to expand to economic size (Para 13.6.5).

(10) In order to introduce some stability in the availability and price of edible oils, a buffer stock of at least two months requirements should be built up, through additional imports if necessary (Para 13.6.4).

(11) The stipulation of use of a minimum of 5 per cent sesamum oil should continue (Para 13.6.6).

13. **Sugar** (Chapter 14)

Findings

(a) In the past, the policy on sugar has — especially from 1967 when the dual price policy was adopted — been attuned to increasing the availability of sugar with a minimum price for sugarcane.

(b) The policy also involved considerable divergences in the cane price from State to State and consequently in the ex-factory price for the controlled portion of sugar.

(c) The policy succeeded in bringing more area under sugarcane and also in increasing sugar production to a point of excess supply.

(d) The decontrol of sugar introduced from August 1978 has brought down the price of sugar to a level below the cost of production for a very large segment of the sugar industry.

(e) While the decontrol of sugar has been accompanied by payment of a cane price by sugar factories in line with the statutory price of sugar as laid down by the Centre, some State Governments have decided to subsidise the cane grower for the cane supply to factories by the difference between the earlier State advised prices and the present statutory prices of cane.

(f) Though this benefit of a subsidised cane price is available in respect of cane supply to sugar factories, the price realised by the growers for cane sold for khandsari or gur production is very much lower.

(g) This policy is not followed by the Southern States where the crushing season for cane is much longer and the cane has also a higher sugar content with the result that there has been some decline in the area under cane in these States.

(h) This policy has thus distorted the optimum location of cane cultivation and of the sugar industry.

(i) There has also been a take over of the management of 10 sugar mills after November 1978 in 'the four States of Uttar Pradesh, Bihar, Punjab and Haryana. The support required to meet even the operational costs of these units is reported to be Rs. 10 crores in 1979-80.

(j) After decontrol the consumption of sugar has gone up quite significantly with benefits of the lower price accruing even to rural areas, but with a decline in the prices and production of khandsari and gur. Over October 1978 to January 1979, the total internal consumption of sugar has been 19.6 lakh tonnes.

Recommendations

(1) In areas where it is possible to continue existing factories through better cropping methods, and the sugar industry can be made viable on a long-term basis, the existing sugar factories should be

converted into co-operatives of cane growers with universal membership so as to establish a nexus between the cane price and the sugar price without the need for Government intervention (Paras 14.7.7, 14.7.8 and 14.7.9).

(2) Such a policy is desirable to avoid both a continuing subsidy on sugarcane as well as a continuing subsidy on sugar production which is implicit in a take over of uneconomic sugar factories (Para 14.7.10).

(3) Where the sugar industry is not likely to be viable, there should be a phased programme for converting sugar units into other industrial units, e.g., cotton yarn spinning mills for supply of yarn to handlooms, even if based on cotton obtained from other States, and other agro-based industries (Para 14.7.11).

(4) For this purpose, a subsidy should be given for conversion of these units from sugar production to other activities (Para 14.7.6).

(5) If the above policy is adopted, there would be a case for Government subsidy for maintaining a buffer stock of sugar which may prevent swings in prices (Paras 14.7.11, 14.7.14 and 14.7.15).

(6) An essential ingredient of this is uniform pricing of sugarcane (based on recovery of sugar) throughout India to bring about an optimal utilisation of the land resources of the country (Paras 14.7.5 and 14.7.16).

(7) Some of the extant controls on sugar, and related items are no longer relevant, and may be rescinded. In particular, there is no advantage in retaining the Sugarcane Pressmud Control Order and the Gur (Regulation of Use) Order (Paras 14.4.2 and 14.4.5).

14. **Textiles** (Chapter 15)

Findings

(a) A major problem of the textile industry arises from the fluctuations in the output and prices of raw cotton.

(b) Neither the "control" of the ceiling price nor the "support price" of cotton has worked successfully, and "support prices" have been too low to lead to any increase in the area and output of cotton.

(c) A large part of the cotton is lost annually because of pests and insects, the estimated loss being as much as around 30 per cent and even 40 per cent in case of an epidemic or pestilential attack.

(d) Although the Cotton Corporation of India was set-up with a view to stabilising the price of cotton through effective intervention in the cotton market, and although various committees have recommended that to be really effective, the Cotton Corporation should buy atleast 30 per cent of the cotton output, the Corporation has failed to do so.

(e) The Cotton Corporation has never been provided the funds with which to achieve the above target, and has also been hamstrung by directives from the Ministry.

(f) The Cotton Corporation has suffered a heavy loss on imported cotton which has had to be subsidised, because of the timing of the import purchases made by the Corporation at the behest of the Government, coupled with the refusal of the textile industry to lift the imported cotton even though it had made a firm commitment at the import prices indicated by the Corporation prior to ordering the imported cotton.

(g) The opportunity of a build up of a buffer stock of cotton was missed last year when cotton was allowed to be exported rather than purchased by the Cotton Corporation for building up a buffer stock.

(h) The textile industry has a total of nine control orders issued at different points of time under the Essential Commodities Act, covering various facets of the textiles industry.

(i) Of these the Cotton Textiles (Control) Order of 1948 – which exercises comprehensive control over the mill sector of the cotton textile industry — has been amended from time to time but has never been up dated and brought out in a manner calculated to indicate the finally amended control system as it exists.

(j) The control low has as a result become quite complex and generally unintelligible.

(k) It has been a policy objective to limit the expansion of weaving capacity in the mill sector in the interest of employment in the decentralised sector.

(l) There are many reasons for sickness in the textile industry including management weaknesses. The hypothesis of limitation of expansion of weaving capacity having led to the sickness of mill industry is not convincing because more than a 100 mills were already sick, long before the production of controlled cloth became a losing proposition for the mills.

(m) The obligation of controlled cloth production imposed on the mill sector has led to economic difficulties of this industry.

(n) Insofar as the decentralised sector is concerned, it — and the handloom weaving class in particular — suffers from many disadvantages and disabilities including the high price and inferior quality of yarn, non-availability of yarn at times, lack of finance and lack of marketing.

(o) Even the policy of reservation of certain categories of cloth for production only by handlooms has not helped because of poaching by the powerloom sector.

(p) There has been steady of unauthorised powerlooms which has been abetted by some States, to the detriment of the growth of handlooms production and disadvantage of the other States which have not permitted the expansion of powerlooms.

(q) With the introduction of synthetics, blended yarn has not been available to the decentralised sector, and mill production has increasingly turned to production of cloth varieties intended for the well-to-do classes.

(r) There is some degree of compartmentalisation of production between different segments of the textile industry, though lately there have been some relaxations which have benefited only some segments of the industry.

(s) In the woollen industry, the decentralised sector has been facing yarn shortage, particularly the indigenous yarn required for carpet weaving and barrack blanket making.

(t) There has also reportedly arisen a shortage of woollen yarn spinning capacity.

(u) The large woollen industry is quite small in comparison with the large scale cotton textile industry, and needs protection from the diversification facility granted to the latter.

(v) Of the diverse clauses of the nine control orders relevant for the textile industry, many are dormant and not in use, and many others irrelevant in today's situation.

Recommendations

(1) The Cotton Corporation of India should be freed from bureaucratic control, given necessary funds and general guidelines, and authorised to buy upto 30 per cent of the cotton crop, and also build up a buffer stock of cotton for which it should be given requisite credit facilities (Para 15.3.11).

(2) The Corporation should be divested of its bureaucratic character,

its shares being held jointly by the Central Government, cotton marketing co-operative federations of the cotton growing States, co-operatives of cotton farmers, etc. (Paras 15.3.14 and 15.3.15).

(3) Cotton ginning and pressing should be reserved for co-operatives of cotton growers with universal or near universal membership (Para 15.3.16).

(4) In order to raise the output of cotton, the spraying of the cotton crop with pesticides should be a national programme, the cost being met from the cotton cess fund (Para 15.3.18).

(5) The cess on cotton should be raised from the present 25 paise per bale to Rs. 50 per bale, or about $1^1/_2$ per cent of the price per bale, in order to pay for the above as well as for the carrying charges of a part of the buffer stock of cotton to be built up (Para 15.3.18).

(6) There should be no canalisation of and no subsidy on imported cotton in future (Para 15.3.13).

(7) The control over the weaving capacity of the mill sector should continue (Para 15.4.5).

(8) The Soft Loan Scheme of the IDBI should not be used for expansion of weaving capacity/reduction of employment in the weaving section of the industry, and for financing the modernisation/replacement of well-to-do mills at interest rates not available to the decentralised sector (Para 15.4.8).

(9) Price stamping of mill cloth is redundant and should be withdrawn except for Janata cloth which is subsidised (Para 15.4.8).

(10) The reservation of spheres of production by handlooms should be enlarged, and the control enforced (Para 15.5.9).

(11) For this purpose, there should be regulation of the sale of looms by the textile machinery manufacturing industry (Para 15.9.8).

(12) Some varieties of cloth production should be reserved for the powerloom sector, though the expansion of this sector should not be allowed (Para 15.5.9).

(13) Excise duty on yarn in cones should be raised *vis-a-vis* yarn in hanks (Para 15.5.9).

(14) The area of reservation of products for the handloom sector should be enlarged to include *sarees* and *dhotis* with border (Para 15.5.9).

(15) Control over production of yarn in hanks should be made more stringent in regard to proportion and quality (Para 15.5.9).

(16) Disbursement of subsidy on handloom (on production of Janata

dhotis and *sarees*) should be speeded up and the procedure and documentation simplified drastically (Para 15.5.9).

(17) The supply of good quality yarn at reasonable prices for the decentralised sector should be ensured, and until sufficient capacity for yarn production, by spinning mills set-up by Government or by the Co-operative sector, is created, there should be a compulsory obligation for producing a certain percentage of yarn in hanks (Para 15.5.7).

(18) Both handloom and *khadi* should be encouraged through compulsory Government purchases as well as a price preference in favour of the khadi handloom sectors (Para 15.5.10).

(19) The multifibre approach should be reduced to one of merely meeting the deficit in cotton availability, and not as a part of conscious policy to encourage the growth of multifibre fabrics (Para 15.6.3).

(20) The supply of blended yarn to handlooms should be ensured (Para 15.5.9).

(21) There is no case for a reduction of the duty on synthetic fibres which may affect the interests of the cotton growers adversely (Para 15.6.5).

(22) There should be encouragement given to the hand made carpet weaving and barrack blankets industry in the same manner as for *khadi* and handlooms, and expansion of capacity for mill made tufted carpets should not be allowed even for export, as they would impinge on the supply of indigenous woollen yarn for the decentralised sector (Para 15.8.6).

(23) Controlled expansion of spinning capacity in the woollen industry should be allowed, to meet the needs of hosiery, and similar knitted woollens industry (Para 15.8.6).

(24) When there is short supply of raw cotton and need for import of man-made fibres, the import should be through the STC on a well regulated basis so that the requirements of the decentralised sector can be met (Para 15.6.5.).

(25) Distribution of controlled cloth should be linked to the distribution of other essential articles to the target group (Para 15.4.12).

(26) The varieties of cloth to be subsidised for distribution should be such as are purchased by the lower income groups, and supplied through shops located in areas where low income people generally live (Para 15.4.13).

(27) A large number of controls at present on the Statute Book in

respect of the textile industry are redundant and should be removed (Para 15.9.8).

(28) The control law should be succintly brought out in a comprehensive document (Para 15.9.8).

(29) The office of the Textile Commissioner should be wound up and the residual control functions — including powers of prosecution for violation of Government orders — should vest with a Textiles Development Board, incharge of the co-ordinated development and regulation of the entire textiles industry, covering *khadi*, handlooms, powerlooms and the mill sector (Para 15.9.9).

15. **Jute** (Chapter 16)

Findings

(a) The major problem of the jute industry is the instability in the price and availability of raw jute arising partly as a result of sharp fluctuations in acreage and partly as a result of vagaries of the weather.

(b) The acreage fluctuations have been inversely related to changes in raw jute prices.

(c) The jute grower does not get a reasonable price for raw jute because of the present defective system of raw jute procurement, the grower being cheated not only on the price but also in the matter of grade of jute, moisture content, etc.

(d) The jute trade is today mainly in the hands of *benami* procurers on behalf of the mills and there is a wide gulf between the price for raw jute paid by the mills officially and the price received by the grower.

(e) Exports of jute goods have been good in spells, as for instance between 1961 and 1965 when raw jute prices and jute availability were relatively stable.

(f) The growth of synthetics has been accentuated and accelerated by the sudden sharp changes in prices and availability of jute goods.

(g) Government policies, particularly in the matter of export duties which have been sticky in the extreme, have also contributed to halting exports and to accentuate problems of the industry.

(h) As a result of cupidity in the matter of raw jute purchase and various other problems indicated above, the jute industry has been in a state of sickness and bad health, and the management of a number of sick mills has had to be taken over the Government.

(i) The need for a reasonable support price for raw jute and for the creation of a buffer stock of raw jute was realised quite early, but in spite of fairly severe control provisions under the Essential Commodities Act, it has not been possible to maintain the price of raw jute at a reasonable level.

(j) The Jute Corporation of India — which was created specifically with a view to stabilising the price of raw jute and to operate a buffer stock for this purpose — has failed to achieve any of the above objectives of policy.

(k) The reasons for the Jute Corporation's have been numerous: it does not have the requisite organisation to intervene effectively in the primary market; it has never been given the requisite finance; and it has been hamstrung by instructions received from Ministry in regard to its operations, which has left generally powerless.

(l) Apart from the Jute Textiles (Control) Order of 1956 and the Jute (Licensing and Control) Order of 1961 — both issued under the Essential Commodities Act — there is control over the jute industry and trade in respect of forward contracts; and there is voluntary registration of export contracts and canalised import of raw jute.

(m) The main control stems from the Jute (Licensing and Control) Order which confers on the authorities wide powers of control over the jute industry.

(n) None of the fairly stringent controls on jute and jute goods, has been able to resolve the basic problem of either the jute grower or of the jute industry, and it is widely alleged that there is considerable pay of unaccounted money in the jute industry particularly in the purchase of raw jute, while the industry continues to be in difficulties.

(o) Forward trading in jute goods is likely to lead only to increased speculation, and is therefore rightly banned.

Recommendations

(1) In order to resolve the problems of both the growers of raw jute and the jute industry, there should be monoply procurement of raw jute by the Jute Corporation of India (Para 16.7.19).

(2) In undertaking this task, the Jute Corporation should seek the help of local authorities and build up an organisation suited to each of

the jute growing areas in consultation with the State Government and other concerned authorities (Para 16.7.19).

(3) In order that the Jute Corporation is made fully responsive to the needs of the situation, it should be converted to a joint sector organisation in which, apart from the Central Government, the Government of West Bengal and other jute growing States may hold shares with possibility of some shareholding also by co-operatives of jute farmers or other organisations of jute growers (Para 16.7.24).

(4) The Jute Corporation should seek the assistance of organisation like the Indian Jute Research Institute for the grading of raw jute (Para 16.7.23).

(5) The Jute Corporation should also be put in a position to build a buffer stock of raw jute so as to stabilise the price and availability of jute to the industry, the carry over stock of raw jute at the end of the season being a minimum of 10 lakh bales (Paras 16.7.25 and 16.7.26).

(6) Prices of raw jute should be determined by an independent body like the Agricultural Prices Commission after careful consideration of price parities between jute, paddy and other competing crops (Para 16.7.19).

(7) The period until the new jute crop should be used for the required buildup of the organisation of the Jute Corporation (Para 16.7.25).

(8) With the above change, a number of formal controls on the jute industry can be phased out (Para 16.7.27).

(9) The scheme for registration of export contracts may be continued (Para 16.6.26).

16. **Fertilisers and Pesticides** (Chapter 17)

Findings

(a) The costs of production of fertilisers vary substantially from unit to unit because of the divergent feedstock allowed by Government to different units, the cost of fuel oil and coal based fertilisers being significantly higher than the cost of naphtha and natural gas based fertilisers.

(b) In spite of substantial increase in production of late, there is still need for sizeable import of fertilisers.

(c) The present consumption of fertilisers in India is heavily weighted in favour of N which, it is recommended, should be corrected for a more balanced use of fertilisers.

(d) The fertiliser industry is both capital intensive and corrosive, and the cost of production of new units is substantially higher than the cost of production of existing units, which however would have a high replacement cost.

(e) There is at present a subsidy on indigenous nitrogenous fertilisers, in order to keep the price low for the farmer; a promotional subsidy on phosphatic fertilisers; a subsidy on imported fertilisers; and a subsidy for internal freight so as to equate the price of fertilisers throughout the country.

(f) The total amount of subsidy given for fertilisers has been increasing rapidly of late.

(g) There is evidence that fertilisers are fairly widely used both by large and small farmers but the use of fertilisers is still generally limited to certain selected areas.

(h) From all available evidence, the return from fertilisers in terms of higher output is several times the cost of fertilisers.

(i) Insofar as imported fertilisers are concerned, there are certain problems which prevent the import of fertilisers in bulk which would be much cheaper than the import of bagged fertilisers.

(j) The cost of distribution of imported fertilisers by the FCI is considerably more than the cost of distribution by other agencies lately asked to handle part of the imported fertilisers.

(k) In spite of numerous efforts, and the facility of a subsidy from the Department of Agriculture, the progress of both construction of *Gobar Gas plants* and compost pits as also of plants for treatment and composting of urban wastes has been very slow.

(l) The loss of crops from pests varies from 10 to 30 per cent on a conservative estimate, and where there is an attack of pests in epidemic form, the loss is significantly higher.

(m) For many crops, it has not been possible to rely on the efforts of individual farmers because pests move from smaller farms where pesticides are not applied to neighbouring larger farms, thus nullifying the effect of the application of pesticides.

Recommendations

(1) Price control on fertilisers has to continue because of the widely divergent cost of production of different units based on different

feedstock (Paras 17.7.5 and 17.7.7).

(2) Some relaxation in the control on distribution/movement of fertilisers is called for so as to have flexibility to the producers to sell outside their command area (Para 17.5.11).

(3) The subsidy on fertilisers on a long-term basis should not continue but cannot be given up suddenly and should be eliminated only in a series of steps over a period of, say, five years (Para 17.7.13).

(4) In the mean time, older plants should be given a special allowance for replacement of equipment by putting the pooled price at a level higher than the weighted average retention price, the difference being funded for replacement of equipment of the older units (Para 17.7.6).

(5) The subsidy on imported fertilisers should be eliminated by reducing the cost of handling and distribution which appears to be feasible (Paras 17.5.8 and 17.5.9).

(6) A separate subsidy for fertilisers could be continued, rather increased, under various Integrated Rural Development Schemes so that the use of fertilisers could be popularised and the benefit of the subsidy reaches the target group already identified (Paras 17.7.13 and 17.10.1).

(7) The subsidy on Gobar Gas plants, compost pits and composting of urban wastes should be increased in order to improve the availability of organic manure and also to save on kerosene and firewood as fuel and for lighting purposes (Para 17.8.3).

(8) The subsidy on Gobar Gas plants should be available for all designs of Gobar Gas plants and not merely for designs approved by the KVIC (Para 17.8.4).

(9) There should be a national scheme for spraying major crops with pesticides, part of the cost of which should be subsidised (Para 17.9.5).

(10) In determining agricultural prices, note should be taken of the totality of subsidies as well as the cost of inputs so that prices are determined on a realistic basis (Para 17.7.14).

17. **Coal** (Chapter 18)

Findings

(a) After nationalisation of the coal industry in 1973, controls on it are "administrative" rather than statutory, though earlier controls still remain on the statute book.

(b) Statutory control on distribution is effective only in regard to soft coke which State Governments control under the Essential Commodities Act.

(c) The administrative control on coal has kept coal prices generally low, involving a subsidy of around Rs. 140 crores in 1978-79.

(d) The spread in the prices of different varieties of coal — based on their heat value — is too narrow, and encourages the demand for the scarcer varieties of coal, and discourages the use of "middlings" and poorer grades of coal.

(e) The supply of coal to all but a few "essential" categories of consumers is irregular, and there is a black market in coal.

(f) The present system makes for a sub-optimal loading/transport arrangement from the point of view of the economy as a whole.

Recommendations

(1) The price of coal should be determined by an independent authority (like the BICP) with a view of discouraging improvident uses of coal (Para 18.7.1).

(2) In the pricing formula, there should be an economic incentive to use slack coal and "middlings", and a disincentive to use the scarcer varieties of coal (Para 18.5.8).

(3) In order to rationalise movement and distribution, as also to resolve disputes as to the price of coal, steel plants should have captive coking coal mines (Para 18.6.3).

(4) Coal dumps should be established at convenient centres (in district headquarters and cities with a population above 50,000) (Para 18.6.5).

(5) The overall cost of distribution should be reduced by using ropeways, and also by loading wagons in outlying mines and shunting the coal to central points for the formation of rake loads, for which Coal India should own and operate wagons and shunters (Para 18.6.4).

(6) Existing subsidies on sand stowing and other development works are inadequate and need to be increased several-fold either by increasing the cess on coal or by increasing the coal price, and making sand stowing a part of the normal operational routine (Para 18.7.4).

(7) The existing legislation on coal, by way of the Coal Mines (Conservation and Development) Act of 1974; the Coking Coal Mines (Emergency Provisions) Act of 1971; and the Coal Mines (Taking Over of Management) Act of 1973, are all redundant now, in view of the nationalisation of the under the Essential Commodities Act, is also redundant; the subsidies now granted through cess/excise collections could also be made a direct charge on the cost of coal (Para 18.5.7).

(8) The Coal Controller's organisation which does not have any really useful function today, should be merged with the CIL (Para 18.5.8).

(9) Coal mining can be selectively allowed to State Governments or Co-operative societies (particularly in hill areas) supported or sponsored by State Governments (Para 18.6.6).

18. **Steel** (Chapter 19)

Findings

(a) Although a very large part of the steel output goes to a limited number of identifiable users, the distribution of steel to the decentralised sector has so far been uneven and the monitoring of the control system has not been satisfactory. As a result, black market premiums have emerged and small users have been at a disadvantage in the matter of steel supplies.

(b) The tight control kept on the price of steel, statutorily until the sixties and administratively thereafter, had led to a situation in which the integrated steel plants have not been able to generate adequate resources for their own modernisation and expansion. The expansion of steel capacity required for the development of the economy, therefore, has to be financed from public savings which involves a subsidy from the general taxpayer to the user of the steel and steel products.

(c) Though formal control was given up in the mid-sixties, there has been a tight administrative control on steel prices, exercised by Government thereafter.

(d) The experiment at dual pricing as operated in the past, from 1973, has involved a subsidisation on steel used by the public sector by other users of steel, and has also encouraged misuse of the cheaper varieties of steel (like plates).

(e) There has been tight control over the use of alloy steel and stainless steel, by way of highly restrictive policy in the past and a prohibitive import duty on some categories of stainless steel of late. This has led to the use of mild steel in lieu of alloy steel in many engineering industries, to the detriment of the growth of such industries.

(f) The main part of the control mechanism — the Iron and Steel Controller's organisation — has lost its utility today, and appears to be redundant. So are bodies like the Steel Priority Committee and the Iron Ore Board, all their planning and advisory functions now properly vesting with the SAIL and the JPC.

Recommendations

(1) The tight administrative control over steel prices should be relaxed. Government should lay down guidelines indicating the priority sectors (which should be kept down to a very few, possibly only Defence needs and export production), the prices to be charged from the priority sectors, and other relevant parameters. For the rest, the SAIL should be free to charge prices as per market demand (Para 19.11.4).

(2) If any department wishes that steel should be made available to any priority sector at a concessional price, it should subsidise the use of steel by that sector out of its own budget, so that the costs and the beneficiaries of the subsidy can be identified (Para 19.11.4).

(3) The present system of distribution has not worked to the advantage of small scale industries and for the decentralised sector. The Small Scale Industries Corporations should improve their efficiency and reduce costs. In any case, the trade would be in a better position to meet the requirements of the small producer and the small user of steel, and should be given a bigger role in steel trade with the safeguard regarding pricing, which would reduce the possibility of the black marketing in steel (Para 19.7.6).

(4) The import of ferrous scrap should be freely permitted under OGL (Para 19.8.2).

(5) The canalisation of steel import should be continued for bulk items, and imported and indigenous steel should be pooled and sold at uniform prices. For all "mismatched" steel sections, free import should be allowed (Paras 19.11.5 and 19.11.6).

(6) The complex system of licensing and approvals by the Iron & Steel Controller in the downstream steel industry may be dispensed with, and the creation of capacity in the steel industry — other than in respect of integrated steel plants — should follow the same procedures as for all other industries, namely, there ought to be a banned list, a free list, and a restricted list to be licensed on merit (Para 19.9.2).

(7) The functions of the Iron & Steel Control organisation should be merged with the SAIL or the JPC, the recommendatory authority in regard to the capacity being the Technical Wing of the Department of Steel. The Steel Priority Committee as well as the Iron Ore Board could also be wound up (Paras 19.9.2, 19.9.3 and 19.9.5).

19. **Non-Ferrous Metals** (Chapter 20)

Findings

(a) In the area of non-ferrous metals, apart from formal controls, there have lately been a number of administrative controls.

(b) Apart from price control, there has been canalisation of import of major non-ferrous metals, aluminium, copper and zinc all being so canalised.

(c) Price and distribution control have been applied extensively in respect of aluminium though other metals have also been subject to controlled distribution through allocations from time to time, and also to prices determined administratively.

(d) In the policy of price control adopted for non-ferrous metals, there has been no consistent approach nor any detailed study of the implications of the controls prior to their being instituted.

(e) In the matter of aluminium, a number of divergent objectives have shaped policy, the consequences of which have not been carefully worked out; and similar lack of any consistent long-term approach has influenced the pricing of copper and zinc.

(f) Copper prices in particular, and also zinc prices have been subject to considerable speculative fluctuations in the international markets which have led to similar fluctuations in domestic prices of these metals, leading in turn to the emergence of speculative changes in the demand for these metals.

(g) The indigenous cost of production of copper — which is a key raw material for a large number of key industries — is significantly higher than the world prices owing to the lean grade of copper ore available in the country.

(h) Some of these industries being capital intensive as well as power intensive, there have arisen serious problems in the matter of pricing for new units as also for different units paying widely divergent rates for power.

(i) These metals being of strategic importance, as also basic inputs for a large number of important industries, there is need to evolve a policy which would both provide a minimal protection to indigenous production for strategic reasons, and also the evolution of a policy which would both insulate the domestic producer against international price fluctuations and not raise the general cost structure too much.

Recommendations

(a) *Aluminium*

(1) In regard to aluminium, there should be a more realistic system of power rates for all aluminium smelters which should be based on the opportunity cost for power and not on the cost of generation of any one power station feeding a particular smelter; the above would in turn require price pooling until this major input cost for all producers is more or less equated (Para 20.2.6.1).

(2) These changes should be made in gradual steps over a period of, say, five years so as to avoid the shock of sudden change, and to allow a period of transition (Para 20.2.6.1).

(3) The divergent capital costs of new and old units could be allowed by way of excise duty rebates or similar fiscal adjustments (Para 20.2.6.1).

(4) This would enable the price of aluminium to be freed from control in course of time, so that there is incentive for greater efficiency of production (Para 20.2.6.1).

(5) In the meantime there should be a uniform pooled price with different retention costs for different units (Para 20.2.6.1).

(6) A buffer stock of, say, approximately 20,000 tonnes (as would appear on *prima facie* grounds) of aluminium should also be built up so that the management of supply could ensure continued availability of aluminium, and a truly competitive price of

aluminium could emerge when control is finally lifted (Para 20.2.6.1).

(7) Production control on the quantum of EC grade aluminium to be produced should continue to ensure availability (Para 20.3.6.1).

(b) *Copper*

(8) In the case of copper, with the only producing unit in the public sector having a higher cost of production than imported copper, a "managed" price should continue (Para 20.3.5.1).

(9) To achieve the above, the canalisation of import of copper — which has in any case proved to be beneficial — should continue (Para 20.3.5.1).

(10) In order to ensure a fair price of copper, which can also be sustained, a buffer stock of, say, approximately 30,000 tonnes (as would appear on *prima facie* grounds) of copper should also be built up, taking advantage of downward swings in international prices for inventory build-up (Para 20.3.5.1).

(11) On the above basis, copper prices should be announced after pooling the prices of indigenous and imported copper, on an annual basis (Para 20.3.5.1).

(12) There should be suitable price differential between special high grade electrolytic copper wire bars and ordinary fire refined copper (Para 20.3.5.1).

(c) *Zinc*

(13) For zinc there is similar need for managed prices and of pooling of prices (Para 20.4.5.1).

(14) In pooling zinc prices, however, distinction should only be made between pricing of zinc based on imported concentrates — which is normally linked to the international price of zinc — and pricing of zinc based on indigenous ore mining, and other considerations should not be brought into play in price determination (Para 20.4.5.1).

(15) A buffer stock of, say, approximately 25,000 tonnes (as would appear on *prima facie* grounds) of zinc metal should also be built up, as for other non-ferrous metals, so as to introduce stability in supply and prices (Para 20.4.5.1).

(16) Canalised import should also continue for zinc for the same

reasons as for copper (Para 20.4.5.1.).

20. **Cement** (Chapter 21)

Findings

(a) Price control over cement in the past has been a strong factor in inhibiting the growth of capacity in the cement industry.
(b) Past control over distribution has given unmerited profit to the middlemen and even the new system of distribution initiated recently is not likely to be free from black market transactions in cement.
(c) There has also been inhibition in regard to creation of capacity in the cement industry by the large houses and licences have been given to new parties who have not succeeded in establishing cement capacity.
(d) Investment by Government in cement industry has also been limited, and in particular there has not been adequate investment in cement industry in the deficit areas.
(e) The above has been accentuated by the freight pooling system, and more particularly, an uniform ex-factory price of cement throughout the country without reference to the cost of transportation.
(f) As a result, there has emerged a substantial gap between the demand for and supply of cement which is currently estimated at between two to three million tonnes per annum.
(g) Import of cement does not provide a solution because apart from the high price of imported cement there are limitations even of port capacity.
(h) One consequence of the controlled price of cement has been the somewhat profligate use of cement and gradual elimination of traditional building materials including lime mortar and other substitutes for cement.
(i) The system of controlled price and distribution has inhibited innovative changes both in production and marketing techniques in the cement industry.
(j) There has also been control in the matter of import of new technology justified on grounds of encouragement of indigenous research which has held up the possibility of increases in output with relatively low investment.

(k) The new system of distribution introduced since October 1978 in some areas and in January 1979 in some others provides for complete allocation of all concerned by governmental authorities and is likely to make for further rigidity in the distribution system.

(l) This would already appear to have happened in some of the areas where it is claimed that the new distribution system has been working well.

(m) In any case the rigid distribution system can only function in a regime of scarcity and is unlikely to function when there is no shortage of cement in the country.

(n) As a result of the control over pricing and distribution of cement, the large users of cement including those whose requirements cannot be deemed to be of high priority have got supplies of cement at concessional prices while cement manufacturers have not got the benefit of high prices, and black market money has been made by distributors and middlemen in respect of a substantial part of cement.

Recommendations

(1) There should be no licensing control in respect of cement expansion (Para 21.2.4).

(2) While price and distribution controls and freight pooling cannot be given up, differential retention prices should be worked out so as to encourage the creation of capacity in deficit areas (Paras 21.4.3 and 21.4.4).

(3) A special allowance of atleast Rs. 20 per tonne of cement should be allowed to producers — increasing the price of cement by Re. 1 per bag — and the proceeds funded, to be released for expansion of the industry (Para 21.8.6).

(4) In the pricing formula, split locations should be encouraged so that grinding plants can be set-up nearer the consuming centres, so as to reduce the burden on the transportation system, through the movement of clinkers in open wagons (Para 21.3.9).

(5) The manufacture of pozzolana cement should be encouraged and Government departments should be asked to use pozzolana cement so as to increase the total supply of cement in the country (Para 21.8.1).

(6) There should be increased emphasis on setting up capacity for grinding cement, to be fed initially by imported clinkers, which

Government is already considering (Para 21.8.1).

(7) There should be free import of technology for purposes such as precalcination of cement with a view to increasing output at minimal investment cost (Para 21.8.5).

(8) Rules regarding building and construction should be changed to permit construction of building with substitute materials like lime mortar, and at the same time, the use of cement for ostentatious and low priority purposes such as the concreting of pavements and construction of fountains in urban areas should be banned; also five-star hotels and similar multistoreyed building may be asked to pay the full import price of cement for their requirements (Paras 21.8.2 and 21.8.3).

(9) To the extent controls are considered necessary on cement price, distribution, etc., the same may be exercised under the EC Act instead of the IDR Act (Para 21.4.2).

21. **Paper and Newsprint** (Chapter 22)

Findings

(a) There are only two controls on the paper industry as of today, one on percentages of different varieties of cultural papers to be produced by mills, and the other an "informal" control over the price and distribution of white printing paper required by the student community.

(b) In spite of the paper industry making frequent complaints as to the rigours of price control it has for some time been making fairly good profits, and yet there has been no marked investment interest in the paper industry.

(c) This has been due partly to the long gestation period of investment and partly to the requirement of large investment funds for this industry; at the same time, investment in the paper industry had suffered because of lack of clarity in licensing policy, a number of schemes prepared by large houses being rejected.

(d) There has also been evidence of the generation of considerable black money in the paper industry inspite of there being no price control over most varieties of paper.

(e) The control over the distribution of white printing paper has been weak and both the system of allocation and the system of distribution have been designed without much thought or preplanning so that the system is open to various leakages.

(f) The informal control over the price of white printing paper — at Rs. 2750 per tonne — has continued since 1974 without any change.

(g) There has been inadequate control over and non-observance by mills of the regulations pertaining to, environmental pollution; the effluent discharge of the large paper mills continuing to pose a serious problem of water pollution.

(h) Inadequate thought has been given to the long-term supply of paper without creating an ecological imbalance through the cutting down of forests, and even short-term export/import policies in regard to this industry have been *ad hoc* and not attuned to long term needs of the industry.

(i) There have been two problems in relation to newsprint control, first in regard to the tight control exercised over newsprint allocation, and secondly, in regard to the pricing of newsprint produced by NEPA Mills.

Recommendations

(1) The control over varietal production imposed on the paper industry should continue (Para 22.5.5).

(2) There is no justification for any "concessional" (and informally controlled) price for Government purchase of paper which has in any case not accrued in practice, and the availability of concessional paper should be limited to meet the requirements of the student community (Para 22.4.10).

(3) The present system of allocation of white printing paper for meeting the requirements of student community should be tightened, and the distribution system in respect of exercise books improved to avoid leakages (Para 22.4.6).

(4) Regulatory measures on environmental pollution by the paper industry should be tightened up, and there should be stiff penalties for infringement of the regulations regarding effluent discharge (Para 22.6.3).

(5) Government should give institutional and other support for the development of the handmade paper industry and also preferential treatment for Government purchase of such paper (Para 22.8.1).

(6) There should be no control over newsprint import or allocation,

and strict regulation of the use of NEPA Mills newsprint should also be done away with, NEPA Mills being allowed to compete in the market after imposition of an appropriate duty on imported newsprint (Para 22.7.5).

22. **Rubber** (Chapter 23)

Findings

(a) The Rubber Act provides wide ranging powers of control, over all aspects of rubber, to the Rubber Board.
(b) In the past, rubber prices have been fixed but have generally not been effective.
(c) Over the past few years, rubber prices have fluctuated widely.
(d) Rubber has been exported over 1976-78 at a loss in order to prevent a slump in prices, requiring rubber to be now imported to prevent rubber prices from soaring to artificially high levels.
(e) A cess has been regularly collected from rubber users, but not fully used for the development of rubber, leaving a large balance in the cess fund.

Recommendations

(1) A realistic support price should be announced for rubber, on the basis of independent studies by a body like the Agricultural Prices Commission or the BICP (Para 23.9.3).
(2) The Rubber Board should enter the market, and purchase and sell rubber to stabilise the market (Para 23.9.4).
(3) The Rubber Board should immediately set about to build up a buffer stock of rubber while the size of buffer stock to be gradually built up should be decided after expert study. On *prima facie* grounds, a buffer stock of around 2 months' requirement, or around 25000 tonnes of raw rubber, should be built up (Para 23.9.4).
(4) The interest cost of holding an inventory of this size would be a little more than half of the money collected annually under the rubber cess, and the financing of the buffer stock of rubber would be a legitimate charge on the rubber cess (Para 23.9.4).
(5) Regulation of prices of rubber should be exercised effectively, without a formal control in the above manner, so as to assist the

sustained growth of rubber plantations as well as rubber using industries (Para 23.9.3).

23. **Gold** (Chapter 24)

Findings

(a) Gold control, which was instituted partly to wean the country away from the gold habit and partly to prevent smuggling of gold into the country, has not subserved either of the two objectives for which it had been instituted.
(b) Amendment to gold control made in September, 1963 provided loopholes for, and later since 1966, permitted the fabrication of gold jewellery, which defeated the first objective of gold control indicated earlier.
(c) Smuggling of gold into the country has continued unabated, there being strong evidence to presume that the current rate of smuggled gold import into India is at least 50 tonnes per annum, if not more, other estimates placing the quantum of gold smuggling at an annual rate of upto 100 tonnes per annum, which would indicate that the second objective of gold control has similarly not been achieved.
(d) At the present international price of gold, the value of smuggled gold into the country would involve a minimum annual foreign exchange outgo of Rs. 300 crores.
(e) Since the Indian price of gold is significantly higher, the savings drain in the economy arising oniy from smuggled gold would be even higher.
(f) The craze for gold ornaments has been fanned by a number of other factors and circumstances, an important factor being the enormous increase in the international price of gold in the last 10 years, from $ 35 per ounce upto March 1968 to something like $ 238 per ounce by the end of March 1979.
(g) This phenomenal increase in the international price of gold has occurred partly because of the loss of confidence in reserve currencies and partly because of the search, on the part of liquid funds generated after the oil price hike of 1973, for a stable asset or store of value.
(h) One result of the above development has been that those who have held gold in the form of gold jewellery have gained through

appreciation in the price of gold more than those who have held other assets which are productive, encouraging the speculative demand for gold as an asset over and above the normal demand for gold as jewellery and for other uses.

(i) Since import of gold has not been permitted since 1939, there has emerged over the years a difference between the international price of gold and the Indian price of gold, both of which have moved in more or less a parallel fashion.

(j) The difference between the Indian price of gold and the international price of gold has been based partly on the cost of smuggling gold, and partly on the facility of foreign exchange payment for purchase of gold abroad for smuggling into India.

(k) The difference between the Indian and the international price of gold has of late widened: from approximately Rs. 50 per 10 grams before 1968 to approximately Rs. 90 per 10 grams between 1970 and 1975 to approximately Rs. 180 per 10 grams over 1976 and 1977, and finally to Rs. 280 per 10 grams in the last few months.

(l) The changes in the broad gap between Indian and international gold prices upto the third quarter of 1978 may be assumed to reflect, by and large, an increase in the cost of smuggling, though the recent sharp increase in the difference appears to reflect a speculative increase in the price of gold in India.

(m) One factor relevant in this connection is the ease with which the smuggling of gold can be financed which depends in turn of the extent to which the exchange rate of the rupee is realistic and export earnings as well as internal remittances tend to flow through normal banking channels or seek non-banking channels for funnelling these receipts.

(n) The gold auctions by the Reserve Bank of India during 1978 did not help to either reduce the price of gold within the country or to raise the resources expected and had to be abandoned after the auctioning of the total of around 13 tonnes of gold.

(o) The international trade in gold jewellery is mainly for jewellery of 9 to 14-carats, the emphasis being on latest fashions and hallmark of quality rather than on the gold content of the jewellery.

(p) To the extent that gold has been regularly smuggled into the country in spite of the controls imposed so far, the policy options are: (i) to permit the free import of gold (subject to an import duty calibrated to the cost of smuggling); (ii) to continue to put a blind eye to the problem of smuggling and to continue with present policies and only intensify the attempt to check smuggling; or (iii) to attempt to change the gold habit both for purposes of making of gold ornaments as well as a form of asset in which to hold savings.

Recommendations

(1) Gold control should be amended and the manufacture of gold ornaments above 18-carat purity should be totally prohibited (Para 24.5.9).
(2) To meet the demand for 18-carat gold, Government should import the required quantum of gold, refine it through the mints and sell 18-carat gold bars freely (Para 24.5.10).
(3) Free import of simple tools and equipment should be permitted to jewellers in order to facilitate working with even lower carat gold, e.g., of 14-carats (Para 24.7.2).
(4) After a few years, when goldsmiths have become attuned to using equipment for production of jewellery with lower gold content, there should be a reduction in the purity of gold to 14-carat for the making of jewellery (Para 24.7.3).
(5) Suitable agencies of the Government like the Hindustan Diamond Trading Company Ltd. H.D.T.C. and the HHEC should be asked to organise the production of gold and studded jewellery for export by importing modern designs, seeking export orders for the jewellery so produced, by exhibiting them abroad through the HDTC and HHEC, and organising production to meet the specific requirements of the international market, by supplying the goldsmiths with simple tools and equipment required to fabricate jewellery with lower gold content (Para 26.6.4).
(6) The Import Replenishment scheme for export of gold jewellery in its present form should be given up (Para 24.6.4).
(7) Better facilities to attract the savings of poorer people should be devised in order to get the people move away from savings in the form of gold ornaments; such savings should be so devised as to be simple, productive — that is carry an attractive rate of interest — and yet be capable of easy encashment, without difficulty in time of need (Para 24.7.11).
(8) "Gold bonds" may be revived but with suitable modifications, with indexation to allow for price changes for gold ornaments of

higher than 18-carat gold content — subject to a value ceiling — in order to break the gold habit as a store of value in the country (Para 24.7.10).

(9) Import of any special tools of trade required by jewellers should be subsidised (Para 24.6.4).

(10) There is need to provide people with a reliable, profitable semi-liquid form of asset which can replace gold. One way would be to allow people to sell gold to the mints (instead of the pawnbrokers as at present) or other nominated agencies (Para 24.7.4).

24. **Decentralised Sector** (Chapter 25)

Findings

(a) There is both urgent need and good economic justification for the promotion of employment oriented production, distribution and construction methods, which may call for protection and subsidy to this sector.

(b) In the background of the present divergence between real and market rates of interest and wages and other disadvantages of the decentralised sector, and the social subsidy enjoyed today by large scale industry in urban conglomerates, some part of the present support or subsidy to the decentralised sector is no more than the social subsidy at present enjoyed by large scale urban industry.

(c) The decentralised sector should be defined to cover not only decentralised production but also decentralised distribution and construction activity.

(d) Various criteria can be drawn up for identifying specific activities for which decentralised economic activity would give relatively the highest output, so as to maximise both employment and output.

(e) The decentralised sector faces a number of problems: (i) unfair competition from organised industry, (ii) inadequate supply of raw materials at high prices, (iii) inadequate supply of finance, (iv) lack of marketing facilities, etc.

(f) The present organisational support for the decentralised sector suffers from a number of inadequacies.

Recommendations

(1) Although there is a very large list of industries numbering 807

reserved for "small scale industries" (which are "modern small scale industries" quite different from village industries), there is a need for a separate list of reserved items for the decentralised sector especially for artisans and cottage industry type workers (Para 25.5.1).

(2) To begin with, there is a case for reserving the following types of production activities for the decentralised sector:

(a) all *dhotis* and *sarees* with border (of any kind or width);
(b) all carpet weaving, shawls, and woollen blankets;
(c) certain types of leather and PVC products (including the stitching of shoes from uppers and sole leather). This policy has to be integrated with the upgrading of tanning techniques, setting up of common facility centres, training, and in fact, some sort of "production cooperation" between the organised and decentralised sectors;
(d) soap, on the basis of supply of "fatty acids" from the organised sector; and
(e) matches, on the basis of supply of potassium chlorate from the organised sector (Para 25.5.5).

(3) For adequate supply of raw materials for the decentralised sector, the Government should ensure that:

(a) a part of the supply of raw materials is available for the decentralised sector, compulsively if necessary;
(b) the cost of these raw materials to the decentralised sector is no higher than to the mill sector through a subsidy, if necessary; and
(c) the quality of raw materials supplied to the decentralised sector is not inferior to the quality of raw materials available to the organised sector, through the imposition of quality control, laying down of specifications and standards, etc. (Para 25.3.5).

(4) State or district or local level institutions of repute should stand guarantee for the production and marketing of the products of the decentralised sector, so that banking funds can flow without any difficulty for the development of this sector (Para 25.3.7).

(5) There should also be a separate list for government and public sector purchase exclusively from cottage and village industries

(Para 25.5.2).

(6) In order to give positive encouragement to the decentralised sector, at least 20 per cent incremental credit to be given by banks should be reserved for the decentralised sector (Para 25.5.2).

(7) Institutions which can act as a link between the artisans and the financial institutions purveying credit, should be organised (Para 25.3.10).

(8) Assistance given under various schemes of integrated rural development (like the MFAL scheme) should be extended for all types of production in the decentralised sector, and not merely for two of the 23 industries falling under the purview the KVIC (Para 25.3.8).

(9) In order to protect employment, effort should be made to integrate private retail distribution into the scheme for public distribution of essential commodities to be introduced; and suitable restraints should be introduced in order to ensure the use of labour intensive methods in construction activity (Para 25.2.2).

25. **Credit Control** (Chapter 26)

Findings

(a) Insofar as the DRI scheme is concerned, the subsidy involved in the grant of concessional finance has in practice set a limit to the total quantum of credit made available to the small artisans and the tiny producers.

(b) Selective credit control has not been able to prevent speculative stock holding in a situation of shortages because of the existence of non-banking funds.

(c) The term lending institutions cannot, as they are themselves not prepared to, replace the licensing system which accords priority for industrial investment.

(d) The grant of concessional finance to large and medium scale industry by term lending institutions can militate against the objective of employment-orientation.

(e) There is a paucity of institutions which can act as a bridge between the lending institutions and the small producer, in particular the small agriculturist and the cottage industry artisan.

Recommendations

(1) Rather than give only a small part of the requirements of funds

required by the small producer at a concessional rate of interest, credit should be made available in adequate volume and with speed to the small producers, at reasonable commercial interest rates at which funds are available to the organised sector (Paras 26.3 5 and 26.3.6).

(2) In order to keep up pressure on the lending authorities to extend credit to the target group, a minimum of 20 per cent of the additional credit grant should be deployed to the decentralised sector (Para 26.3.7).

(3) Although selective credit control cannot replace direct physical control over stocks in a situation of scarcity, it should nonetheless be used discriminatingly and carefully to ensure that supply of credit is available in a manner calculated to meet the genuine requirements of trade as may be necessary (Para 26.2.9).

(4) In order to ensure that industrial licensing is able to direct investment to priority and preferred sectors, there should be greater interaction between the policy-makers and the financial institutions, and the latter should be represented on the Licensing Committee (Para 26.4.10).

(5) Concessions on capital for large scale industry should be given only with very great circumspection and care, so that this policy does not militate against labour intensive forms of production (Para 26.4.11).

(6) There should be a build-up or strengthening of institutions which can act as a bridge between the banks and the small borrowers, so that the requisite volume of capital can be made available to the really small producer (Para 26.4.3).

(7) After providing clear guidelines in regard to purposes for which credit may be given, Reserve Bank approval of loans by nationalised banks to accounts of more than Rs. 2 crores each may be dispensed with, and the nationalised banks should be asked to report regularly as to the status of these large accounts to the RBI (Para 26.4.5).

26. **Price Control** (Chapter 27)

Findings

(a) The issues that arise in regard to agricultural prices and prices of industrial products are somewhat different.

(b) With agricultural products, the control over prices has not succeeded in the past, and lately the focus has shifted to the determination of minimum support prices so as to assure a reasonable price to the grower.
(c) In agriculture, the management of supply is a function of the necessary inputs for increasing productivity, of rainfall, and also of relative prices of competing crops.
(d) For industrial prices the management of supply is partly a function of plan priorities and plan investments, partly a matter of private investments which in turn depends on restraints and other conditions for private investment and also on the pricing policy for industrial products.
(e) In the past, the fixation of industrial prices has suffered from diverse lacunae with the result that the supply of most essential consumer goods, the price of which has generally been regulated, has persistently fallen short of demand.

Recommendations

(1) In the fixation of agricultural prices, due attention should be paid to price parties between competing crops (Para 27.2.8).
(2) In order that a support price policy can succeed, an adequate buffer stock may be created so that stability of supply is assured (Para 27.2.7).
(3) The support prices should be announced ahead of sowing and based on recommendations of an independent jurisdical high power technical body, and not based on political pressure and influence, and that for this purpose, the Government should, as a matter of convention, accept the recommendations of such technical authorities like the Agricultural Prices Commission and the Bureau of Industrial Costs and Prices (Para 27.2.8).
(4) In fixing industrial prices, due note should be taken of replacement costs of capital and not merely of historical costs of capital (Para 27.3.11).
(5) While this is necessary in order to expand industrial output, distributed profits should be regulated, and if necessary, a part of the price should be separately funded for replacement, modernisation and expansion (Para 27.3.13).
(6) In fixing industrial prices, there should be realistic assumption of capacity utilisation based on past averages of consumption and

other cost norms; and there should be a suitable escalation clause of avoid problems arising from lags in price fixation based on historical costs of production (Para 27.3.12).

(7) The price control should be avoided as far as possible and where resorted to, should be combined with a package of measures calculated to increase supply in the long run (Para 27.3.15).

27. **Distribution Control and Buffer Stocks** (Chapter 28)

Findings

(a) Control over prices is meaningless without control over distribution.
(b) Proper distribution control cannot be achieved without an effective machinery for distribution.
(c) An effective public distribution has been unanimously recommended by all Chief Ministers, on the basis of which Government has already announced a new policy frame for public distribution.
(d) Such a frame has to start with proper supply management and end with effective monitoring.
(e) The maintenance of an adequate buffer stock of all essential items is essential in any rational policy of supply management, so as to provide stability in the supply and prices of all the essential items, both in the interest of the producers as well as in the interest of the consumers.
(f) Different States have adopted different, and additional, schemes for meeting the requirements of the vulnerable sections of the population.
(g) One of the difficulties of the public distribution system in the past has been the narrow coverage of items sold from ration shops.
(h) The cost of public distribution has been somewhat higher than the cost of private distribution partly because of the above, and partly because of the higher wage, rates and allowances for Government servants.
(i) Even in Kerala, where the public distribution system has worked well in the past, the system has been running rather than after the letting of restrictions on movement control.

Recommendations

(1) The adequacy of supply of essential commodities should be en-

sured through proper supply management and through operation of buffer stocks and through well planned imports where necessary. This would be an essential pre-requisite to the success of an efficient distribution system (Para 28.4.1).

(2) This should be buttressed by adequate storage capacity in far-flung and hilly areas to ensure adequate supply of the essential commodities throughout the country and throughout the year (Para 28.4.10).

(3) Adequate buffer stock should be built up, based on the degree of fluctuation in the availability of different products and the degree of stability and protection from fluctuations in availability and prices that is required (Para 28.4.4).

(4) The costs of buffer stock operations would be a legitimate charge on the consumers for certain items and on the taxpayer in general for certain others, as recommended variously in the two Chapters on Non-Ferrous Metals and Foodgrains respectively (Para 28.4.4).

(5) As eclectic approach should be adopted and the private distribution system should be used wherever possible, to function under strict discipline (Para 28.4.6).

(6) The co-operative form of management should be adopted wherever possible in order to reduce the cost of distribution (Para 28.4.7).

(7) The public distribution system should be geared to move quickly into any item in which shortages appear suddenly, for which purpose the distribution system should be in a position to commandeer a reasonable part of the supply (Para 28.4.8).

(8) The vulnerable sections of the population, especially those below the poverty line, should be subsidised through the public distribution system (Para 28.4.1).

(9) The public distribution system should be made economically viable not only by reduction of the overhead costs but also by arranging for the supply of a wider variety of essential commodities than customary; however, it may not be possible to combine all items to be sold from the same shop (Para 28.4.7).

(10) A proper system of monitoring of the public distribution system should be adopted, by organising committees of consumers and citizens at large (Para 28.4.11).

(11) In order that the vulnerable sections of the population can be supplied essential commodities at subsidised rates, a special ration-

card system should be devised so that the benefit of the subsidised supplies reaches only the target group (Para 28.4.9).

28. **Generation of Black Money** (Chapter 29)

Findings

(a) The controls have been an important source of black money.
(b) Price control without an adequate machinery for distribution and speedy arrangement for increasing supplies is potentially a source of black money generation.
(c) Leakages in the distribution system are another potential source of black money.
(d) Significant generation of black money has been involved in cement and paper industries.
(e) Rent control is yet another source of black money generation.
(f) Harassment to the public and petty corruption stem from the large number of licences required by the small shopkeepers and traders.

Recommendations

(1) To the extent possible, other alternative policies like buffer stock operations and fiscal policy should be used, and non-discretionary controls should be imposed (Para 29.2.2).
(2) It would be desirable to have as small a list of restricted items involving individual discretion as may be possible (Para 29.2.2).
(3) There should be suitable monitoring of the control administration as well as of the working of the controls (Para 29.3.2).
(4) Controls should not be prolonged where leakages and the generation of black money cannot be prevented (Para 29.3.2).

29. **Implementation and Monitoring** (Chapter 30)

Findings

(a) The basic requirement of monitoring of controls is an efficient data system in regard to which, numerous expert bodies have already made various recommendations.
(b) The efficacy of controls and the monitoring of controls are closely linked together and depend also on the number of points

of controls, the possibility of leakage being directly linked to the number of points of control which need monitoring.

(c) In the matter of distribution control, the control system has to reach down to a very large area where a public distribution system is likely to be useful.

(d) At present consumers are not properly organised and the consumer movement is in its infancy.

(e) This also stems from the fact that the consumers who need protection also constitute the weakest sections of the society.

(f) At present the chambers of commerce and industry in India do not adequately represent either manufacturing establishments or trading units.

(g) Existing chambers act primarily as grievance lobbies to make representations to Government and are doing little to regulate the conduct of their own members with the result that there is widespread distrust of the business community among consumers in general.

Recommendations

(1) On a national level, all controls and subsidies should be monitored by the Planning Commission in a monitoring unit to be set-up, so that the adjustments required in plans and programmes as also in the operation of controls can take note of the problems thrown up by the functioning of the controls (Para 30.6.2).

(2) The monitoring unit in the Planning Commission should function as a co-ordinating unit for monitoring (Para 30.6.4).

(3) Similar monitoring of controls should be undertaken by State Planning Boards for the Central as also State level controls and subsidies are concerned. The actual working of controls implemented by the State Civil Supplies departments should be the special concern of State monitoring agencies (Para 30.6.3).

(4) The monitoring of controls and subsidies should be devised on a multi-level pattern, the primary monitoring agency being the control authority (Para 30.6.1).

(5) The price and distribution controls can be monitored by developing a vibrant consumer movement which should be encouraged and funded by the Government (Para 30.7.3).

(6) The monitoring of price and distribution controls could be made easier and made more efficient by organising citizens councils in

each area, and to begin with they could be asked to oversee the functioning and working of fair price shops (Para 30.7.3).

(7) There should be organised effort on the part of the Government to educate the public and to give wide publicity in regard to the actual entitlements, so that consumers councils can oversee the functioning of the distribution system (Para 30.7.3).

(8) The chambers of commerce and industry should undertake voluntary regulation of the conduct of their members (Para 30.8.7).

(9) A beginning could be made by attempting, in respect of specified industries, crafts and trade that membership of a chamber should be compulsory for all those who participate in that profession, such chambers being organised at the local level with at least one chamber in each district and a city and these chambers should be required to draw up a code of conduct which they would be required to enforce on all members; they should also be vested with powers to deregister errant members, (Paras 30.8.7 and 30.8.8).

(10) If the experiment succeeds, the coverage of such compulsory membership could be extended to other industries, in crafts and trade so as to ensure voluntary regulation and the observance of a code of conduct by all members (Para 30.8.8).

4

COMMITTEE ON NATIONAL EMPLOYMENT SERVICE, 1978 — REPORT[1]

Chairman Shri P.C. Mathew

Members Shri S. Abdul Qadir; Prof. (Miss) Malathi Bolar; Shri I.C. Kumar; Shri L.S. Mishra replaced by Shri P.S. Rao; Shri K.G. Verma; Shri R. Shankarappa; Shri H.C. Malkani; Shri Vijay Merchant

M. Secy. Shri K.S. Baroi.

Appointment

Employment Exchanges, in spite of their large network covering the entire country, have been increasingly unable to meet the expectations of the millions of job-seekers registering with them every year. There has also been a growing volume of complaints regarding corruption and incompetence in their working and criticism has frequently been made both in and outside legislatures on their unsatisfactory performance.

Criticism have been made from time to time regarding the working of Employment Exchanges. Government are keen to have the various aspects of the problem comprehensively examined and have, therefore, decided to set-up a Committee to go into the working of Employment Exchanges and to suggest suitable remedial measures. Vide Government of India in the Ministry of Labour Resolution No. DGET-5(9)/77; E.E.I. dated March 1, 1978.

Terms of Reference

(i) to study various aspects of employment service with a view to

1. New Delhi, Ministry of Labour, Directorate General of Employment and Training, 1979, p. 222.

making it more responsive to the changing circumstances and needs and to make recommendation there on;

(ii) to examine nature and scope of complaints of malpractices in Employment Exchanges and to suggest suitable ways and means to eradicate them in order to improve the image and efficiency of the Employment Service;

(iii) to devise and recommend suitable measures and to increase placement of registrants in Employment Exchanges, both in Governments (Centre and States) as also public and private sectors, as well as to secure maximum and effective utilisation of Employment Service by employer;

(iv) to examine and recommend special steps, if any, to be taken in the matter of placement services to the disadvantaged and handicapped sections, such as Scheduled Tribes, minorities physically handicapped, etc.;

(v) to examine the possibilities of involvement of Employment Service for dealing with rural employment problem arising out of the changed strategies of the Government in giving primacy to the rural employment problem under the reorientation of planning strategies;

(vi) to prescribe minimum basic norms of the amenities, conveniences and welfare measures which are required to be provided at the Employment Exchanges for the public and to suggest ways and means for the implementation of the same; and

(vii) to consider any other matter of relevance and to make recommendations thereon.

Contents

Introductory; National Employment Service in India—A Historical Survey; Complaints about Employment Exchange Organisation; Multiple Recruiting Agencies; Compulsory Recruitment through Employment Exchange; Job Development and Public Relations; Rural Employment; Employment Service to Disadvantaged and Handicapped persons; Vocational Guidance; Individual Counselling and Employment Market Information; Research and Staff Training; Centre-State Collaboration in the Operation of Employment Exchanges; Proposed Organisation; Summary of main conclusions and recommendations; Note of Dissent, Appendices from I to XXII.

Recommendations

A summary of the main conclusions and recommendations made in the earlier chapters of this report is given below.

The Committee Recommends

1. Adequate inspection staff should be provided to conduct regular inspection of Employment Exchanges and to look into complaints. (Para 3.12)

2. The legality and propriety of existing restrictions imposed by State Governments on registration at Employment Exchanges in each State should be reviewed and residential restrictions, if any are needed, should be imposed by Central enactment in accordance with Constitutional provisions. (Para 3.12)

3. Employment Exchanges should be provided with access to testing facilities at establishments which enjoy public confidence. (Para 3.12)

4. The accommodation and amenities and communication facilities available at Employment Exchanges should be improved. (Para 3.12)

5. The specific recommendations for operational improvement of the National Employment Service suggested by Study Groups, such as the one constituted in 1969 by the National Labour Commission, should be taken up and implemented, wherever necessary, in the course of the reorganisation and expansion recommended in this report. (Para 3.12)

6. It is not necessary to ban private recruiting agencies, but there is need to regulate their operations by means of a statute which should also prohibit the collection of fees by them from job-seekers. (Para 4.7)

7. The Central and State Governments and their establishments and undertakings should make the fullest use of Employment Exchanges to recruit persons to fill their posts, more particularly posts of Grades III and IV. (Para 4.7)

8. Where they consider it necessary to set-up a special recruitment board for an establishment, the Employment Exchange Organisation should be closely associated with it as its Secretariat and entrusted with the task of preparing lists of candidates from the Employment Exchange registers, arranged in order of merit on such criteria as the recruitment board may prescribe. (Para 4.7)

9. In any State where the bulk of recruitment to Class III and Class IV posts is carried out by special recruitment boards from the open market, without making full use of the Employment Exchange Organisation, Government may consider whether it will be worthwhile to continue the Employment Exchanges in the concerned States. (Para 4.7)

10. Government should examine whether, in view of the undertaking to maintain a free public employment service implied in India's ratification of I.L.O. Convention No. 88, it is legal or proper for Service Commissions and recruiting boards, who select candidates to fill jobs in the Public Sector, to charge fees from the large number of people who apply for every job that is advertised. (Para 4.7)

11. Instead of making it compulsory for employers to make appointments exclusively from panels of names sent by Employment Exchanges, employers may be allowed to visit Employment Exchanges, inspect the registration cards in the required category and make their own panels (not necessarily based on date of registration) containing candidates whom they would like to send for interview, provided they notify in advance the general scheme of selection, namely the criteria on the basis of which the selection is to be made. This facility would apply not only to Clerical and Class IV jobs, but also to all other categories of jobs for which lists are maintained by the Employment Exchanges. (Paras 5.7 and 3.12)

12. The legal obligation on both Public and Private Sector employers to notify vacancies and send periodic returns may continue. While a new legislation has been recommended for the purpose of ensuring full use of Employment Exchanges, it is felt that it need not be extended at this stage for compelling job-seekers to register themselves at Employment Exchanges or prohibiting employers from appointing persons not registered at Employment Exchanges. There seem no justification to impose on Public Sector Undertakings restrictions from which similarly situated Private Sector units are free. Both classes of employers should have full freedom to appoint qualified people according to their job requirements and predetermined criteria. They should first approach the Employment Exchanges where they will have all the facilities of self-service as suggested in paragraph 5.7 of this report. In case they do not find any candidates suitable, they should report this fact to the Employment Exchange concerned and may fill up the vacancy from other sources, provided they send within seven days a return in the prescribed form regarding the manner in which the

vacancy has been filled and the particulars of the person with whom the vacancy has been filled. If the employers so wish, the Employment Exchange should issue advertisements on their behalf, scrutinise applications and assist in conducting tests/interviews. To achieve these objects, a new Section 4A (Appendix XIII) may be added to the Employment Exchanges (Compulsory Notification of Vacancies) Act, 1959. This will necessitate deletion of sub-section (2) of Section 3 and sub-section (4) of Section 4 and amendment in Sections 5 and 7 of the Act. This will also require a change in the title of the Act so as to be called, "The National Employment Service Act". The new legislation will apply only to Class III and Class IV vacancies. (Para 5.9)

13. Employment Exchange Organisation should do everything possible to change its public image as a bureaucratic organisation bound by procedural red-tape. It should develop the image of an agency which studies the requirements of its employer-clients in the form of assistance to recruit employees satisfying certain requirements and try to provide quality service efficiently and promptly. The placement function involves the finding of a suitable job for a given man (or woman) and a suitable man (or woman) for a given job. Acceptance of the job or the man should be voluntary for the client job-seeker or employer. There should be frequent personal contacts between Employment Exchange Officers and Employers for this purpose. Similarly, Employment Exchange Officers should meet and advise the job-seekers about different job requirements and trends in employment market. (Para 6.6)

14. A full employment policy should aim at filling all stomachs and not merely keeping all hands busy. The only possible remedy to rural unemployment and poverty is to create more opportunities for productive employment to rural workers during non-agricultural seasons when they are unemployed. The Employment Exchange Organisation should undertake registration, collection of employment and unemployment intelligence, dissemination of information and guidance and thus assist in the creation of off-season employment opportunities at Block level. (Paras 7.1 and 7.12)

15. The Employment Exchange Organisation should act as an early warning device for the organisation of relief works in rural areas and help in recruiting legal persons to such works during seasons of local severe unemployment. (Para 7.12)

16. While the National Sample Survey Organisation may be charged with quinquennial surveys of employment and unemployment

to study long-term trends and analytical features, the Employment Exchange Organisation should prepare monthly/quarterly reports of the state of employment/unemployment at State levels to assist employment planning at those levels; it may also assist the National Sample Survey in organising its quinquennial employment and unemployment surveys. (The staff should be temporarily strengthened when such special tasks are undertaken). (Para 7.12)

17. The Employment Exchange Organisation should itself undertake detailed local surveys on unemployment during seasons of severe unemployment, with the help of additional technical staff sanctioned for the purpose. (Para 7.12)

18. The Employment Exchange Organisation should not be made responsible for the management of unemployment cash benefit disbursement schemes introduced by State Governments, although they will supply such factual information as is available in their records. (Para 7.12)

19. There is a need to undertake studies to identify various types of paid employment and self-employment which could be filled by different categories of the handicapped persons and to design special training and adaptation courses and fixtures and gadgets that could throw open new vistas of employment to such persons. Self-employment schemes with public assistance should also be designed for suitable cases. (Para 8.7)

20. It would be desirable that reservation of jobs for the disadvantaged categories of Scheduled Castes, Scheduled Tribes and the Physically Handicapped are extended to Private Sector also and that the reservation should be made statutory. A technical difficulty should be overcome, if necessary, by amending the Constitution to extend the coverage of Article 31-C to legislation in pursuance of Article 16. (Para 8.8)

21. Corporate units should be asked to indicate in their statutory annual reports the extent to which reservation of jobs for Scheduled Castes, Scheduled Tribes and the Physically Handicapped has been fulfilled. Auditors should also be required to comment on this aspect as part of their social audit in the course of the annual statutory audit. (Para 8.8)

22. Arrangements for special training should be made for all categories of posts to the candidates belonging to Scheduled Castes and Scheduled Tribes, designed to increase their employability on a competitive basis. Besides, in every Employment Exchange there

should be a Special Cell to advise the candidates of this category to go in for trades and vocations in which entry will be easier for them. (Para 8.9)

23. The National Employment Service should assist in implementing any recommendations made by the Special Commission for Scheduled Castes and Scheduled Tribes in regard to improving employment opportunities and employability of these persons. (Para 8.9)

24. More Creches and Day-Care Centres for Children and more Hostels for working girls should be set-up to assist more women to take up jobs. (Para 8.10)

25. There is also need for more training courses for girls and women, particularly short-term modular courses which aim at general competence rather than specialisation in trades such as typing, etc. (Para 8.10)

26. The cause of women's employment can be served better by Government if they pay more attention to expanding training facilities and job-opportunities for women in occupations and areas where women would naturally receive more favourable consideration for employment than by compelling or inducing employers to exclude men who would otherwise have been preferred by the employers and to appoint women in those places. (Para 8.10)

27. It is for the Central and State Governments to decide whether any reservation of jobs is necessary for any class of persons, e.g., minorities and backward classes. No action is due by Employment Service Organisation till Government decided on who are the minorities and backward classes entitled to such reservation and clear instructions in conformity with law are issued by Government to public employers regarding the extent and manner of the reservation; it should be the responsibility of employing authorities to ensure that their requisitions to Employment Exchanges conform to these instructions. (Para 8.11)

28. The existence of both unfilled jobs and qualified job-seekers side by side is partly due to unrealistic expectations of both employers and job-seekers. Both of them should be counselled to temper their expectations with a realistic awareness of the conditions of the present day employment market. (Para 9.6)

29. Regular collection of data under Employment Market Information Programme should be confined to those establishments only which fall within the purview of the Employment Exchanges

(Compulsory Notification of Vacancies) Act, 1959 and the time of the staff thus saved should be utilised in keeping the Employers' Register comprehensive. The studies in respect of establishments employing 10 to 24 workers in Private Sector need be made only on a biennial basis and that too on the basis of a limited number of industries or regions being taken up on each occasion. (Para 9.11)

30. While there is a constant need to educate the employers about their obligations under the Employment Exchanges (Compulsory Notification of Vacancies) Act, 1959 through mass media habitual and incorrigible defaulters should be prosecuted. (Para 9.12)

31. The quality of work and effectiveness of Central supervision to maintain standards in all States in the fields of Vocational Guidance, Individual Counselling and Employment Market Information can be improved if there is more effective inspection and evaluation by the Directorate General of Employment and Training Organisation. The exclusion of agriculture and rural sector, which also constitutes a grave omission, needs to be remedied. These aspects should be taken into account by the Employment Exchange Organisation in planning its future work. (Para 9.14)

32. Employment Exchange Organisation should consider developing a system of monthly labour force reporting in the rural areas and quarterly labour force reporting in the urban areas and the substance and form of these reports should be settled in consultation with the Central Statistical Organisation and improved progressively. For such a scheme, additional staff would have to be appointed. (Para 9.15)

33. The data collected through Employment Market Information Programme and the recommended monthly quarterly labour force reports are of the utmost importance and should be utilised while determining employment and job-training policies for each area and in making-policy changes from time to time. The data should also be fed to Government to assist them in designing projects intended to create local opportunities for self-employment. (Para 9.15)

34. Every item of research of survey undertaken at the National or State Directorate's level should receive the approval of Technical Committees for Research and Surveys and the design of such items should also be cleared by technical experts, before resources are allocated to it. The results of the various items of research and survey should also be discussed by the concerned technical committee with special reference to the users and the specific uses to which they will

put the results; abstracts of research and survey results should be sufficiently well circulated for information and utilisation. (Para 10.8)

35. The Central Institute for Research and Training in Employment Service (CIRTES) should exclusively be made responsible for:

(a) research to develop procedure, technique, methodology, training material and guidance/selection tests;
(b) surveys/studies;
(c) coordination of work pertaining to research/surveys/studies done at State level; and
(d) training of officers and supporting staff. (Para 10.10)

36. To have a sufficiently qualified and technically experienced person to head the Central Institute for Research and Training in Employment Service, the post of Director, CIRTES should be equated to that of Director of Employment Exchanges, Directorate General of Employment and Training. (Para 10.10)

37. To undertake the work of pre-service, in-service and refresher training of officers and other supporting staff, including Statistical Assistants and Clerks, Central Institute for Research and Training in Employment Service should be set-up Regional Institutes which will also feed-back material in respect of functional and problem-oriented research. The Regional Institutes will be under the administrative and technical control of CIRTES. (Para 10.10)

38. Central Institute for Research and Training in Employment Service should have hostel facilities and training programmes organised by the CIRTES should be residential courses for all Officers/supporting staff deputed for training. (Para 10.10)

39. Modern teaching methods and techniques, including audio-visual methods, should be used by Central Institute for Research and Training in Employment Service while imparting training. (Para 10.10)

40. No staff, either at Officer's level or at other levels, should be entrusted with the work relating to Employment Exchange/Bureau unless and until he/she has undergone pre-service training successfully. Besides, there should be regular programmes for in-service and refresher training. (Para 10.10)

41. Implementation of the recommendations made in this report is of crucial importance for social and economic development. Therefore, the strengthening and expansion of the National Employment Service should be accepted as a Central Plan Scheme during the Sixth Plan and

the necessary tied funds allocated to it on 100 per cent basis. After the expansion programme ceases to be a Plan scheme, recurring cost which will be a part of Non-Plan expenditure will be shared by the Central and State Governments on 60:40 ratio. Implementation may be carried out through the State Governments, as in the case of other schemes of national importance, like the National Highway Scheme. The disbursement of the Central Grant will, of course, be conditional on the implementation of the scheme according to guidelines to be given by the Central Government in consultation with the States. (Paras 10.10, 12.9 and 12.20)

42. For improving the effectiveness of Central direction, the Employment Service should be made a National Service and there should be a separate Ministry of Manpower Planning and Employment at the Centre (and corresponding Departments in the States) together with the normal executive field staff or a Directorate General (or a statutory National Manpower Commission as in the United Kingdom) which combines both executive and secretariat functions at Government level in respect of the subjects concerned. (Paras 12.9 and 12.10)

43. The work of Employment Exchanges should be extended to rural areas and skeleton staff be provided for this work at the block level. (Para 12.12)

44. In small and medium district towns, the registration and submission can be done by Employment Exchange at one place. In large district towns and metropolitan cities, there could be more than one office for registration, renewals and vocational guidance to avoid crowding and inconvenience to the job-seekers, wherever necessary, and the technical section of the Employment Exchange, dealing with registration and submission for technical vacancies, should be located in places where there is high enough concentration of industry, or it could be located as a separate section in an Industrial Training Institute, so as to facilitate testing. (Para 12.13)

45. The officer of the Employment Service at district level should be of Class I status and his scale of pay stepped up on the basis of the norms suggested in Appendix XII. (Para 12.14)

46. The University Employment Information and Guidance Bureaux, Special Employment Exchanges and Vocational Rehabilitation Centres for the Physically Handicapped, Coaching-cum-Guidance. Centres for Scheduled Castes and Scheduled Tribes and Professional and Executive Employment Offices at State capitals need to be strengthened and expanded without prejudice to their quality.

However, the registration of professional and executive types of applicants may be done at University Employment Information and Guidance Bureaux, but placement should exclusively be done by the State Professional and Executive Employment Offices by maintaining the live register and providing interview facilities to employers at common central places. (Paras 12.15 and 8.7)

47. In case of Vocational Rehabilitation Centres for the Physically Handicapped the evaluation and guidance part of their work should be looked after by the Employment Directorate, but the training part should be taken care of by the Training Directorate who should depute Training Instructors and other technical staff for the administration of the programme. There should be a Committee consisting of representatives of Employment and Training Directorates and also of Medical and Social Organisations which should meet every month and prepare tailor-made training programmes to meet the needs of individuals or homogeneous groups of disabled persons. (Para 12.15)

48. Each Vocational Rehabilitation Centre for the Physically Handicapped should have a hostel with free lodging and boarding facilities for the clients to stay during evaluation and training. (Para 12.15)

49. The facilities and amenities available at Employment Exchanges should be improved and augmented, if the Exchanges are to function efficiently and smoothly and prove more popular with employers and workers. The following items deserve special attention:

(i) Standard lay-outs which provide for all essential requirements of space, including waiting halls for job-seekers and interview rooms for employers, should be drawn up for Employment Offices with different work-loads by the Directorate General of Employment and Training. These standards should be kept in view while hiring or constructing accommodation for Employment Exchanges;

(ii) The accommodation should have adequate furniture according to norms to be fixed by the Directorate General of Employment;

(iii) Each District Office should be provided with a Jeep. Field Officers should be paid a fixed conveyance allowance to be fixed by the Directorate General of Employment according to State rules, provided they maintain a scooter and utilise it for visits to establishments, etc. Provision for loan on easy terms to purchase the scooter should also be made;

(iv) Office equipment, such as typewriters, duplicators, calculators and filing cabinets should be provided to the offices as per norms to be fixed by the Directorate General of Employment;

(v) All State Directorates having live register of over one lakh many consider the provision of modern data processing facilities; and

(vi) The quality of staff at higher levels should be upgraded and work methods and procedure improved.

5

RAILWAY ACCIDENT INVESTIGATION REPORT ON COLLISION OF NO. 7 DOWN BOMBAY-AHMEDABAD JANATA EXPRESS WITH THE REAR OF NO. 537 DOWN CHURCHGATE–VIRAR SUBURBAN TRAIN AT KM. 49/15-16 BETWEEN NALGAON AND VASAI ROAD STATIONS ON THE CHURCHGATE–VIRAR SUBURBAN SECTION OF WESTERN RAILWAY AT ABOUT 20.15 HOURS ON APRIL 18, 1978[1]

One Man Commission Shri P.M.N. Murthy

Appointment

The Commission was Constituted under Ministry of Tourism and Civil Aviation (Commission of Railway Safety) in accordance with Rule 4 of the Statutory Investigation in Railway Accidents Rules 1973 Vide Notification No. RS 13-T(8)/71 dated April 19, 1973 on April 18, 1978.

Terms of Reference

To enquire into the Collision of No. 7 Down Bombay-Ahmedabad Janata Express with the rear of No. 537 Down Churchgate–Virar Suburban Train at Km 49/15-16 between Nalgaon and Vasai Road Stations on the Churchgate–Virar Suburban Section of Western Railway at about 20.15 hours on April 18, 1978.

1. Delhi, Controller of Publications, 1983, 31 p.

Contents

Conclusions

54. On careful consideration of the available evidence factual, material and circumstantial and on the basis of observations and tests carried out, I have reached the following conclusions:

Cause

(a) The Collision of No. 7 Down Bombay – Ahmedabad Janata Express with the rear of No. 537 Down Churchgate–Virar Suburban train at Km. 49/15-16 between Nalgaon and Vasai Road stations on the Churchgate–Virar broad gauge suburban section of Western Railway at about 20.15 hours on 18th April, 1978, was the result of the Express train being driven past a blank Automatic Signal [No. A 216] into the section beyond, without requisite care and at such a speed as did not enable the Driver to stop short of the obstruction.

The rear of the Suburban train had not been protected with detonators (or a lighted fusee) and its tail lamp had been extinguished prior to the collision, but its Guard had, after some minutes of stoppage at that location, switched 'on' and 'off' his rear headlight in the *bona fide* belief that this would adequately caution the Express Driver of the presence of his train ahead.

Responsibility

(b) (i) The Primary responsibility for this accident lies on the Driver of the Express train who failed to stop at the Automatic Signal whose light was extinguished and exercise due precautions enjoined by regulations. He contravened the provisions of General Rules 76, 82, 277, 279 and the Subsidiary Rules framed thereunder – [reproduced in Annexure-IV].

(ii) The Assistant Driver should also share some responsibility for this mishap for his omission to keep a vigilant lookout and advise the

Driver well in time of the danger signal shown and the obstruction ahead. The contravened the provisions of General Rule 122 [Reproduced in Annexure-IV].

A brief bio-data of the Driving Crew is at Annexure VI.

(iii) The accident may have been averted or its consequences rendered less severe, had the Suburban train been protected in rear in accordance with the requirements of General Rule 280. The roles of the Motorman and Guard of the Suburban train in this connection have been detailed in para 51-I.

Relief Measures

55. (a) Section II of the Report contains a brief description of Relief Measures provided. My observations on some major items of criticism voiced during the Inquiry are at para 53, on which action may be taken as necessary.

(b) There is little doubt that invaluable services were rendered to the victims of this accident by fellow commuters, members of the public living in the neighbourhood, and the railway staff resident in the proximity who ungrudgingly rushed to the site on coming to know of the accident [and engaged themselves in providing succour, in a spirit of anonymity].

The Railway Administration may acknowledge these services and convey their appreciation *inter-alia* to:

(i) The Private Doctors from Vasai Road, Virar and Nalla Sopara who attended to the injured at the station and at site;

(ii) Chief Medical Officer of the Sanjivini Hospital, Virar and his staff;

(iii) Co-operative Societies of Vasai Road – 'Sarvodaya Machhimar Sahakari Society', Pachu Bandra; Arnala Machhimar Multipurpose Society; and Pan Marketing Co-operative Society;

(iv) Individuals who (from their evidence) could be deemed to have rendered great service in rescuing the injured – Shri Albert Micheal Almeida of Bangli Naka; Shri Marshal I. Mechado of Jeewan Wadi; and Shri Sanjay Ambadas Bhavsar of Majlekar Chawl. [The list is obviously not exhaustive];

(v) The Railway staff resident in the vicinity who rushed to the station/site on hearing the news and offered their services – S/Shri A. Vanderhyde, Senior Electrical Foreman (OHE)/Bombay Central [See Para 7(b) (ii)], Michael T. Carvelho, Assistant Electrical Foreman

(TRS), Bandra; B.P. Khaladkar, Divisional Catering Inspector, Bombay Central, and H. Ram Kumar, Commercial Controller, Bombay Central – to mention only a few who appeared at the Inquiry and tendered evidence. There may be many others meriting appreciation; and

(vi) Dr. M.R. Dạs, Divisional Medical Officer, Valsad, who alighted at site from No. 24 UP Express and rendered first-aid to many of the injured under trying circumstances.

Recommendations

56. Five Immediate Recommendations were appended to my Preliminary Report on this Accident. These have been included in this Section.

57. The severity of the impact may have been considerably less and the telescoping possibly avoided had the end coach of No. 537 Down Local train been provided with side buffers. Whereas side buffers exist on the extreme coaches of most Suburban trains, one rake of 1963 Jessops make and 4 of 1951 origin, which have Alliance Couplers with centre buffers, do not have this provision. It is desired that these 5 rakes on the Western Railway and similar rakes if any, on the Central Railway be equipped with standard side buffers with suitable centre couplers, on top priority.

58. The extant designs of Electric Multiple Unit Stock may be reviewed with a view to improving their crash-worthiness.

59. At present, the headlights as well as the tail lamps in the cabs of Suburban trains are controlled by a single switch in such a manner that when one is lit the other is extinguished. Arrangements may be made urgently to provide separate switches located on opposite sides.

60. (a) This accident underscores the need for evolving without further delay a more effective last vehicle indication particularly on Suburban sections where trains follow each other at very close intervals. Towards this end, an additional tail lamp may be provided to Guards of Suburban trains, either as a fixed installation in the cab or as a portable one, which could be flashed towards the rear in cases of stoppage. In this context, the arrangement suggested by the Chief Electrical Engineer, Western Railway to provide on the end panels of EMUs a scotchlite acrylic moulded reflector and a flasher light unit (in addition to the existing tail lamp) is commended for consideration.

(b) A 'proving light' may be provided in the cabs of EMUs to indicate to Guards the condition of tail lamps – whether burning or extinguished.

61. Apropos para 7(b) (ii) of the Report, the incidence of paint in the affected coach getting a flame and starting a minor fire, indicates the need to ensure the use of only fire retarding/resistant paints of proper quality in EMUs (and other passenger carrying stock).

62. Since children also travel in Ladies compartments, such compartments may be provided in the middle of EMU rakes (as on some Suburban trains on the Central Railway), instead of at the end (as is now down on the Western Railway).

63. The feasibility of providing doors in intermediate partitions of II Class compartments in existing rakes which could be opened by passengers in an emergency, or even doing away with such partitions, may be examined.

64. The manufacture of a batch 6 DC EMU rakes with provision of vestibules on trial basis, vide Railway Board's O.M. No. 76/Safety (A&R)/1/4 dated 20th January 1977, may be expedited.

65. Signal posts on the Suburban sections may be coated with luminous paint (with alternate stripes of yellow and black) to improve their visibility during night.

66. The system of surveillance on signalling installations, including check on the quality of bulbs and bulb holders needs to be improved to obviate the incidence of blank signals – intermittent and otherwise.

67. (a) The integrity of signalling installations in the Suburban sections should be further strengthened by providing throughout 'red lamp protection', 'cascading facility' and by replacing 3 aspect Signals by 4 aspects wherever the inter-signal distance warrants it.

(b) Adverting to Para 41 of the Report, the adequacy of the infrastructure available at present for maintenance of installations in the Suburban section should be reviewed and suitably buttressed with necessary inputs of additional manpower, means for greater mobility and communication.

(c) The signalling gear on Suburban sections is put to much more intensive use than elsewhere. As such, a separate schedule (as distinct from the one in vogue) needs to be framed for their replacement (on time-cum-condition basis).

(d) It may be verified if 'broken rail protection' is available in the Automatic Block Territory. If not, means may be adopted to provide the same.

(e) Location/Relay boxes and signal lamp housings may be adequately secured and locked to prevent unauthorised access.

68. (a) This accident highlights the need to provide a means of verbal communication between the passengers and running crew (Guard and Driver/Motorman) and between the crew, so that passengers could be alerted to get off the train in an emergency. The evolution of a suitable Public Address (PA) system for this purpose, which could be operated either by the Guard or Driver/Motorman, appears to be a necessity which can no longer be delayed, a beginning being made the EMUs in the first instance.

(b) Till the evolvement of such PA system is possible, the adoption of the suggestion made vide Para 29 of my Report on the Accident due to fire on No. 274 Up Borivli-Churchgate Suburban train which occurred on the Western Railway on 18-10-1975, to provide Guards and Motorman of Suburban trains with Loudspeakers (which did not find favour with the Railway Board) appears to merit reconsideration. The provision, as an alternative, of even a siren may be useful to alert the commuters in an emergency.

69. The provision of an Automatic Warning System to EMU trains in the Bombay Suburban sections is an approved work and it is understood that requisite materials are being collected by the Western Railway. While it is necessary to push through this work with a greater degree of urgency, it is essential that the scope of the work is enlarged to cover, in addition to EMUs, all locomotives running on the Suburban sections. Without this, the purpose of this provision will not be fully served.

70. The practice of switching 'on' and 'off' the rear headlight tail lamp by Guards of Suburban trains as a cautionary indication to a train in rear, which is not authorised and which under certain circumstances is likely to cause confusion, may be prohibited.

71. With reference to Para 53 (vi) of the Report, the Railway Board, had in connection with the Commission's Report on the Collision accident at Charni Road station of Western Railway on 13-10-1964, remarked that the Railways were 'being asked to impress upon the Traffic Controllers to give intimation of the accidents ,to Power Controllers without delay so that the latter would take necessary action for switching 'off' the power in the affected section'. The omission to switch off power in the present case up to 23.05 hours may be probed into and suitable corrective action taken.

72. (a) Considerable concern was expressed in the Press as well by some witnesses, about the delay in making over the bodies of those

who died in this accident to their next of kin. Although, this does not fall strictly within the ambit of their duties, considering the humanitarian aspect and the moral obligation involved, Railway Administrations may in such major accidents detail a Senior Railway Officer to liaise with the Police and other agencies concerned and help in expediting the process, so that the relatives of the dead may be saved from further anguish.

(b) On the same grounds, the Officer so nominated may also render necessary assistance in finding suitable transport to convey the dead to the houses of next of kin or burial/cremation grounds as required.

73. A few other cognate matters and suggestions made by the Public during the Inquiry, have been separately referred to the Railway Administration.

Railway Board's Comments on Various Paras of the Report

Para 57 – On Western Railway the end coaches of a rake of 1963 stock have been replaced by MAN coaches having side buffers. As for the end coaches on 4 rakes of 1951 stock, it has not been found possible to fit side buffers. However, in consultation with the RDSO, the rubber sandwich block used on Escorts Schaku coupler is being tried out.

Para 58 – This has been examined by RDSO and it has been found that it would not be possible to increase the crash-worthiness of EMU stock without increase in tare weight and/or reduction in carrying capacity, as the maximum axle loads for which the EMU coaches have been designed are already exceeded under actual loading conditions during peak hours in Bombay area. Further efforts will be called upon to be made by RDSO as a directed effort at weight reduction.

Para 59 – This has been implemented by the Western Railway. Necessary instructions on the subject are also being issued to other railways.

Para 60 (a) – Action is being taken by the railway administration to provide an additional tail lamp with flashing device as a fixed installation in the cabs. In regard to a portable lamp to be displayed by the Guard, re-chargeable battery type lamp of design approved by the RDSO are being procured and their utility will be assessed.

(b) – It is considered that any circuitry for a 'proving light' to indicate the condition of the tail lamp, will involve the risk of failure of the tail lamp. Aperture has, however, been made in the cassing of the tail lamp so that Guard from inside the cab can visually observe whether the tail lamp is burning or not.

Para 61 – RDSO has been asked to look into it and make suitable recommendations.

Para 62 – As advised by the Railway, the proposal for shifting the ladies compartments to the middle of the EMU rakes was examined earlier in consultation with the Suburban Railway Users Committee, but the proposal was not found feasible for reasons that the Motorman/Guard would not be able to keep a watch on these compartments and render assistance in case of an emergency.

It is seen that Chief Commissioner of Railway Safety has accepted the position explained by the Railway.

Para 63 – The suggestion of the Commissioner of Railway Safety is being implemented by the Railway progressively as and when coaches return to shops.

Para 64 – The proposal to build vestibuled EMU trains in the Suburban areas of Bombay, Calcutta and Madras has been carefully considered by this Ministry. It has been decided not to pursue the matter in view of the possibility of commuters occupying the vestibuled area due to overcrowding, and thus proving a source of danger and extreme inconvenience to the travelling public.

Para 65 – Signal posts are not land marks and even the present practice of white paint gives enough visibility in the head lights of locomotives. If luminous paint is used, too many luminous posts would be encountered, which would distract the attention of the driver. The railways are being advised that proper white painting of signal posts is ensured in automatic signalling territories on Suburban sections.

Para 66 – Instructions have been issued to Western Railway to provide cascading of Signals in Automatic Signalling Territories, i.e., when green bulb fuses, yellow should light and when yellow bulb fuses, red should light and if red light fuses, the Signal in rear to be thrown to red, if there is a train in the concerned signalling section. This would eliminate occurrence of blank signals except in remote cases where the red lamp of a signal fuses after the train has passed the signal in rear.

Para 67 (a) – Accepted. The work costing Rs. 22.5 lakhs has already been approved for execution of blank signal protection. As for conversion of 3 aspects signalling into 4 aspects signalling, work on a portion of the section is under completion and the work on the balance portion would be taken up in due course.

(b) – A continuous review of the maintenance procedures of various types of equipments is undertaken and necessary inputs provided, where required. The railway administration are considering the proposal of strengthening the maintenance cadre, as necessary.

(c) – The aspect of linking the effective life of signal equipment with train schedules on time-cum-condition basis has been engaging the attention of this Ministry for sometime and the matter is under consideration.

(d) – Broken rail protection with the help of track circuit cannot be guaranteed mainly because track circuit can function through leakage in ballast even though there is break in rail. Further this is not possible at all in multiple tracks due to cross bonding.

(e) – Location/relay box is provided not only with inbuilt 'E' type locks but also, depending on the location, with suitable strapping all round, and in some cases with RCC location huts. While no uniform policy can be laid down in this regard, strengthening and making the box pilfer-proof is done depending on the location and incidence of outside interference.

Para 68 – RDSO has been asked to look into this and make suitable recommendations.

Para 69 – The work of providing automatic warning system in a phased manner as per the recommendations of the RAIC-68 is being progressed with the following priorities.

(a) Suburban sections.
(b) Trunk routes where the speed of trains exceeds 120 kmph
(c) Other trunk routes and main lines.

At present, the works sanctioned are for Howrah-Mughalsarai and Mughalsarai-Delhi sections, and for the Suburban sections of Western and Central Railways.

Para 70 – Instructions have been issued by the Railway to prohibit the practice of switching 'on' and 'off' the rear headlight tail lamp by Guards of Suburban trains. Instructions on the subject have been issued to all the Railways vide letter No. 78/Safety (A&R)/1/3 dated 20-8-79.

Para 71 – The railway administration is being asked to investigate as to why the power controller was not asked to switch off the power supply to OHE earlier, and take steps to avoid recurrence thereof.

Para 72 – In this case, the railway administration remained in close touch with the Civil and other authorities and assisted them in making available transport for taking dead to the residences or burial/cremation grounds, as desired by next of kin. Necessary instructions for making adequate and prompt relief to the victims of accidents have been issued vide Board's circular letter No. 79/Safety (A&R)/5/2 dated 17-10-1979 (copy enclosed).

Relief Measures

Para 55 – The appreciation of the administration has been duly conveyed to the individuals for rendering invaluable services to the victims of the accident. Action has also been taken to recognise the commendable services and action of the railway staff cited by the Commissioner of Railway Safety.

Para 53 – It is noticed that much of the criticism regarding relief/rescue operations which appeared in the press in connection with the accident was not founded on facts, and that no material complaint could be found by the Commissioner of Railway Safety regarding medical attention and relief. Instructions have, however, been issued to all railways vide Board's letter No. 66/Safety I/18/7 dated 29-4-1978 that in Metropolitan cities no time should be lost in summoning the assistance of fire brigades with their salvage equipment.

6

COMMITTEE ON THIRD LEVEL AIR SERVICES, 1978 — REPORT[1]

Chairman Mr. Bhagwan S. Gidwani
Members Miss A. Mehta; Shri A.K. Sarkar; Shri G.D. Mathur; Shri J.K. Choudhury, Shri S. Ekambaram

Appointment

It will be recalled that Indian Airlines submitted two reports on the operation of Third Level Air Service. These reports were examined and submitted to the Minister after certain tentative conclusions were reached. The Minister had observed that the reports received from Indian Airlines are incomplete and many aspects have been left out which have to be investigated. For this purpose the Minister has directed that a Committee on Third Level Air Services may be constituted. Therefore, the Government of India, in the Ministry of Tourism and Civil Aviation constituted the Committee vide its No. AV 14011/1/77-A dated April 19, 1978.

Terms of Reference

The Committee will examine the two reports regarding Third Level operations prepared by the Indian Airlines and also the schemes of operation of such services in other countries and prepare a detailed Project Report. The Committee would *inter alia* examine and make recommendations in respect of the following points:

1. How should the phasing of the scheme of Third Level operations be done keeping in view the requirements of different regions, present traffic, traffic potential, etc., – which places should be taken in

1. New Delhi, Ministry of Tourism and Civil Aviation, 1978, 194 p.

the first phase for being connected by air services and which should be taken subsequently and in what order?

2. Out of the various available small aircrafts suitable for Third Level services, which will be the most suitable from the technical and economic point of view?

3. Examination of the pros and cons of the following alternatives for operating the Third Level services with a view to recommending the one found most suitable for acceptance:

(a) Operation by Indian Airlines;
(b) Operation by a subsidiary of Indian Airlines;
(c) Operation by a separate public sector corporation of the Central Governments; and
(d) Operation by a Joint Sector Corporation of the Central and the State Governments concerned.

4. What should be the administrative structure, rate structure, pay structure, route pattern, etc., for the proposed Third Level services so as to ensure their proper operation and also minimise costs and maximise revenue?

5. Projections of estimated income expenditure, profit/loss over the next few years indicating when would the operations break even (This is on the assumption that in the initial year the Third Level operations may not be entirely self supporting).

6. Details of the minimum developmental works required at aerodromes for Third Level operations, their estimated costs and phasing.

7. Examine whether the Third Level operations can be subsidised by grants from the Civil Aviation Development Fund until such time they become self-sustaining.

Contents

Note by Chairman of the Committee on Third Level Air Services – Presentation of Report and a Summary of its findings; Introductory Aspects – The need for expansion of domestic air network; Operator of Third Level Air Services; Concessions recommended for Third Level operations; Administrative Structure and related aspects – Subsidiary of Indian Airlines; Capital cost of the Project; Technical and economic evaluation of the aircraft of Third Level operations; Projections of estimated income, expenditure and profit/loss; Need for repayable loans from Government; Phasing of Third Level Operations; Source of Funds for Third Level activities.

Recommendations

Note by Chairman of the Committee on Third Level Air Services

Presentation of the Report and a Summary of its Findings.

The Committee on Third Level Air Services was appointed by order of the Minister of Tourism and Civil Aviation, communicated to the members of the Committee on 19th April 1978. A copy of this communication is attached at Appendix-I to this Chapter, which also indicates the Terms of Reference of the Committee.

Subsequently, recognising that establishment and growth of Third Level Air Services would have a positive influence on a systematic programme of manufacture of indigenous aircraft in the country, we co-opted a representative of Hindustan Aeronautics Limited (Dr. S.M. Ramachandra, Deputy Chief Design Engineer, HAL) to be associated with the Committee's deliberations. Besides, a representative of Air-India (Major S.G. Srinivasan, Regional Director) was also associated.

4. While the Report speaks for itself and deals exhaustively with certain aspects, the subsequent Paragraphs in the Chapter are intended to summarise some of the main decisions taken by the Committee. An attempt has also been made to explain the method of our approach and the measure of agreement that we have reached in respect of those decisions.

I. *The Main Conclusion of the Committee – and the Majority Proposal*

5. The main conclusion which the Committee has unanimously reached is that it is not only practicable but also essential to establish Third Level Air Services in India on an immediate basis and, to begin with, at least 50 new population centres (which are specified in the Report) should be served in the very first phase itself.*

The Committee is also satisfied that the establishment of Third Level Air Services will eventually be economically viable and will not

* Excluding international tourists.

impose any burden on the scarce financial resources of either the Central Government or the States.

6. The Chairman of the Committee and the majority of its members have also evolved a specific proposal (see Chapter XI) which will ensure that neither initially nor at any subsequent stages will the Government have any responsibility or liability for meeting any expenditure for or on behalf of the Third Level Air Services and that these services will, throughout, remain self-sustaining. Briefly stated, the majority proposal simply involves raising funds by establishment of Embarkation Charges within the framework of Aircraft Rules at the rate of 10 per cent of the fare paid by domestic passengers on Indian Airlines and ploughing back most of this amount back to Indian Airlines for Third Level Air Services to be operated through a subsidiary organisation. By this means, an amount of about Rs. 143 crores can be collected over a period of 10 years, enough for the present and future needs of Third Level Air Services. It has to be recognised that nearly 98 per cent* of Indian Airlines passengers travel on 'expense account' or company or government account, and the Chairman's view supported by the majority in the Committee was that there is merit in accepting the principle that the 'rich must pay for themselves and to some extent, for others'. We have of course noted the objections of the members from Indian Airlines that these charges would restrict their present and future flexibility for increasing fares. We however, feel that inasmuch as similar charges area regular feature in respect of international passengers on Air-India and foreign airlines, there is rationale for imposing them on domestic passengers in respect of the twin objective of establishing Third Level Air Services and improving our aerodromes and navigational facilities. Besides in so far as the question of flexibility for increasing fares is concerned, our view is that any such increase in fares has to be justified independently and separately on its own merits, quite apart from the question of Embarkation charges.

In any case, the proposal by the Chairman of the Committee and the majority emanates from the consideration that there are competing claims for limited funds that Government has. Although air transport has an ever-increasing role to play in revitalising economic activity, it is unlikely that Third Level air services would receive priority over food, agriculture, health, etc., to permit demands to be made on the limited resources of the Government to an extent sufficient to meet their requirement. In a country where the basic wants of people – for food, shelter, clothing and employment – have yet to be met, it would be odd to suggest that Government should allocate its scarce funds for establishment of air services. It is necessary, therefore, to locate alternative sources of these funds. The Chairman and the majority of the Committee were, therefore, convinced that in order not to burden the Government the source of funds for these activities should primarily emanate from affluent users of air transport and that the most appropriate method of financing the project would be by way of introducing Embarkation Charges. Side by side with it, the proposal by the Chairman of the Committee and supported by the majority also envisages that the Government will be fully absolved of all expenditure needed in this regard for aerodrome development, provision of communication facilities and other related infrastructural improvements of ground and air navigational services, needed for Third Level Air Services. Besides, by acceptance of this proposal, sufficient funds would be available for continuous growth of Third Level Air Services, far beyond the immediate goal of connecting 50 new population centres, since the Committee is convinced that keeping in view the size of India's land area and its outlying territories as also economic, social and related factors, its present recommendation of serving 50 new centres represents no more than a modest beginning.

It must be clarified that this majority proposal, while it does not place any financial burden on public funds, ensures that Government will have full control over policies and goals in respect of Third Level Air Services, since the Chairman of the Committee and the majority of its members are convinced that the task of setting goals and policies cannot be left merely to those who operate the Third Level Air Services.

The Chairman of the Committee and the majority do not agree that the proposal to raise funds by means of Embarkation Charges in unorthodox, considering that the international passengers embarking in India are subject to such charges and also to the travel tax. In any case, ultra orthodox methods have not produced for us in the decades gone by since independence and nationalisation, a network of air services or aerodromes and related facilities which a country of India's size and status should have.

An apprehension was expressed that while Government might not disapprove the system of Embarkation Charges, it might wish to divert the funds arising the reform into General funds and not for the benefit of the Third Level Air Services. The Committee as a whole did not share this apprehension – which in any case had been tentatively voiced – and also felt that such diversion of funds would be unwise in the interests of the country.

7. Irrespective of whether the proposal for financing the Third Level Air Services as evolved by the Chairman of the Committee and the majority cf its members is accepted, rejected or modified, the Committee remains unanimous on the need to establish Third Level Air Services on an immediate basis.

II. Principal objective of the Committee – Economic viability

8. The Committee was unanimously of the view that we should set up, economically, a strong and viable system of Third Level Air Services which should adequately respond to consumer demand, enable long-term market growth and eventually permit profitable operations by efficient carriers. The Committee recognised that even far beyond the considerations of economic viability, there are strong factors which emphasise the need for establishment and development of Third Level Air Services – and much will be said later in this Report about those factors. Even so, the Committee felt that factors which undercut the economic viability of such air services will not benefit the travelling public or the shippers and will eventually defeat the programme of development of Third Level Air Services.

The Committee, therefore, concluded that the Third Level Air Service system should be so established as to respond efficiently to market conditions and requirements and that it should be provided at such population centres where substantial potential for air transportation exists. In short, the strict test of economic viability must be applied.

It is after having applied this test that the Committee has recommended unanimously that 50 new population centres qualify for establishment of Third Level Air Services.

III. Main Consideration before the Committee – Present Unsatisfactory Position of the Domestic Network

9. The Committee noted the unfortunate fact that although during the period between Independence (1947) and Nationalisation (1953), the domestic airlines of India were serving 55 points in India, the present position is that Indian Airlines is serving a total of 61 points

on its domestic network.

Thus, in the quarter century since Nationalisation, all we have achieved is the net gain of additional 6 points on the domestic network.

Few countries, if any, of the size of India can be charged with such slow coverage of the domestic network.

10. This unparalleled stagnation is by no means the fault of Indian Airlines. Indian Airlines has a proud and enviable record of achievement. It provides a safe, efficient air transportation system at as low cost as is economically justified. It has responded effectively to technological changes and is using the most modern aircraft as far as possible. It has increased its capacity and frequencies of services. By any standard, it must be regarded as a successful airline, which apart from its record of safety and efficiency, is also able to earn profits despite mounting burdens of excessive fuel costs, sales taxes, landing and navigational charges.

Still, the fact remains that Indian Airlines' concentration has been on an intensive network, covering a limited number of points and that there has been no worthwhile effort towards an extension of that network.

11. This unfortunate state of affairs has arisen obviously due to an overemphasis and somewhat total commitment to the guideline provided for in Section 9 of the Air Corporation Act of 1953 whereby the airline is to act "so far as may be" on business principles – an instruction that has been construed to direct the airline to concentrate on commercial routes with proven existing traffic or immediate potential traffic.

Somehow, the foregoing guideline has over-shadowed as imperative – the imperative provided for in Section 7(2)(j) read with Section 7(1) which directed the airline to "take such steps as are calculated to extend the air transport services, including the development of feeder services" – a clear cut instruction directing the airline to open up new routes, cater to new markets and to bring more communities into the stream of air commerce, thereby extending the air transportation network.

12. Apart from the consideration that the fleet of Indian Airlines has been heavily weighted with aircraft types that are not well suited to economic operation on minor air routes and small aerodromes, the fact also remains that in order to get a better hearing from the Government and the necessary sanctions from the Finance and the Planning Commission, the policy in respect of establishing the route network has

been such that the guideline in Section 9 of the Act has prevailed, in a large measure, over the imperative of Section 7(2)(j) and accordingly no emphasis has been given to development of feeder and regional routes, since the possibility of their being immediately remunerative was regarded as doubtful.

13. It is not as if all the routes presently served by Indian Airlines are remunerative. Far from it, many of them, judged individually without reference to overall utilisation and other factors of inter-relationship, are losing routes. However, they are there not on account of any conscious adherence to the imperative of Section 7(2)(j) but due to other considerations. The original network was inherited by Indian Airlines from the predecessor companies and except for modest variations, by and large, the old network pattern has been essentially maintained. The few new points that have been added owe their existence to the fact that they were expected to be immediately remunerative without the tedious need to experiment or because there were certain important pressures, not altogether connected with commercial aspects.

Thus, it is that the evolution of the route network has been painfully slow and from 55 points served prior to Nationalisation, the Indian Airlines network today serves 61 points – an addition of 6 points in the period of two and a half decades. Clearly this is due also to disregard of Section 7(1) of the Air Corporation Act which suggests that the Corporation is to be regarded as a public utility with the obligation to secure that air transport services are developed to the best advantage.

14. It is not intended to locate any blame for this slow process with Indian Airlines. The airline has had its compulsions in appearing before the Finance, Planning Commission and other bodies which often have to base their judgements on financial aspects and profitability. Government directors on the airline Board have also almost invariably adopted the financial yardstick. There has all along been limited, if any recognition of the fact that the guideline of Section 9 of the Act – "to act as far as may be on business principles" – is subject and subordinate to the principles of Section 7, and not the other way round. In any case, an airline by its very nature and particularly when it is monopolistic, would like to operate for immediate profit as far as possible, and cannot be expected to set for itself the tasks and goals which Section 7 of the Act envisaged, and it was therefore open to Government to make wider use of its powers under Section 34(2). Government, on the other hand, while it has given attention, after nationalisation, to efficiency of the enterprise, economic self-reliance, profitability, im-

provements in capacity and frequency, has not been so attentive to extension of the network to widen the aerial scope of mobility which would have achieved the goals envisaged in Section 7 of the Act.

Be that as it may, what is clearly necessary is to cure the present acute stagnation of the aerial network. It is with this in view that the Committee has suggested that 50 new population centres must be added to the aerial network, in the first phase itself.

IV. The Need and Rationale for Third Level Air Services

15. The preceding paragraphs spoke of the stagnating aerial network of Indian Airlines and of the need to extend and augment it by adding 50 population centres in the first phase and many more in the subsequent phases.

The reasons for such extension of the network are obvious and have been briefly touched upon in the Report. However we should clarify that it is not merely to seek an academic adherence to the provisions of Section 7(1) and 7(2)(j) of the Air Corporation Act, that a large scale extension of the route network is rendered necessary. The fact is that the reasons and the rationale which motivated these Sections in the 1953 Act have become so pronounced – even paramount – that the extension of the domestic air network (and establishment of the Third Level Air Services to serve such tended network) has become an inescapable necessity.

Rising expectations must be regarded as a continuous process in a developing society – and throughout, this process manifests itself in every phase of development. Nevertheless, the extent and intensity of these expectations, ever since the new Governments came into power, has reached such proportions that it would be unwise to ignore them. Keeping this aspect in view, it would seem that unless the domestic aerial network is extended and Third Level Air Services are established, the charge will often be often that Indian Airlines represents an *Urban Phenomenon*.

The Indian Airlines lives upto the world airline standard is a matter of some significance for the professionals. As for the rest, they would naturally like to see that the domestic network is extended beyond the present thresholds so as to bring the benefits of air transportation to many more urban and rural communities. Apart from the substantial economic benefits that such extension of air transportation system will undoubtedly usher for these communities, one must take into account the psychological factor. Transport improvements do achieve a sense of national purpose through demonstrational methods. There was a time when even the building of a road for a village came to be regarded as a symbolic act of some importance and served to alter the attitude of the villagers towards the Government, giving them a greater sense of identity. What was true of the village roads then, applies in modern times to the establishment of air services, particularly in the context of the emerging hopes that there is to be a fundamental shift in policy which would call for greater response and sensitiveness to the needs of smaller communities.

Neither in this Chapter nor in the Report itself, can we attempt to explain all the benefits that will flow from the establishment of Third Level Air Services. Limitations of time and space would not permit such an attempt. But it is clear that the hopes with which the nationalisation of air transport services was ushered in, have not been met. It cannot be said that the air transportation system in India has become an integral part of India's economic and social life. Nor can it be said to have contributed to national integration by opening up new areas.

An efficient and extensive air transportation system has always been recognised as a vital factor in building up and strengthening political institutions and certainly it helps in bringing about economic and social integration. It is for this reason that various countries refer to *political cohesion* as an objective of air transport policy and regard an air transportation system as a principal means of achieving national integration and unity.

16. It is not a question only of regional prestige which calls for the need to establish Third Level Air Services. The fact is that *isolation perpetuates poverty*. Access is indispensable to any economic activity. If we have to redress the unevenness of economic development and locate economic activity more evenly, obviously there is need to raise the input of entrepreneurs and enterprises into neglected regions of the country and also to increase the proportion of output coming from those regions. Otherwise it would not be easy to achieve the goal of industrial dispersion and regional economic development. Air Transport in India can do far more than it has done so far to serve development programmes. It can carry industrialists and businessmen quickly to areas presently starved of an airlink and also doctors, medical aid, government officials and others. It has at times been said that Time is not of essence in a developing country and that where there is exten-

sive unemployment or underemployment the time savings merely make the situation worse. The reverse is true. The time savings for entrepreneurs and industrialists who wish to develop new markets and industries in the region are of essence. Stretching the supply of technicians, movement of raw materials coupled with the need to discover and exploit natural resources, is yet another example. In fact, even in respect of shipment of goods time saving is more valuable in the less developed regions than in the advanced regions, for the simple reason that cargo tied up in transit is capital and is therefore of particular importance where capital is in short supply. Delay can immobilise a small scale industry far more. Also, it is clear that in opening up new markets and expanding the existing markets, time saving should be regarded as essential to the process of production and distribution, apart from the fact that transportation of commodities previously sold locally but now transported to markets where a better price can be obtained, will lead to definite economic advantages for the rural and regional areas.

Thus, we are satisfied that the establishment and development of Third Level Air Services will extend the frontiers of employment for labour, capital and enterprise.

17. Also, it has to be recognised that we have a large body of unemployed pilots and Aircraft Maintenance Engineers in reserve. They have spent large sums of money and time in securing these qualifications but their prospects of obtaining employment are limited. The establishment of Third Level Air Services would no doubt help in relieving unemployment problem of these trained personnel. There is, also, a larger Issue. For a variety of obvious reasons, India should build up a large number of trained personnel who should, at the same time, not find it too difficult to find employment. It is not only a question of building up our strength for the needs of air transport, of defence and security but obviously, creation of such reserve power and having it gainfully employed marks an important phase in the transition from a developing into a developed state.

18. Summing up, the provision of Third Level Air Services would serve numerous national objectives and goals and amongst them are, the regional prestige coupled with economic self-reliance; national unity, identity had integration; access to previously in accessible areas; equalisation by locational dispersion including efficient resource allocation and natural resource discovery and development; development and modernisation of skills, industries, agriculture, arts and institutions in smaller towns and communities; promotion of a high level of in-

dustrial activity; trade and tourism; national security; swift delivery of mails, messages and newspapers; movement of raw materials; greater employment for trained technical personnel and workers in the rural areas; and besides it will serve many other material and social objectives, making also welfare activities, health services and cultural amenities available to smaller communities.

What needs to be realised is that countries and regions with low standards of living are characteristically countries and regions with inadequate means of air transportation.

V. Third Level Air Services – A Modest Attempt in the First Phase

19. Having regard to the fact that Indian Airlines is presently serving only 61 cities and that our proposal aims at adding 50 new population centres to the existing domestic network in the first phase itself, it might appear on the face of it that we have something ambitious in view. This is not so. In fact, the proposal is extremely modest as the following aspects will show:

A fleet of 20 small aircraft which may eventually be required for operating the Third Level Air Services in the first phase, involving the addition of 50 new population centres, would provide approximately 164 million seat kilometres as compared to 4846 million seat kilometres provided by the existing fleet of the Indian Airlines in 1977-78.

Thus in the first phase of the Third Level Air Services, only about 3.5 per cent of the capacity now generated by the Indian Airlines' fleet would be provided.

The capital cost for a fleet of 20 aircraft to serve about 50 new population centres will be approximately 50 per cent of the cost of single Boeing 747 aircraft. Or, to put it differently, the cost will be just about as much as constructing and providing facilities for a single major domestic aerodrome (non-international).

Even the capital cost, spread over a period of three years for building aerodromes, developing infrastructure and providing communication and navigational facilities to serve these 50 new population centres would not exceed Rs. 19 crores.

In any case, the new population centres have been selected on the basis of their immediate traffic potential and the Committee has been careful to select only such centres which hold a definite promise of becoming economically viable.

Besides, as has already been clarified, at no time, neither initially nor in the later phases, will Government be called upon to shoulder any financial burden for the cost of establishing Third Level Air Services or for building the necessary infrastructure for them, since we have located an alternative source for these funds.

The State-wise distribution of the new population centres (next Section) will also show how little is proposed to be done in the first phase.

VI. State-wise Distribution of New Population Centres for Third Level Air Services

20. The State-wise distribution of the population centres which have been selected unanimously by the Committee is given hereunder:

Andhra Pradesh
1. Cuddapah
2. Warangal
3. Rajahmundry

Arunachal Pradesh
1. Itanagar
2. Along
3. Ziro
4. Passighat
5. Tezu
6. Daborijo

Assam
1. Rupsi

Bihar
1. Gaya
2. Muzaffarpur
3. Jamshedpur

Goa, Daman and Diu
1. Diu

Gujarat
1. Amroli
2. Mithapur
3. Surat
4. Kandla

Haryana
1. Karnal

Himachal Pradesh
1. Simla
2. Kulu

Karnataka
1. Hubli
2. Mysore
3. Raichur

Kerala
1. Kozhikode (Calicut)

Lakshadweep
1. Kavaratti

Madhya Pradesh
1. Kanha

2. Jagdalpur

Maharashtra
1. Ratnagiri
2. Kolhapur
3. Nanded

Meghalaya
1. Shillong

Mizoram
1. Aizawal

Orissa
1. Puri
2. Rourkela

Pondicherry
1. Pondicherry

Punjab
1. Ludhiana
2. Jullundur

Rajasthan
1. Ajmer
2. Jaisalmer
3. Bikaner
4. Kota
5. Abu Road

Sikkim
1. Gangtok

Tamil Nadu
1. Ramanathapuram
2. Thanjavur
3. Tuticorin

Uttar Pradesh
1. Pantnagar
2. Dehradun

West Bengal
1. Cooch Behar

There are indeed many other places which would eventually qualify for Third Level Air Services. For the moment, however, the Committee having gone into the question of competing claims of all the population centres, recommends the above for inclusion in the first phase. We fully appreciate that the subsequent phases of the development of the Third Level Air Services will have to be far more ambitious taking into account not only the success of the first phase but also our large geographical area, the tempo of economic development and the need for a dispersal which should be both equitable and economic.

VII. Operation by a Subsidiary of Indian Airlines

21. Terms of Reference for the Committee required us to examine alternatives for operating the Third Level Air Services with a view to

recommending the one found most suitable for acceptance:

(a) Operation by Indian Airlines;
(b) Operation by a subsidiary of Indian Airlines;
(c) Operation by a separate public sector corporation of the Central Government; and
(d) Operation by a Joint Sector Corporation of the Central and the State Governments concerned.

The relative merits of entrusting operation of Third Level Air Services to Indian Airlines itself or to a subsidiary of Indian Airlines or to a separate public sector corporation or to a joint sector corporation of the Central and State Governments were considered in depth by the Committee and the unanimous conclusion reached by us was that the most appropriate course of action would be to set up an airline which would be a subsidiary of Indian Airlines for the operation of Third Level Air Services, having regard to the attendant circumstances associated with the proposal and the advantages which the public would derive from such a project.

22. Amongst the advantages for entrusting this work to the Subsidiary of Indian Airlines, are the following:

– If the establishment of Third Level Air Services is to be regarded as a continuing and a developing scheme – and we do so regard it – there will be occasions when some of the third level routes will come to achieve a higher classification both in terms of greater traffic demand and the need for bigger aircraft, requiring possible integration with the routes of Indian Airlines. It will be difficult to achieve this kind of improvement in the Third Level Air Services unless there is a close coordination between Indian Airlines and the new operator.
– Implicit in the foregoing also is the consideration that in several cases, Indian Airlines itself may, with its own fleet, be called upon to operate some of the routes on behalf of the Third Level operator or *vice versa*. It will be easier thereby to achieve expansion.
– Advantages of know how, expertise, booking offices, travel agency connections, telexes and telephones with Indian Airlines have, will be a close coordination, be made more easily

available to the Third Level operator, at incremental cost only. Such an arrangement can subsist only with a Subsidiary.

- Wasteful competition would be avoided.
- Indian Airlines would be able to provide better facilities for training of pilots and technical personnel.
- There would be maximum utilisation of aircraft and minimum duplication of workshop facilities and senior staff.
- Indian Airlines will feel greater responsibility to support the new unit with connections on their own trunk routes, if the subsidiary relationship is maintained.
- Investment for Third Level Air Services will be drawn from the Embarkation Charges collected from Indian Airlines passengers.
- In any case, with the present development of having one common Chairman for our two nationalised carriers (Indian Airlines and Air-India), we do not see why we should move away from the concept of coordinated development.

As the final consideration, it must be pointed out that public confidence would be greater if Indian Airlines, with its established image is entrusted with the task of operating these services through its own Subsidiary.

23. For these reasons and also taking into account the high costs, we ruled out the possibility of entrusting the Third Level Air Services to a separate public sector corporation or to a joint sector corporation of the Central and State Governments. Also, it is not feasible to recommend that Indian Airlines itself should directly operate these services because of larger overheads resulting in high costs, accounting problems and conflict of policy with the possibility of inattention or indifference to Third Level Air Services.

VIII. Role of Private Enterprise

24. The question relating to the role of private enterprise was not posed to us specifically and the Terms of Reference required us to consider the alternatives of entrusting the Third Level operations to Indian Airlines or to a new public sector organisation or to a joint sector Corporation or to a subsidiary of Indian Airlines. Even so, while choosing the last alternative (Subsidiary), we did consider:

(i) if private enterprise could be entrusted with the main task of operation of the Third Level operations, or

(ii) if private enterprise could have an important supplementary role to play in respect of such operations.

In respect of (i) above, we were unanimously of the view that for reasons stated in the previous section, the main task of operating Third Level Air Services would have to be entrusted to a Subsidiary of Indian Airlines and not to private enterprise.

While commercial air transport in India owed its initial development almost entirely to the initiative, resource and vision of private enterprise, the fact remains that ever since nationalisation of scheduled air transport services in 1953, the role of private operators has been dwindling and they have almost disappeared from the scene. In the absence of indigenously produced small aircraft and with the restrictions imposed on importing aircraft from abroad, private operators did not find it possible to operate many feeder routes or even non-scheduled services, although statutory provisions exist since long enabling Government to permit private operators to operate routes not served by Indian Airlines.

Let us look at the figures of their operations. In 1976, Private operators carried 9,326 passengers on scheduled and non-scheduled services, and in 1977, they carried 1,457 passenger, as against over 4 million passengers carried by Indian Airlines on scheduled services. The activity in respect of non-scheduled air transport by private operators has almost diet out. How different was the picture prior to nationalisation! In 1953, nearly a hundred thousand passengers were transported by private operators on non-scheduled services alone, representing roughly 25 per cent of what they carried on scheduled services. Year by year, there has been a noticeable decline in the activities of the private operators until they have reached a stage that all that they carried in 1977 were 1,457 passengers. It would, therefore, not be easy for them to undertake a large scale operation of Third Level Air Services. Besides, some of the considerations which weighed in favour of nationalisation can be said to be valid for application to Third Level Air Services as well.

Nevertheless, there is no doubt that having regard to the issue at (ii) above, private enterprise can be utilised to a great extent to serve a supplementary and complementary role even though the main task is to be entrusted to the Subsidiary of Indian Airlines. Private enterprise had at one time a leadership role in the development of domestic air transportation. If the objective of spreading and expanding the network of air services in the national interest is to be achieved, the regulatory regime to be imposed by the Government should be such as to encourage private enterprise and to give them necessary incentives for playing the supplementary role. Often, a private operator can more easily adapt his air transport product to public demand. A well managed private carrier, with low overheads, who can flexibly respond to such public demand, can possibly make a profit and at the same time offer improved services at a low cost.

25. There could be a variety of ways in which private enterprise can, given the necessary incentives, assistant in the task of development of Third Level Air Services since, as we have said, in many cases, privately owned and managed companies could provide efficient and consumer responsive services. Thus:

– It should be open to private enterprise to continue to operate on routes not served by Indian Airlines and its Subsidiary. It is of course recognised that the award of a route carries with it the responsibility for adequate performance and service.
– Besides, privately managed companies could also operate certain Third Level Services by a collaborative arrangements with or on behalf of Indian Airlines or its Subsidiary. This collaborative management could take the form of a *Charter* or *Sub-Charter* or even *Agency relationship* or *Associateship*. (An example — though not a strict parallel — of such an arrangement is Air-India's sub-charters mostly to the Gulf. In the past, Air-India rarely, if ever, entered into such arrangements with Indian non-Scheduled or private operators. It has now become a common (feature.)
– Privately owned and managed companies can enter into arrangements with State Governments, possibly on an *agency basis* or otherwise for an intensive network of Third Level Air Services in their own regions. This will have to be within the strict framework of the statutory regulations and policy as promulgated by the Director General of Civil Aviation and it will need to be ensured that both Indian Airlines and its Subsidiary are kept will into the picture so that on the one hand, the services of such private carriers are operated with strict adherence to safety and security and on the other, undercut-

ting, duplication and wasteful competition is avoided. As has already been said, our own proposal for the first phase of Third Level Air Services is so modest that there would not be too much satisfaction for many State Governments who may wish to make their own arrangements for establishing such services. For this purpose, collaborative arrangements with private operators might be worthwhile on their part and the routes could accordingly be awarded by Director General of Civil Aviation if the necessary conditions in respect of such operations can be met by these operators.

26. As to the specific *incentives* for private enterprise, since their effective participation will be important to the establishment of Third Level Air Services in the national interest, the following measures would be worth considering:

- Private operators could get the treatment in respect of import of aircraft and spares as would be accorded to the Subsidiary of Indian Airlines.
- Besides import of aircraft and related equipment, private operators could also be granted the same concessions by the Centre and the States in respect of excise duties, sales taxes, and landing and housing charges.

While there can be no question of giving private operators any direct financial aid from the Centre, it is felt that if the foreign concessions and facilities are given, the private operator could turn out to be a significant participant in the Third Level activities.

IX. Concessions for Third Level Air Services

27. The concessions that we have in view for the Third Level Air Services are not many.

All we are seeking is that Government should not treat, at least in the initial stages, these Third Level Air Services as *a new course of revenue.* Thus, the concessions that we have in view are:

(i) Exemption from the requirement of D.G.C.A. for paying landing, housing and parking charges and route navigation facility charges;

(ii) Exemption from or reimbursement of sales tax by State

Governments on fuel and oil uplifted;

(iii) Exemption from or reimbursement of excise duties by Central Government on fuel and oil uplifted; and

(iv) Exemption from Customs duty by Central Government on aircraft and spares imported.

Tax holidays are not unknown and are in fact a common feature in respect of pioneering and developmental activities. In any case, the concessions that we have suggested do not involve depriving the Centre or the States of any existing revenue. Nor are we suggesting the continuance of these concessions for ever. An initial period of ten years should suffice.

As already stated, these concessions could be made available not only to the Subsidiary of Indian Airlines but also to Indian Airlines itself in respect of its own new Third Level Air Services that they might introduce as also to private operators who might engage in this activity.

X. Routes for Third Level Air Services

28. While selecting 50 new population centres for the Third Level Air Services in the first phase, the Committee also gave consideration to the routes to be operated, the number of aircraft to be based at a particular central point and aspects related to utilisation of such aircraft. The Committee's recommendations are given in Appendix X-A (Chapter X). It is of course appreciated that several adjustments might need to be made and the recommendations are therefore tentative since the operator (Subsidiary of Indian Airlines) will have to take several factors into account including the need to coordinate the routes and schedules with the connections provided by Indian Airlines.

The basic consideration, however, which the Committee unanimously had in view while determining the table of Routes, was the commercial viability of the service on that route and its impact on the total domestic route system.

XI. Choice of Aircraft

29. The Committee is unanimously of the view that we should for several obvious reasons and in order to achieve economy, go in for a homogenous fleet of a single type of aircraft. For the moment we will have to rely on imported aircraft until a stage is reached when an in-

digenously manufactured aircraft is available.

The Committee also went into the question of the choice of aircraft with some thoroughness and a co-ordinated study was also carried out by the Technical Centre of the Civil Aviation Department in conjunction with Indian Airlines assisted by the Representative of Hindustan Aeronautics Ltd., and other members of the Committee. This study can be seen in Chapter VII and the Appendices attached thereto which except for the few minor aspects specified therein, have the unanimous approval of the Committee. Basically, this study examines the merits and demerits of seven different types of small aircraft from the operational, economic and other related aspects. The study also furnishes an assessment of the operating cost and estimates of break-even points.

The Committee is of the view that this study would provide considerable assistance for the final selection of aircraft to be used for Third Level Air Services.

Thus, the Committee itself has not made the final choice of the aircraft, feeling that it would not be correct to do so on account of the following considerations:

- The Committee felt that the final recommendations on its part to identify and select the aircraft for Third Level, if it leaks out, would stand in the way of the negotiation of the pricing formula and other terms and conditions of purchase. For instance, the manufacturer of the aircraft which has been finally selected by the Committee would be in a stronger bargaining position and it might also be somewhat embarrassing to the operator to deviate from the recommendations of the Committee.
- In any case, such a decision for final selection of aircraft should rest with the operator and since in this case the operations would be by the subsidiary of Indian Airlines, there would naturally be the usual Government scrutiny and adherence to established procedures at appropriate stage.

For these reasons — but mainly to avoid pressure lobbies and raising hopes in one direction or the other — the Committee felt justified in preparing a detailed study in respect of several aircraft but has not considered it fit to saddle the operator with the final recommendations. Incidentally, the Managing Director of Indian Airlines had also suggested to the Chairman of the Committee that it was the view of Indian

Airlines that the final evaluation of aircraft would be premature at this stage and would need to be undertaken by the designated operator.

XII. Effect on Indigenous Production of Aircraft

30. A systematic programme of establishment of Third Level Air Services which has been proposed in the Report will certainly have a positive impact on accelerating the development of indigenous production of aircraft, with all its consequential advantages for the country. We have been assured by H.A.L. that they have the capacity and plans to produce a suitable aircraft for Third Level Air Services within the period of next few years. This must be regarded as a happy development, since apart from the other obvious advantages of manufacture of indigenous aircraft, it will also accelerate the expansion of Third Level Air Services in India.

XIII. Integrated Development

31. Obviously, the establishment and growth of Third Level Air Services cannot be considered in isolation from the problem of infrastructural development at our aerodromes. A safe and efficient system of airports, airways, ground equipment, navigational and communication facilities has to be provided.

In the past, there has been some lack of co-ordination in the sense that at times when Indian Airlines charged their schedules or particularly when they introduced the Airbus, its impact on the cost of aerodrome development was not considered simultaneously. In the case of an extensive system of Third Level Air Services, it would be worthwhile to evolve measures for greater co-ordination so that an integrated approach is achieved.

It is with this mainly in view that the Committee gave consideration to the cost and scheduled of the infrastructural development for making the 50 new population centres that have been proposed. The total cost, including construction of some new aerodromes and provision of communication and navigational aids, will come to Rs. 18 crores spread over a period of three years. This cost, as has already been pointed out, will be met from the Embarkation Charges, within the framework of Aircraft Rules, 1937.

In so far as the time schedule is concerned, out of the 50 population centres which we have selected for linkage by Third Level operations, services to 40 of them can begin within a period of one year, the remaining 10 Centres where new aerodromes have to be constructed will take somewhat longer.

XIV. Area of Agreement

32. Most of the decisions of the Committee have been unanimous. The only major point on which there has been a difference of opinion relates to financing of Third Level Air Services in respect of which members from Indian Airlines felt that the Embarkation Charges did not represent the appropriate method of financing. This difference of opinion has been explained in Section (I) above of this Chapter and Chapter XI of the Report.

(In parenthesis, it must be mentioned that the DGCA is in any case thinking of imposing embarkation charges in respect of Indian Airlines domestic passengers even if the proposal for the Third Level Air Services does not materialise. It is possible that the scale of those charges might be slightly lower if the proposal for Third Level is scrapped. However, the question of imposing Embarkation Charges has arisen in DGCA's mind not because of the proposal for Third Level Air Services alone but on account of the need to recover from users the cost of services provided. In the Civil Aviation Department, we have taken certain steps to increase progressively our revenue so as to meet our increasing commitments for improving facilities at our aerodromes and in respect of air navigation and communication services. In 1976-77 and in preceding years, the revenue used to be about Rs. 3 crores per annum. Due to certain recent measures, it has been possible to increase that revenue with effect from last ear from Rs. 3 crores per year to Rs. 20 crores per year. This amount is hardly sufficient to meet our rising commitments and in any case in order that the Seventh Five-Year Plan in respect of Civil Aviation should be self-sustaining, the Embarkation Charges will have to be imposed well ahead of it).

33. Besides the foregoing difference of opinion, the only aspects on which the Chairman and the majority of the Committee differed with representatives of Indian Airlines were the following:

(1) *Depreciation:* The majority view was that the depreciation should be based on 15 years life for an aircraft keeping in view an annual utilisation of 2000 hours while Indian Airlines felt that a life-span of 10 years economic life should be provided for purposes of deprecia-

tion, having regard to high landing cycles and several important related aspects. The other members did not agree with this view, for the following reasons:

- Indian Airlines themselves provide for 15 years depreciation for Airbus.
- Air-India provides for 15 years depreciation.
- Manufacturers' view on the small aircraft is that 15 years life should be expected.
- A lesser life expectancy based on "obsolescence concept" is not realistic under Indian conditions.

(2) *Hull insurance:* While the majority view was that provision for Hull insurance should be at 3 per cent, Indian Airlines felt that it should be at the rate of 5 per cent. The majority noted that Hull insurance made by Air-India and Indian Airlines for different types of imported aircraft varied from 0.80 per cent and above and that it is not unusual in unprofitable years for an airline even to resort to selfinsurance for "Hull".

(3) *Spares:* Indian Airlines felt that spares support should be taken at 15 per cent of the fly-away price of the aircraft. The view of the other members constituting the majority was that if not more than one type of aircraft was used in the Third Level operations, there would be a homogenous fleet and the need for spare support could then be reduced to 10 per cent, since the manufacturers' view also lends support to provision of spare support at the rate of 10 per cent.

(4) *Spare engines:* Primarily based on the view given by the manufacturers, and on the basis of the view expressed by the representative from the Hindustan Aeronautics Limited, the members of the Committee other than from Indian Airlines, felt that the number of spare engines and propellers should be 25 per cent of the installed engines and propellers, though members from Indian Airlines thought that the principle should be based on a minimum of 35 per cent of the installed engines and propellers.

However, the foregoing are not such major or serious differences and even assuming that the views of Indian Airlines are accepted substantially, the impact on the cost of operations would not be so significant and all it would mean is that the break-even point would be shifted somewhat.

(XV) Presentation of the Report

34. While presenting of the Report, I should particularly like to thank Indian Airlines for their assistance. The Committee was able to draw much from the material already submitted by them in their two earlier reports on Third Level Air Services. Besides, the member from the Indian Airlines on the Committee — Shri G.D. Mathur, Deputy Managing Director, along with Shri J.K. Choudhury, Planning Manager and other officers of Indian Airlines prepared several studies based on which we have identified the 50 new population centres which should be served in the first phase. Our estimates of the cost of the Third Level Project assessments in respect of aircraft and the administrative structure of the Subsidiary airline are also based on these studies. Among the officers of the Indian Airlines who helped us in preparation of these studies are Capt. R.K. Sen, Shri V.D. Ganguli, Dr. G.K. Agarwal and Shri M.S. Balakrishna.

The Committee received tremendous help from Shri K.B. Ganesan, Head of the Technical Centre of the Civil Aviation Department and from Shri P.R. Chandrasekhar, Director of Research and Development and Shri R. Saha, Scientific Officer. I must also mention the valuable contribution by Dr. S.M. Ramachandra, Deputy Chief Design Engineer of the Hindustan Aeronautics Limited and Major S.G. Srinivasan, Regional Director, Air-India.

The Committee is particularly thankful to Shri I.R. Menon, Deputy Director of Regulations and Information who took upon himself organisational and secretarial burdens of the Committee including the preparation of preliminary drafts.

Particularly I must thank each and every members of the Committee. It is due to their extraordinary zeal and co-operation that this Report has been prepared within the period of three months allotted to the Committee.

7

NATIONAL TRANSPORT POLICY COMMITTEE, 1978 — REPORT[1]

Chairman Shri B.D. Pande
Members Air Chief Marshall Shri P.C. Lal; Shri G.P. Warrier; Dr. F.P. Antia; Dr. M.Q. Dalvi.
Co-opted Member Dr. V.G. Bhatia
M. Secy. Shri S.P. Bagla

Appointment

In view of the socio-economic changes that have taken place in the country during the past decade on the new priorities and objectives set out in the Draft 1978-83 Plan, the Planning Commission have decided to set-up a high-level Committee to formulate a national transport policy tailored to meeting the new plan priorities. The policy approved by Government will serve as basis for developing a transportation system for meeting the transport requirements of the communities as also of agriculture, industry and trade at the minimum social cost. The Government of India Planning Commission appointed the National Transport Policy Committee vide Resolution No. T & C/3(15)/77 dated April 26, 1978.

Terms of Reference

(1) To propose a comprehensive national transport policy for the country for the next decade or so, keeping in view the objectives and priorities set out in the Five-Year Plan. In formulating such a policy, the Committee will:

(a) to recommend an optional inter-modal mix of different systems

1. **Delhi, Controller of Publication, 1980, 393 p.**

and also suggest appropriate technical choices within each system, keeping in view the need to generate maximum employment potential; and

(b) to suggest organisational, administrative, fiscal and legal measures required for planning, implementing, monitoring and evaluating programmes formulated for giving effect to relevant components of the national transport policy by the Central and State Government and major transport agencies at both the National, State and local levels.

(2) To identify the areas in which the data base of the transport system should be strengthened in order to be able to formulate integrated transport plans, and to suggest procedures and methodologies for formulating and appraising such plans at the Central, State, District and Block Level.

(3) To recommend areas in which research and development in the transport field should be undertaken and the institutional framework for carrying it out.

(4) To suggest measures for improving training facilities in transport planning and management.

(5) To recommend any other measures which the Committee may consider relevant in relation to items (1) to (4) above.

Contents

Introduction; Objectives of National Transport Policy – Main issues; Transport Development in India – A Review; Determination of Optimal Inter-Modal Mix; Taxation, Pricing and Subsidy; Freight Equalisation; Machinery for Transport Co-ordination; Transport Planning and Data Base; Transport Research and Training; Railways; Road Development; Road Transport; Urban Transport; Air Transport; Coastal Shipping; Inland Water Transport; Ports and Harbours; Ropeways and Pipelines; Conclusion; Note of Dissent by Dr. F.P. Antia, Member; Comments on the Note of Dissent; Summary of Recommendations; Appendices.

Recommendations

Objectives of National Transport Policy

1. Long gestation periods are involved in building up transport capacity. A long-term view has, therefore, to be taken and funds allocated for creating transport capacity ahead of demand. (Paras 1.15 and 1.5.5)

2. Passenger transport should be given adequate attention to improve travel conditions. (Para 1.2.2)

3. Attention must be given to transport needs of rural areas together with inter-urban and intra-urban passenger travel of an essential character. (Para 1.2.3)

4. When planning new transport facilities it is essential to ensure a realistic appraisal of traffic demand. Efforts should be made to reduce delays in planning and execution of transport projects. (Paras 1.41 & 1.4.2)

5. Transport is an essential element of an integrated plan for area development. Inadequacy of transport may at times serve as an inhibiting factor in the development process. (Para 1.5.4)

6. The issues to be considered in evolving an integrated framework for transport policy are determination of the size of total transport investment, distribution of these resources between various transport modes and the fixation of tariffs for transport services. (Para 1.6.1)

7. Transport should be included in the priority sector for determination of interse priorities for the plan. The allocation of funds to the transport sector has perforce to be larger than of those sectors where the incidence of lumpiness of investment is not so heavy. (Para 1.6.2)

8. There has been a progressive decline in the share of transport in the total plan outlay, and if this trend continues, it could damage the nation's economy. There is also need for maximum economic use of all available capacities in the transport system. (Para 1.6.6)

9. Investment policy for an optimal inter-modal mix should be based on comparative resource cost analysis of various transport modes. Transport investment decision should also take into account social costs such as caused by congestion, pollution, accidents and noise. (Paras 1.7.1 to 1.7.3)

10. Every transport undertaking should at least, cover its short run operating costs. Attempts should be made to avoid subsidies unless there are weighty considerations for their retention on social grounds in which case they should be direct. (Paras 1.8.2 and 1.8.3)

11. Transport agencies should be given freedom to fix their own fares and freight rates on the basis of their cost so long as they do not violate the broad pricing guidelines set by the Government. (Para 1.8.5)

12. Energy conservation should be the over-riding consideration in determining an optimal mix of our future transport system.

(Para 1.9.1)

13. Impact of environmental objectives on transport should be considered. Sound traffic management and effective land-use policy can help in reducing the adverse effect of environmental pollution and hazards. (Paras 1.10.1 and 1.10.2).

Transport Development in India—A Review

1. Railways and roads have been the principal modes of transport. In 1950-78, passenger traffic increased from 66.5 to 177 b. pkms. and freight traffic from 44 to 163 b. tkms. by rail. On roads, it is estimated that in the same period passenger traffic increased from 23 to 250b. pkms. and freight from 5.5 to 77 b. pkms. (Paras 2.3.3 and 2.3.10)

2. A significant development is the marked shift in the relative share of rail and road transport in the total traffic carried. The share of road transport in both passenger and goods traffic increased at a much faster rate than of railways, although in absolute terms, traffic increased substantially on both the modes. (Para 2.5.1)

3. Despite continuous efforts made since 1951 to augment the capacity of various modes of transport, the transport sector has generally experienced bottlenecks and capacity shortages. The imbalances between the demand and supply of transport facilities has adversely affected the smooth functioning of the economy. (Para 2.5.5)

4. The imbalances underline the need for creating transport capacity ahead of traffic demand, so that some cushion in the system exists to meet unexpected spurts or shifts in transport requirements.

Determination of Optimal Inter-Modal Mix

1. For determining an optimal inter-modal mix the resource cost analysis of the main transport modes should be considered. The policy aim should be to create a transport system which provides service at the least resource cost to society. (Paras 3.3.2 and 3.1.4)

2. The role of employment generation in determining an optimal inter-modal mix is minimal. (Para 3.1.5)

3. Energy conservation should be given the over-riding consideration in determining inter-modal mix. The energy efficient modes should have a bigger role to play in future. (Para 3.1.9)

4. Movement of commodities are generally economical by road for shorter distances up to 300-350 kms., beyond this range, cost advantage lies with the railways. (Para 3.2.15)

5. Movement by block loads are more economic than movement in wagon loads by railways. Break-even points of distance over which rail transport becomes economical reduce further with an increase in the price of diesel and with better utilisation of capacity. (Para 3.2.13)

6. Rail passenger resource costs are higher than those of highway transport although if value on time saving, comfort and convenience are made, cost advantage would be in favour of railways for long distance movements. (Para 3.2.20)

7. Total passenger traffic is expected to increase to about 1344 b. pkms. by 2000 A.D. Road transport's share will continue at about 60 per cent and it would be 800 b. pkms. Rail share would be 520 b. pkms. Air transport's share at under 2 per cent would be 23.6. b. pkms. (Para 3.5.11)

8. At the present price of diesel and its consequential impact in break-even levels and assuming a shift to rail of only 50 per cent of traffic moving by road beyond break-even levels, the share of rail and road in freight traffic changes from 67:33 observed in the past ten years to 72:28. The share of railways would increase further with a rise in diesel prices and if the assumed share of shiftable traffic is increased in favour of rail. (Para 3.7.1)

9. Total freight traffic is estimated to increased to 550 b. tonne-kms. by the turn of the century. In the suggested inter-modal mix railways will be expected to carry 468 b. tonne-kms. and road transport 182 b. tonne-kms. in 2000 A.D. (Para 3.7.2)

10. Rail and road transport would require annually 14.7 m. tonnes of diesel in 2000 A.D. At current prices (dollar 30 per barrel) this will cost about Rs. 2800 crores. The projections for diesel given by the Working Group on Energy Policy for 2000 A.D. are 33 m. tonnes at reference level and 23 m tonnes at optimal level forecasts. In comparison with these estimates, the savings would amount to over Rs. 3500 crores per annum in relation to the reference level and Rs. 1650 crores in relation to optimal level forecasts. (Para 3.7.5)

11. A major break-through in technology in the foreseeable future to replace petroleum products for traction in the transport sector is not yet visible. The requirement estimated is the minimum which must be met on priority basis. (Para 3.7.6)

12. Government should try to change the inter-modal mix in the desired direction, through investment and pricing mechanism rather than through regulation and physical control. (Para 7.7.7)

Taxation, Pricing and Subsidy

1. Taxation in transport has three broad functions : as a user price in lieu of service provided, as part of general revenue collection and as a shadow price for scarce resources used. Taxation and pricing policies should maximise generation of internal resources. (Paras 4.1.1 and 4.1.2)

2. Generally, transport services should cover their short-run marginal costs. Large-scale investment in transport projects which are not economically viable on a long-term basis and do not cover the opportunity cost of capital should not generally be undertaken. Surpluses generated by any transport service should accrue to the national pool of investible resources rather than to its own account separately. While there is no need for any general subsidy in transport sector, there is on objection to cross-subsidization to a limited extent. (Para 4.1.3)

3. Fuel taxation should not only serve as a means of raising revenue, but also as a shadow price for ensuring socially efficient use of this scarce resource. (Para 4.1.5)

4. Railway fare and freight structure need to be revised to bring it in line with costs and to correct anomalies and undesirable subsidies. (Paras 4.1.6 and 4.2.2)

5. The railways have been incurring losses on sub-urban systems on account of concessional monthly season tickets even after the upward revision of fares made in April, 1979. These fares should be further raised to wipe off the losses to enable the railways to provide better services. (Para 4.2.3)

6. The railways charge lower freight rates than their costs for certain commodities of mass consumption as a part of their social obligation and incur losses. About 50 per cent of these losses are on account of foodgrains. Since the influence of transport costs on their prices is marginal, the economics of "cost-plus" basis of fixing rail freight rates for these commodities may be examined in greater detail by the Rail Tariff Enquiry Committee. (Para 4.2.5)

7. The location of the North Eastern region, now linked with the rest of the country through a longer route, should not put people of that area to a disadvantage. A suitable freight policy needs to be devised for this region. (Para 4.2.6)

8. Indian Airlines should enjoy appropriate freedom and flexibility for suitably revising and adjusting its fare structure to meet costs and generate maximum internal surpluses. (Para 4.3.2)

9. There is hardly any evidence to show that the overall tax-burden on the road transport industry is heavy to inequitous or it has

adversely affected the industry. While the contention that total tax raised from any source should be spent on that source is not tenable, taxes paid by road users as a whole bear a close relationship to public expenditure on road construction and maintenance. (Paras 4.4.3 and 4.4.4)

10. There is considerable scope for and urgent need to reduce the multiplicity of road transport taxes, rationalise the rate structure, simplify the methods of assessment and centralise collection for smooth inter-State road movements. Tax structure should have uniform basic rates between States so that the incidence of taxation, at least between neighbouring States, is comparable. (Paras 4.4.5 to 4.4.7)

11. Passenger and goods taxes need to be integrated with the motor vehicles tax and collected at a flat rate and at a single point (as is already done in some States) rather than vehicle-wise and as a percentage of fare in case of passenger buses. (Para 4.4.8)

12. There is no justification for charging a uniform composite fee of Rs. 700 for national and zonal permits. These permits should be issued liberally but full fee applicable to each of the States to which they relate, should be charged at a single point in the home State. (Paras 4.4.9 and 4.4.10)

13. In the interest of smooth inter-State road transport and for reducing wide disparity in taxation as between States, Centre may consider the desirability of introducing a suitable legislation. (Para 4.4.12)

14. There is need for adjusting excise duty on diesel so as to reflect its true cost to the economy. (Para 4.4.13)

15. Fares of public sector road transport undertakings often do not cover short-term marginal costs. These should be revised and brought in line with the cost-structure except in certain special cases where, if necessary, a direct exchequer subsidy may be provided. (Paras 4.4.14 and 4.4.15)

16. Octroi should be abolished in stages starting with small localities of say 25,000 population or less. While this is primarily the responsibility of the State Governments, Centre should use its persuasive powers and encourage the States to abolish octroi even by extending financial assistance to them. (Para 4.5.6)

Freight Equalisation

1. Freight equalisation is not the only instrument to achieve balance regional development. Other measures such as licensing policy, appropriate fiscal and credit facilities, provision of essential infrastructure are also equally important. (Para 5.2.4)

2. The beneficial effect in terms of regional dispersal as a result of freight equalisation was more than offset by increase in real transport costs. (Para 5.3.2)

3. Freight equalisation has had little effect on generating employment activity in backward regions. There is a case for phasing out existing freight equalisation scheme. (Para 5.3.3)

4. For commodities of mass consumption freight equalisation will not make a significant difference in the final price paid by the consumer. This can be better achieved through a comprehensive distribution system. (Paras 5.4.3 and 5.5.2)

Machinery for Transport Co-ordination

1. The purpose of transport co-ordination is to create technical, economic and other conditions for allocation of traffic among transport modes and to help development of transport facilities in each mode in the required proportion at the least cost to the society. (Para 6.2.1)

2. Procedures for approval of investment projects are different for different transport modes and applicable only to Governmental investment. The criteria for appraising transport projects should be common irrespective of the mode or agency. (Para 6.2.4)

3. There is need for a centralised pricing authority to recommend common criteria for fixing fares and freight rates for different transport modes. The constitution of a National Transport Commission with persons having wide and varied experience is proposed. The three main functions of coordination—pricing, investment and regulation could be entrusted to this Commission. (Paras 6.2.7 and 6.3.7)

4. The National Transport Commission could study traffic flows and demand to frame an appropriate inter-modal transport mix and examine fiscal and taxation policy, monitor functioning of the transport system identify imbalances in the availability of services and advise Central and State Governments in the matter of transport policy. (Para 6.3.6)

5. Similar arrangements are recommended for coördinating transport policies and programmes at the State and local levels, within the overall policies prescribed by the Central Government. (Para 6.3.14)

Transport Planning and Data Base

1. Transport Planning requires development of a systematic methodology for projecting traffic demand and its allocation on the

basis of resource costs of different modes of transport. Continuous research will be required on these aspects in order to improve the reliability of traffic forecasts. National Transport Commission should encourage research on methodology of transport planning and appraisal. (Paras 7.2.1 to 7.2.7)

2. Methodology and the framework evolved by RITES for computation of resource costs and compilation of traffic flows are in right direction. Information on traffic flows and resource costs should be periodically collected, preferably once in every five years. (Para 7.3.2 to 7.3.5)

3. Transport Projects generally involve large-scale investments and generate considerable amount of secondary and non-user benefits. There are also complex problems of quantification of social costs such as pollution, environmental effects, accidents costs, etc., and other intangibles. These costs and benefits cannot be properly assessed by applying financial feasibility criteria. Their assessment requires a broader frame of social-cost benefit analysis. Transport projects in future should be appraised within such a wider framework. The present appraisal methodology adopted by the Project Appraisal Division of the Planning Commission is satisfactory for road investment projects but needs to be strengthened for projects in rail, port and other sectors of transport which involve large-scale investments. (Paras 7.4.1 to 7.4.10)

Transport Research and Training

1. An inter-disciplinary centre should be set-up to stimulate research, conduct studies and impart training in transport planning and management. It should enjoy autonomy on the lines of the Institutes of Management and Institutes of Technology. (Paras 8.2.1 and 8.2.2)

2. Efforts should be made to encourage research and training at the universities and other specialised institutions. Necessary financial support should be provided. (Para 8.2.3)

3. A wing or a unit should be organised as part of the National Transport Commission to function as a central forum for co-ordinating the research and development efforts undertaken by different institutions for various modes of transport. This wing should be appropriately advised by a group of experts. (Para 8.2.5)

Railways

1. Growth of both passenger and freight traffic on the railways has been steady, utilisation of assets has improved, density of traffic

per route km. has increased over the years. There is need to augment both rolling stock and line capacity to meet the projected demand of traffic and avoid bottlenecks in the system. (Para 9.2.1 to 9.4.1)

2. The growth of passenger traffic has been faster than what was provided for in the successive five year plans. It is necessary to plan for a realistic growth to meet the requirements of growing population and of new centres of economic activity. (Para 9.5.3)

3. Railways should not expand their services for short distance passenger traffic except between pairs of points where the density of traffic is very high. For short distance traffic, feasibility of introducing more buses in certain States needs to be explored. (Paras 9.8.1 and 9.8.3)

4. Railways should increase loading in train loads and running of point trains to ease pressure on marshalling yards and to improve wagon turnround. (Para 9.11.3)

5. Railways have lately not been able to meet the demand of traffic. Freight traffic on railways is likely to grow to over 460 b.tkms by 2000 A D. Capacity has to be augmented for handling this traffic. There should be enough resilience in the system to provide for spurts of traffic and changes in pattern of movement. (Para 9.14.1)

6. Vigorous steps will be necessary to increase capacity on important routes. It may be necessary to plan alternative routes especially for coal movement to relieve congestion on existing routes. This could help also in reducing the distance between pairs of points and consequently the transport effort. (Para 9.16.2)

7. Rationalisation of terminals, mechanisation of loading and unloading of bulk goods, running heavier trains from siding to siding, clubbing of 'smalls', creation of dumps for coal, steel, cement and other commodities needs to be undertaken. (Para 9.16.3)

8. Coal traffic is likely to grow substantially. It will be necessary to review coal loading arrangements and pilot working, remodel coal yards and developments of new ones to enable operation of unit trains. (Para 9.17.2)

9. Railways should reduce the differential in speeds between freight trains and mail/express trains to improve line capacity. (Para 9.19.1)

10. Railways should develop containerised traffic and introduce piggy back system. This would also speed up the movement from one gauge to another. (Paras 9.20.1 and 9.20.2)

11. With the completion of the microwave network, railways

should now go in for computerised wagon control and passenger reservations. (Para 9.21.1)

12. Separate parcel terminals should be planned particularly at metropolitan cities. Parcel trains could also clear 'smalls' traffic. (Para 9.22.1)

13. Priority should be given to dieselisation of important sections on metre gauge. Also rolling stock and track structure need to be improved to move heavier trains at faster speeds on meter gauge. (Paras 9.24.3 and 9.24.4)

14. Fast express trains should be introduced between pairs of points on metre gauge. (Para 9.24.5)

15. Although technological inputs would improve operation of metre gauge sections, it is necessary to gradually convert to broad gauge high density freight routes which involve heavy transhipment. Major ports should be connected by the broad gauge system. (Para 9.24.6).

16. While taking up metre gauge conversion schemes it should be ensured that the through link in the all-India network of metre gauge is not disrupted. (Para 9.24.8)

17. All narrow gauge sections except the central India narrow gauge system and some narrow gauge hill sections should be closed down. A system approach should be adopted where their conversion to either metre gauge or broad gauge may form part of a network and is justified on traffic potential. (Para 9.25.2)

18. Formation and other permanent assets of these narrow gauge sections should be handed over free to State Governments. However, before closing, it should be ensured that adequate and efficient road transport is available to serve those areas. (Para 9.25.3).

19. Programme of electrification on railways has been slow. An electrification programme of at least 350 kms. per year to cover the main trunk routes is necessary. (Para 9.27.7)

20. 5750 kms. of new rail lines have been constructed since 1950. Most of the new lines have served the purpose for which they were conceived. (Para 9.28.2)

21. Investment criteria for new lines should take into account the financial return and benefits to the economy. A wider social cost-benefit criteria for appraisal needs to be applied. Construction of new lines should be taken up to fulfil the following objectives:

(a) as project-oriented lines to serve new industries or tap mineral and other resources;

(b) to serve as missing links which can form alternative routes to relieve congestion on existing busy rail routes;

(c) on strategic considerations; and

(d) as developmental lines to establish new growth centres or give access to remote areas. (Para 9.31.1)

22. Any region where natural resources are available an integrated plan should be evolved to develop new growth centres and promote economic activity, the provision of a new rail line being an element in such developmental plans. (Para 9.31.1)

23. Reducing total transport effort and relieving congestion on the existing saturated network are important criteria for construction of new lines. There is urgent need for developing alternative routes on which traffic can be diverted, reducing leads and consequently total transportation effort. (Para 9.31.2)

24. Where existing routes are heavily congested, even after doubling tracks, building an altogether new route between the main modal points will give the system a better viability than addition of a third track. This will enable alternative routes to operate during dislocations caused by natural calamities. (Para 9.31.4)

25. During the next two decades, the railway network will need to be expanded by at least 5,000 kms. (Para 9.32.1)

26. Adequate investment on the railways must be ensured to enable them to fulfil the assigned task. (Para 9.33.2).

Road Development

1. Since Bombay Plan of road development (1961-81) is about to end, there is need for formulation of another perspective plan for the next 20 years. The new plan should be comprehensive and should take into account road requirements in rural, hilly and tribal areas in different regions of the country, traffic needs and national priorities. (Para 10.1.7)

2. The existing functional classification of roads as national and State highways, districts roads and village roads, is satisfactory and we do not suggest any change except that minimum standards should be prescribed for 'project' and 'urban' roads which presently are not covered by the standard classification. (Paras 10.2.1 and 10.1.7)

3. Roads should be built keeping in view the traffic requirements for 10 to 15 years instead of the present practice of planning on the basis of five years. There is also the need to prepare suitable road and

bridge inventories for all categories of State roads particularly the state highways and major district roads, and to update them at regular intervals. (Para 10 10.2.3)

4. National highways which constitute about 6 per cent of total surfaced road-length in the country and carry over 25 per cent of road traffic, are inadequate in route length and load carrying capacity. Inadequacy of certain selected stretches needs to be urgently remedied. (Paras 10.3.2 to 10.3.4)

5. Apart from the existing criteria, substantial reduction in travel time and distance may also be included for declaring State roads as national highways. On this basis, 37 missing links and direct connections comprising a length of about 13,000 kms. have been identified for possible addition to the national highway grid. (Paras 10.3.5 and 10.3.6)

6. Around 30 per cent villages in the country had an all-weather road connection on 31 March 1978 while another 16 per cent had fair-weather roads. The estimated requirement of funds to connect all village with all-weather roads at 1978 prices, is around Rs. 11,000 crores which may not be easy to find. The low-cost alternatives considered by us include integrating the rural roads programme with the Integrated Rural Development Programme, tapping supplementary sources of finance, planning for all weather road communication through provision of cross-drainages, culverts on kutcha roads, and taking up of works according to district-wise master plans. (Paras 10.4.1 to 10.4.6)

7. For State highway, district roads and other categories of roads, it is essential that master-plans are drawn up in accordance with a long-term perspective and works executed in a phased manner, avoiding delays in completion of works. Traffic surveys and forecasts must be conducted for determining inter-se priority of road schemes under master plans. (Para 10.5.1)

8. Adequate land area should be earmarked in the master plans for urban areas and a system should be devised whereby unnecessary digging up of roads is minimised and repair-work expeditiously completed. (Para 10.6.1)

9. Maintenance of roads in coal-field areas and feeder roads must receive special attention of the State Governments. Rates of road cess may be suitably enhanced to generate resources for the purpose. The entire proceeds of coal cess should be utilised for proper upkeep of these roads. (Para 10.6.3)

10. Union and State Governments should acquire appropriate legal authority for prevention of ribbon development and encroach-

ments on highways. These provisions should be strictly enforced. (Paras 10.7.1 and 10.7.2)

11. Maintenance of roads leaves much to be desired. This is mainly due to inadequate financial provisions. We recommend that road maintenance should receive the highest priority in preference to new construction. Necessary financial provision should be made in accordance with the prescribed norms which should be updated periodically to take into account rising costs of labour and material. (Para 10.8.4)

12. Utilisation of the Central Road Fund should be limited to programmes of road research and intelligence, training of engineers, traffic surveys and provision of way-side amenities. (Para 10.10.1)

13. There is urgent need for augmenting research and development effort for road development. Mobile field laboratories should be strengthened and attention paid to reduction in road construction costs through use of locally available materials. Regional soil testing centres should be set up in the country under the aegis of the Central Road Research Institute. Private agencies may be associated with road research and transport engineering work. (Para 10.11.1).

Road Transport

1. In 1977-78, mechanised road transport handled 77 b. tkm and 250 b. pkm of goods and passenger traffic respectively. This is expected to go up to 185 b. tkm and 800 b. pkm by 2000-01 A.D. (Para 11.1.1)

2. There is no reliable evidence to show that a single truck operator is not a viable unit. Reorganisation of the structure of the trucking industry is not called for. (Paras 11.4.2 and 11.4.3)

3. The Motor Vehicles Act needs to be replaced by a coherent legislation for promoting adequate, efficient, safe and economic road transport. (Para 11.5.3)

4. The Act provides for a minimum strength of three members including the Chairman for State and Regional Transport Authorities but maximum strength is not prescribed. This should be fixed at not more than seven and should include non-official members with professional backgrounds. Public sector road transport undertakings could be relied upon to determine the need for transport services in an area or on a route operated by them and reference to transport authorities is not necessary. (Paras 11.6.2 to 11.6.4)

5. As the Inter-State Transport Commission was not empowered

to discharge the functions for which it was created, it should be discontinued. (Para 11.6.6.)

6. Fees charged for private carriers should be the same as for public carriers. (Para 11.6.7)

7. The permit system for intra-State goods transport should be abolished wherever it exists. (Para 11.6.8)

8. In the interest of smooth inter-State freight traffic, there should be no restriction on the issue of national, zonal and other inter-State permits put full taxes for all concerned States should be realised at one point in the home State. (Paras 11.6.14 to 11.6.16)

9. For intra-State passenger services, the procedure for grant and renewal of permits should be simplified so that it does not take more than 3 to 4 weeks for an applicant to secure a permit. (Para 11.6.9)

10. For inter-State passenger services, public sector undertakings should be authorised to enter into reciprocal agreements on behalf of the State Governments and the procedures in this regard should also be simplified. (Para 11.6.17)

11. The system of issue of temporary permits for goods and passenger transport needs to be rationalised. The Act should provide for a distinction between a temporary permit purely for short-term requirements, and the one needed for a route or an area which has traffic potential. (Para 11.6.20)

12. Apart from improvement in the terms of bank finance such as reduction in margin money stipulation and the repayment period, quantum of bank finance to road transport industry should be increased so that its dependence on private financiers is minimised. (Paras 11.7.2. to 11.7.6)

13. Public sector road transport undertakings should be allowed to raise fares to economic levels. When they are required to operate services on losing routes and charges low fares as a social obligation, they must be compensated by a direct exchequer subsidy. (Paras 11.7.9 and 11.7.10)

14. Truck terminals should be constructed by State Governments. (Para 11.7.11)

15. Licensing of goods booking agencies should be expedited. (Para 11.8.4)

16. Passenger bus fares should fully cover marginal costs. (Para 11.9.6)

17. Nationalisation of goods transport is not called for. (Para 11.9.3)

18. Although the performance of public sector road transport undertakings has been by and large satisfactory, there is still scope for improvement. (Para 11.9.11)

19. Before any further nationalisation is undertaken, the existing services should be improved and consolidated. A limit of one year should be prescribed during which if a State transport undertaking is not able to run a service already notified, the notification should automatically lapse so that the travelling public does not suffer. (Para 11.9.12)

20. For effecting fuel economy in road transport, improvement and proper maintenance of roads, reduction in the number of check posts, improvements in vehicle design, proper vehicle operation and maintenance are called for. (Paras 11.10.2 to 11.11.5)

21. Recycled engine oil should be exempted from excise duty. (Para 11.10.6)

22. There is need to encourage the development of non-mechanised intermediate public transport modes. (Para 11.10.7)

23. It would not be opportune to dieselise taxis in view of the pressure on diesel. (Para 11.10.10)

24. The bullock cart has assumed added significance in view of severe energy constraint. Research and development to improve cart design should be intensified. (Paras 11.12.3 and 11.12.4)

25. Pedestrian and cycle traffic should receive greater attention in road traffic planning. Intensification of road safety drive, driver education and strict enforcement of traffic regulations are called for. (Paras 11.13.3 to 11.13.6)

26. Traffic Engineering cells should be set up in public works departments of every State. Road surveys should be conducted regularly to identify accident-prone sections for remedial action. (Para 11.13.8)

Urban Transport

1. Urbanisation in inextricably with the process of our economic growth. A certain minimum growth of urban population is, therefore, unavoidable. Proper planning is required to develop new urban centres, with employment opportunities, housing and other civic amenities so that people do not migrate to the existing urban conglomerations and cause deterioration in the quality of urban life. (Para 12.3.4)

2. While urbanisation rate in India has been quite modest, concentration of population in a few selected cities is a matter of concern.

(Para 12.3.5)

3. Transport policy has only a limited role to play in determining population growth in metropolitan cities. Restrictions on intra-urban transport facilities cannot limit or reverse population growth in these cities. (Para 12.5.14)

4. In the foreseeable future bus transport will continue to be the principal means of intracity movements. Priority should therefore be given to strengthen and optimise bus services. (Para 12.6.7)

5. Every effort should be made to divert traffic from personalised modes of motor transport to the public transport system. Electric traction based public transport systems should be preferred. (Para 12.6.8)

6. Comprehensive traffic studies have shown that traffic in metropolitan cities cannot be handled by road-based transport system. (Para 12.7.1)

7. In the metropolitan cities the volume of traffic is growing daily and existing public transport facilities are under severe strain. Over-crowding is becoming unbearable and even maintaining the existing transport facilities is posing great difficulties. Augmenting the existing sub-urban rail facilities and providing new electrified intra-urban rail services are essential to meet the traffic demand. (Para 12.7.2. to 12.7.11)

8. The substantial growth of Intermediate Public Transport (IPT) indicates the inadequacy of public transport facilities in small and medium size cities. This will continue to be important as a supplement to public transport. More attention should be paid to it. (Para 12.7.18)

9. Electric trams and trolley buses have an important role to play mainly on considerations of energy conservation. (Paras 12.7.19 and 12.7.20)

10. A suitable organisation should be established at the Centre preferably as part of the National Transport Commission to supervise and monitor the traffic-cum-land-use studies for various cities. (Para 12.7.21)

11. For medium and small size cities bus services are essential. Proper traffic cells should be set up in the States for conducting traffic surveys on a regular basis. (Para 12.8.8)

12. Improved traffic management methods and control should be given priority. The basic approach needs to be changed and priority given to movement of pedestrians, cyclists and public bus transport system. (Paras 12.9.1, 12.9.2 and 12.9.14)

13. A single transport authority should be set up as part of the regional development authority in the metropolitan cities for overall charge of all modes of transport including metropolitan rapid rail transit systems. At operational level these regional authorities could appoint separate boards for separate modes or activities. (Para 12.11.4)

Air Transport

1. Air transport offers substantial savings in time over long distances and plays an important role in areas where surface transport is not adequate due to the terrain. In respect of the latter, a separate air line has been recommended for the north eastern region. Special consideration has also to be given to the provision of air services along the west coast, in the Saurashtra region and to Kavaratti (Lakshadweep). (Paras 13.5.4 and 13.5.7)

2. Private operators could be allowed to run short haul services to such places as are not served by Indian Airlines, provided infrastructural facilities could be made available with small investments. In case a private operator runs a service on any route at the instance and direction of the Government, subsidy should be provided to him on the same manner as for Indian Airlines. (Para 13.5.7)

3. There is a big gap between seating capacities and operating costs of turbo-prop and jet aircraft presently used by Indian Airlines. There is need to consider acquisition of a more efficient aircraft of suitable capacity. (Para 13.6.3)

4. Indian Airlines should be given more freedom in formulation of its fare structure. Fare revision proposals could be examined by the proposed National Transport Commission. (Para 13.7.2)

5. Tariffs charged by Indian Airlines are not cost oriented, Long haul services subsidise short haul services. The telescoping of fares between long and short hauls is not sharp on Indian Airlines compared to airlines elsewhere. Indian Airlines should rationalise its fare structure to make it cost oriented. (Para 13.7.3)

6. Infrastructure facilities have not kept pace with development of air transport. Capacity for handling both passenger and cargo particularly at international airports should be augmented. (Paras 13.10.2 and 13.10.3)

7. IAAI should devise a tariff structure which should not only pay for investments already made but also finance expansion programme on a long-term basis. (Para 13.10.4.2)

8. Civil Aviation Department should carry out cost benefit analysis by taking into account the likely investment required for improvement of infrastructural facilities and the increase in revenues through landing and navigational charges. (Para 13.10.5.1)

9. Air transport infrastructural facilities are subsidised by the general exchequer if servicing of capital, depreciation and development expenditure are taken into account. This is not appropriate. Airport charges should be so fixed as to fully pay for investments made for services to airlines and air passengers. Department of Civil Aviation should maintain its accounts on commercial principles. (Para 13.10.5.2)

10. Civil Aviation Development Fund need not be continued. The development programme of Indian Airlines should be financed by internal generation of resources and any further assistance required should come from general revenues as in the case of other modes of transport. (Para 13.11.1).

Coastal Shipping

1. Coastal traffic has declined and is now insignificant. Number of vessels and GRT have remained static. (Paras 14.1.1 to 14.1.3)

2. With steep increase in operating costs and port delays, this mode has lost its competitiveness to rail and road transport. (Para 14.2.4)

3. Freight rates prescribed by Government for coal and salt are below operator costs. (Para 14.2.10)

4. Shipping costs for traffic originating and terminating at ports, without involving any transhipment for overland movement, are lower than rail and road costs. (Para 14.3.3)

5. Future of coastal shipping lies mainly in catering to project oriented traffic, involving close-circuit, 'merry-go-round' movement, like transport of coal to power plants or clinker to cements plants. (Paras 14.5.2 and 14.6.2)

6. With an improvement in capacity utilisation of vessels and decrease in port stay and removal of various constraints, coastal shipping could move more tonnage as there is larger quantum of cargo offerings. (Paras 14.2.10 and 14.3.4)

7. For future growth of coastal shipping, the measures suggested are : (i) co-ordination of coastal operations, (ii) modernisation of coastal fleet, (iii) freedom of operations, (iv) simplification of custom pro-

cedures, (v) improvement in port facilities, (vi) priority berthing for coastal vessels, (vii) simplification and rationalisation of the procedures adopted for revision and fixation of freight rates and (viii) improvement in operation of coal dump at Calcutta/Haldia. (Paras 14.4.1 to 14.4.14 and 14.9.1)

8. Since coastal shipping can relieve pressure on surface transport, this mode will continue as an essential adjunct to surface transport. However, as their operating costs are high, this mode will have to be subsidised. (Para 14.9.2)

9. It is necessary for Government to allot an assured quantity of traffic to coastal trade on long-term basis. (Para 14.5.1)

10. Sailing vessels have declined in number so has the traffic carried by them. But because they conserve energy, financial incentives should be given to operators. (Para 14.7.1)

11. There is a special need for providing adequate steamer services between the mainland and Andaman — Nicobar and Lakshadweep groups of islands. (Para 14.8.2)

Inland Water Transport

1. Inland water transport although functionally important in regions in which it offers natural advantage is now almost extinct in the country. (Para 15.2.7)

2. Being location specific, it has only a limited role to play in the transport system of the country. (Para 15.3.1)

3. Most waterways suffer from navigational hazards and lack navigational aids and terminal facilities. (Para 15.3.3)

4. Inter-modal cost comparison shows that IWT has cost advantage for direct movement of cargo only from the terminal to another on the water-front and if it does not involve transhipment to another mode. (Para 15.4.9)

5. Despite the present deficiencies, because of its energy saving aspects and relief to surface transport, this mode can play a useful role in some parts of the country. Therefore, some waterways should be declared as national waterways. (Paras 15.1.1, 15.5.8 and 15.5.28)

6. A proper conservancy policy needs to be followed. (Para 15.5.11)

7. A statutory authority named Inland Water-ways Authority of India (IWAI) should be set up for properly developing IWT. (Para 15.5.18)

8. IWT will need considerable Government support.

Ports and Harbours

1. Congestion at ports adversely affects the competitiveness of country's exports and the growth of its national output. (Para 16.1.3)

2. Planning of port capacity expansion must be undertaken long before congestion actually builds up at ports. (Para 16.6.3)

3. Since demand for port capacity is by and large location specific, port planning should be related to the traffic projected a each port. (Para 16.7.1)

4. In view of non-interchangeability of berths, capacity of port must be assessed separately in relation to three broad categories of cargo, namely, (a) wet or liquid bulk, (b) dry or solid bulk, and (c) break bulk. (Para 16.7.3)

5. A norm of 75 per cent berth occupancy may be adopted for planning of port capacity. (Para 16.7.4)

6. While the estimates of port capacity and traffic for 1982-83 show surplus capacity for handling wet bulk and dry bulk cargo, the capacity for handling general or break-bulk cargo is likely to be short of demand at most major ports particularly at Bombay. (Para 16.7.6)

7. None of our ports has proper container handling facilities. As a result, it has not been possible to get full benefits of containerisation. For this, specialised facilities should be provided. Complementary rail and road facilities should be created. (Paras 16.8.6 and 16.8.8)

8. The long-term solution to Bombay port's congestion will be by significant additions to its capacity. Such capacity expansion is not feasible in the existing port. There is an urgent need for the development of a deep draft port in the country which can receive modern ships, particularly those carrying container and bulk Cargo. Nheva Sheva is the only site technically suitable for the development of a deep-draft port. (Paras 16.9.5 and 16.9.6)

9. As a short-term relief measure, the Bombay Port Trust should on priority basis explore the economic feasibility of mid-stream discharge. (Para 16.9.8)

10. A special Working Group should be set-up to examine the availability of handling equipment at major ports and suggest remedial measures. (Para 16.10.2)

11. The inadequate rail and road transport links have adversely affected traffic handling capacity at some major ports. These ports

should be provided with adequate broad gauge rail and road facilities. (Para 16.10.4)

12. Labour should be involved in all schemes of port modernisation.

13. Port charges must be fixed to cover fully the operational cost at each port. (Para 16.11.12)

14. Port trusts should be given greater freedom in the management of ports to improve their efficiency. (Para 16.12.4)

15. A Central Port Authority should be set up and entrusted with the responsibility of overall planning of port development in the country. (Para 16.12.5)

16. Intermediate and minor ports can play an important role in meeting the requirements of coastal and sailing vessels and to help in reducing pressure on the major ports. (Para 16.13.6)

Ropeways and Pipelines

1. An efficient transport service in hilly terrain is essential for accelerating development. In this context, construction of ropeways, particularly in steep, rocky and rugged areas, has to be examined. (Para 17.2.1)

2. Ropeways have a distinct advantage in hilly areas and can be functionally useful in selected plain areas as well. This mode of transport can be gainfully utilised for short distances or small stretches for close circuit movement of bulk materials such as cement, coal, clay, limestone and clinker. (Para 17.2.26)

3. The capital cost of pipelines is high, but their low cost of operation makes it financially viable, given an adequate volume of traffic. The consumption of energy by pipelines is lowest as compared to other modes. (Para 17.3.7)

8

EXPERT COMMITTEE ON THE REORGANISATION OF CENTRAL REVENUES LABORATORIES, 1978 — REPORT[1]

Chairman Shri A.N. Sattanathan

Members Shri S. Venkataraman; Shri Daya Sagar; Dr. V.S. Ramanathan; Dr. D.R. Gupta; Shri E.K. Ramachandran; (replaced Shri A.K. Bhattacharya); Dr. Madhavan Nair, Dr. A.F. Chhapgar; Dr. L.P. Pandey; Shri J.B. Shah.

M. Secy. Shri V.R. Ranganathan.

Appointment

The Expert Committee on the Central Revenues Laboratories was constituted by the Government of India, Ministry of Finance (Department of Revenue) Vide their Resolution F. No. A-11019/18/78-Ad. IV dated May 31, 1978.

Terms of Reference

(a) The adequacy or otherwise of the number of laboratories under the Central Board of Excise and Customs;

(b) Adequacy or otherwise of modern testing facilities and improvements in the apparatus, equipment, fittings and literature needed in the context of technological innovations and the wide range of products that the Departmental Laboratories are called upon to test;

(c) The procedure for and frequency of sampling;

(d) Measures aimed at reducing delays in testing or advising the department on specific issues referred to the laboratories;

(e) Utility or otherwise of tests carried out by outside

1. New Delhi, Ministry of Finance (Department of Revenue), 1979, 2 Vols.

laboratories;

(f) Feasibility of identifying areas where with suitable training, the departmental field staff can themselves conduct tests which might not require elaborate equipment or expertise as to warrant a reference to the laboratories;

(g) Organisational and administrative set-up of the laboratories with particular reference to :

(i) requirements of staff at each laboratory including leave reserve;
(ii) different grades with channels of promotion;
(iii) minimum qualifications;
(iv) pay and emoluments;
(v) buildings; and
(vi) in-service training.

(h) Any other matter germane to the enquiry.

Contents

Preface; Introduction; Summary; Laboratory Services; The Role of the Laboratories in the Assessment of "Goods"; Procedure for drawal of samples their testing, Reporting, etc., frequencies for drawal of samples; Tests conducted by outside laboratories; Mini kit for on-the sport testing; Rationalisation of the customs and excise tariffs; The role of testing in the settlement of drawback claims; Departmental laboratories in Refineries; Central Revenues control laboratory at headquarters; Reorganisation of the control laboratory set-up at head-quarters; Reorganisation of regional-laboratories and the proposed set-up; Implication of the reorganisation from the staffing angle; Special apparatus and equipment; Laboratory accommodation and infrastruc-ture; Opium and Alkaloid works; Ghazipur and Neemuch; Staff Morale — suggestions for improvement; Staff structure and pay scales, recruitment, training and promotions; Measures for reducing delays in testing and reporting; Model laboratory for Multipurpose work — Regional Research Laboratory, Hyderabad; and Annexures from I to XIV A.

Recommendations

We give in this chapter not complete summary of recommendations as such. In a report which is partly technical it is difficult to summarise recommendations there are several descriptive portions which have to be read in full and a summary may be inadequate. However, we are enumerating here serially most of our precise recommendations, and where this cannot be done indications are given as to the trend in the chapter. It is only fair for the report to be read in its full text; this summary can at best serve as a guide.

Role of Laboratories

1. Laboratories' technical opinion is called for regarding classification of several items, viz. Greyplasticine, Ethylbenene, polyblend, Balsamotolu, Magnesium oxide, Incol (MORL), Acrylic bulked yarn, Bata compound, etc. etc. Furnishing technical opinion adds to the work load of the Chemical Service Officers at all stages. (Para 3.5)

Sampling

2. Certain guidelines are suggested for drawal of samples. (Para 4.4)

3. The Drawing Officers and Testing Officers should be familiar with the Indian Standards Procedures of drawal of samples of several commodities published by them. (Para 4.5)

4. Sampling of Drugs and fine chemicals should be done with clean instruments. (Para 4.7.2)

5. The nature of containers in which the samples are packed should be indicated in the register at the time of drawal itself. (Para 4.7.2)

6. The Bombay Custom House instructions on drawal of samples may be adopted by other ports also, so as to ensure uniformity. (Para 4.8)

7. There should be a periodical exercise for reviewing the orders on drawal of samples. (Para 4.9)

8. The frequency would necessarily vary with the types of goods and standing of the particular manufacturer. A continuous study has to be undertaken for this purpose by a Standing Committee consisting of the Director of Inspection, the Director of Drawback, the Chief Chemists' representative and the representative from an organisation like Indian Standards Institution. (Para 4.10)

9. The 1977 Board's instructions on drawal of samples on the

Central Excise side required to be reviewed. The discretion vested with the Assistant Collector for drawal of samples should not be exercised by the Inspectors. (Para 4.10)

10. A case exists for acceptance by the Department of manufacturer's declaration of Indian Standards Institutions certified goods, Medicines of reputed firms and 'Agmark' label products. (Para 4.10)

11. The attention of all the Collectors should be drawn to the recommendations of the Committee headed by Shri V.R. Mehta of the Ministry of Shipping and Transport on the congestion in parts and accumulation of samples in laboratories. (Para 4.11)

12. Steps should be taken to deliver the samples lying in sheds or in the collection points in the docks to the laboratory atleast twice a day. (Para 4.12)

13. Samples (Import), containing volatile organic solvents such as Paints and Varnishes, Resin solution and Milk Powder and products thereof, Fish oil, Tallow, V.N.E. Oils, Alcoholic Beverages, and preparations, Petroleum products, Surface Active Agents, Starch and Starch products should be despatched to the laboratory with greater expedition and care, and should be tested on priority basis. (Para 4.12)

14. The test validity period for the branded goods or proprietary products of reputed manufacturers may be extended thereby reducing frequency. (Para 4.12)

15. On the Central Excise side, the samples drawn from Patent and Proprietary Medicines, Food products, Aerated waters, V.N.E. Oil and perishable goods should be despatched to the laboratory with greater expedition and should be tested on priority basis. (Para 4.12)

16. The major Custom Houses should pool their experience and adopt a uniform procedure for reducing the frequency of sampling in the light of Committee's observations. (Para 4.13)

17. When a consignment arrives just before and after the time of expiry of the validity of the earlier test report, the cleaning agents may be provide to ask for a test well-ahead of the expiry date of the previous test so that the fresh period of validity commences without delay. (Para 4.14)

18. If the precautions for packing, sealing and registering recommended by us are strictly followed there should not be any objection to the importers/exporters/clearing agents representatives carrying a sealed sample to the laboratory. However, this practice should not be encouraged if there are sufficient departmental staff to do this work.

Para 4.15)

19. The samples drawn should be properly recorded in the laboratory registers and delivered in the shortest possible time to the proper desk in the laboratory. (Para 4.16)

20. The appraising officer should ensure importers/clearing agents/manufacturers supply the printed literature of the products giving information helpful for testing at the time of filing the papers so that this could be forwarded alongwith the samples to the laboratory. (Para 4.17)

21. In disputed cases only, the details of the first test or/and of the retest can be given to the aggrieved party in the interest of natural justice. This cannot be supplied as a matter of routine. (Para 4.17)

22. The various facilities for testing should be made known to all the Trade associations with necessary precaution to ensure that such facilities are not taken undue advantage of. (Para 4.18)

23. On the Central Excise side, ordinarily the retest should be allowed only on remnant samples, as is done on Custom side subject to the observation in S.No. 25 below, regarding quality and content. After the remnant sample is retested and reported on by the Chief Chemist, the field officer should desist asking retest on duplicate or triplicate sample on the plea of natural justice. (Para 4.19)

24. In respect of retest in the original laboratory (a) retest should be done on the remnants samples and (b) retest should be done by different analysts and test results should be checked by the Head of the laboratory. (Para 4.19.2)

25. The first sample should be drawn in adequate quantity. The remnant should be preserved with greater care and precaution to ensure its complete identity in quality and content. If the goods are not cleared, then the Assistant Collector in his discretion may permit drawal of fresh samples in appropriate circumstances. (Para 4.19.3)

26. In the event of Collectorate laboratories having doubts about the method of analysis, adequacy of local equipment used, etc., it should be open to them to send the samples for retest to the Control Laboratory. (Para 4.19.4)

27. On the Central Excise side the contents of the test report alone may be communicated to the party, if sufficient reasons are given for the request. (Para 4.19.5)

28. If the trade desires more frequent sampling, it could be allowed on textile samples particularly yarn samples; the Collector and the Head of the laboratory could arrive at an acceptance norm of fre-

quency. (Para 4.24)

29. The test reports must be devoid of ambiguity and some procedure may be evolved to communicate the testing procedure to the Trade associations. (Para 4.25)

30. The Board might examine in consultation with the Textile Commissioner, the "TEX" system for determining the fineness of the yarn and suitably modify the Textile Tariff. (Para 4.26)

31. A small study group should go into the matters connected with the textile tariff in detail so as to reduce the complicity of the tariff. (Para 4.29)

32. The laboratory officers should be associated with the drawal of samples from bulk goods such as Ores, Oils, including Petroleum Products, Tallow, Paper, Textiles, Steel, Synthetic Rubber, Rubber Chemicals, Organic Surface Active Agents, bulk chemicals, Plastics, resins, etc. (Para 4.30)

33. The Committee does not favour acceptance of private laboratories' reports by the Customs and Central Excise Authorities. The practice, once conceded, could lead to abuses. (Para 5.6)

34. The additional expenditure on equipment proposed is not excessive compared with the advantages derived by having the Revenue Laboratories self-sufficient. (Para 5.7)

35. In extraordinary circumstances the Committee recommends that samples can be sent to the nearest National or Government Laboratories for test, in case necessary facilities are not available in the Revenue Laboratories. (Para 5.8)

36. In extreme cases of congestion, if the reports are required urgently, samples could be tested in reputed private laboratories by the Departmental Chemists. (Para 5.8)

Mini-Kit-Test

37. The concensus of the opinion is against the departmental field staff themselves carrying out simple tests even on a trial basis. The potentialities for misuse and errors might be immense. (Para 6.7)

Tariff Rationalisation

38. The Committee recommends that action may be taken to prescribe alcoholometry units in metric system in both the tariffs. (Para 7.5)

39. The mineral oil items in the Customs Tariff should be amended as per the existing Petroleum Act thereby giving the flashing point in full degree avoiding decimals. (Para 7.6)

40. The use of the word 'Bituminous sustance' in the mineral oil items in the Tariffs causes difficulties in testing. (Para 7.6.1)

41. The Resins and plastic items in the Central Excise Tariff should be worded exactly the same as in the Customs Tariff so as to avoid difficulties in interpretation. (Para 7.7)

42. Non-precise terms like "flats" used in Iron and Steel items should not figure in the Central Excise Tariff. (Para 7.14)

43. The other anomalies pointed out in the Customs and Central Excise Tariffs in this chapter should be examined, so that similarity may be brought about in the wordings of similar or common items in both the tariffs. (Para 7.16)

Drawback

44. Where either Drawback rate is uniform for the sub-grade, sub-Sr. No. and is not related to any material composition, normally samples are not required for test, for example, Aggarbatti, Corrugated Board Boxes, flat files, paper cones, etc. (Para 8.5)

45. Where either the Drawback rate itself is based on material composition or where though the rate is on Free on Board value, and there are different slabs of rates depending upon the material composition, normally a sample is to be drawn for test from each consignment and more declaration of the composition is not acceptable. (Para 8.5)

46. Tests are being carried out on samples of Textile, not drawn by Customs Officers, in the Textile Committee laboratory. The desirability of discontinuing this practice must be examined. (Para 8.7)

47. The procedure for calculation of quantum of drawback should be simplified and constantly revised. (Para 8.13.1)

48. When the difference in the quantum of drawback depending on the main components or use is not very significant from the revenue point of view, a flat rate could be adopted. (Para 8.13.2)

49. When the export consignment is small, as in the case of fancy goods, presentation articles, etc., test can be avoided if flat rates are fixed with reference to the percentage of contents. (Para 8.13.3)

50. The drawal of complicated samples should be handled by a chemist. (Cables etc.) (Para 8.13.4)

51. Avoidance of referring samples to Alipore Test House or out-

side laboratories has to be ensured by additional equipment and staff in the departmental laboratories. (Para 8.13.5)

52. As the bulk of drawback shipments takes place from Bombay, if it is decided that all tests particularly with reference to textile should be done in the departmental laboratory, adequate staff should be sanctioned as temporary measure and the position reviewed every year. (Para 8.13.6)

Departmental Laboratories in Refineries

53. The department should follow uniform policy in the matter of testing of imported crude oil for all the refineries. (Para 9.4)

54. As mineral oil products are of great revenue importance, it is desirable to have the departmental chemists associated with the drawal of samples. (Para 9.10)

55. The drawal of samples in the Refineries should be by surprise and the frequency of drawal of samples in the beginning should be once in a fortnight from final clearance tanks according to the standard procedure. (Para 9.11.1)

56. Surprise samples should be drawn from petroleum products at the distribution and also, and it is better that a departmental chemist is associated with sampling and gauging work, to the extent possible. (Para 9.14)

57. The Committee favours the continuance of the dip system of gauging instead of flow metre. (Para 9.15)

58. The transit loss during movement of petroleum products should be studied for a couple of years and correct quantum of tolerance prescribed. (Para 9.15)

59. The departmental laboratories attached to the Refineries should not depend on the Refineries for the apparatus but instead have their own equipment. (Para 9.17)

60. Clear scientific specifications should be mentioned for speciality products if any tests are to be purposeful. Names presumed to indicate end use may be misleading. (Para 9.18)

61. It would not be advisable to fix standard density as suggested by the Study Group set up by the Collector of Customs and Central Excise, Cochin for various petroleum distillates. (Para 9.19)

62. The instruments used for ascertaining density should be checked by competent authority and both the Refinery and the departmental laboratory should use similar instruments. (Para 9.20)

63. The Committee recommends that the temperature for mineral oil accounting be kept at the temperature as advised by Indian Standards Institution instead of the present 15°C. (Para 9.20)

64. Departmental chemists by closer association with Refinery Control Laboratory Chemists should be encouraged to develop expertise in the field of Petroleum Chemistry. (Para 9.26)

65. The Committee recommends additional departmental Refinery Laboratories for the following Refineries:

1. Haldia Refinery;
2. Indian Oil Corporation Refinery Noonmati and Bongaigaon;
3. Mathura Refinery (when goes into stream). (Para 19.27)

66. The staff complement recommended for these laboratories will be one scientific officer, one laboratory assistant, one stenographer and one sepoy. When the laboratory deals with more than one Refinery, a post of analyst be given instead of a laboratory assistant. (Para 9.27)

Central Revenues Control Laboratory

67. It would be improper to shift opium assay work from Central Revenues Control Laboratory to the factories of Ghazipur and Neemuch. Analysis is bound to lose its impartial and natural position in that event. (Para 10.28)

68. At Ghazipur and Neemuch the rooms where opium estimations are done should be air-conditioned for controlling the temperature at 20°C for obtaining better results. (Para 10.28)

69. The Gas liquid chromotograph method adopted by United Nations Narcotics Laboratory, Geneva can be tried out as a replacement to the conventional British Pharmacopoeia method which is more time consuming. (Para 10.29)

70. The Committee recommends that the opium section of the Central Revenues Control Laboratory should have more working chemists. (Para 10.33)

71. For disposal of the accumulated arrears of opium samples (about 400), *ad hoc* provisions should be made for more chemists at the junior level. (Para 10.34)

72. The Central Excise Wing of the Central Revenues Control Laboratory, New Delhi should be separated from the Control

Laboratory and shifted to another location under Collector of Central Excise, Delhi to serve as Regional Laboratory for the North India Collectorates. (Para 11.1)

73. The Director should pay more visits to the field of laboratories and keep liaison with Collectors. (Para 11.2)

74. The Control Laboratory should have a Director, two Joint Directors, i.e., Joint Director — Technical and Joint Director — Narcotics and general administration. Their duties are outlined. (Para 11.2)

75. The Headquarters Laboratory should undertake (a) Research and Development activities particularly relevant to analytical work, and (b) simplification and standardisation of analytical procedures and keeping and instrumentation and equipment modern. (Para 11.2)

76. In order to make the Headquarters Laboratory more purposeful and effective, following should be attended to more effectively:

(i) Inspection of subordinate laboratories and carrying out Research and Development work;
(ii) Modernising testing facilities; and
(iii) Preparation of a Test Manual. (Paras 11.2 and 11.5)

77. In view of the larger concentration of testing work at Bombay, the Committee recommends appointment of a Joint Director for the Bombay Custom House Laboratory who in addition will inspect all the laboratories in the Western Zone and Southern Zone. (Para 11.3)

78. The Inspection of the technical work of the scientific staff posted to the opium and alkaloid factories will be the special responsibility of the Director. (Para 11.4)

Reorganised Set up

80. The Committee after examining the statistics of the samples from various Collectorates, feels that it would be wasteful and premature to provide every Central Excise Collectorate with a laboratory. (Para 12.2)

81. The following existing laboratories should be recognised as regional laboratories:

(i) Central Excise and Customs Wing of the Control Laboratory, Delhi completely separated from the Control Laboratory;

(ii) Customs House Laboratory, Bombay.
(iii) Central Excise Laboratory, Bombay.
(iv) Customs and Central Excise Laboratory, Calcutta.
(v) Customs and Central Excise Laboratory, Madras. (Para 12.3)

82. The Committee recommends four new Laboratories to be set up soon (1) a Central Excise Laboratory at Kanpur to cater to the Collectorates of Kanpur and Allahabad, (2) a Laboratory for the Central Excise at Hyderabad, (3) at Paradeep Port to handle the Customs samples as well as the samples of Bhubaneshwar Collectorate, and (4) at Gauhati. (Para 12.4)

83. This Laboratory at Gauhati will test the samples of the Indian Oil Corporation Refineries at Noonmati and Bongaigaon, besides excise samples of the Shillong Collectorate. (Para 12.4.4)

84. The Committee recommends at a second stage laboratories at Bangalore, Ahmedabad, Indore, Amritsar, Poona and at the Bombay Air Port, say two or three years after setting up laboratories at Kanpur, Hyderabad and Paradeep. (Para 12.5)

85. The two major laboratories at Bombay, namely Customs and Excise Laboratories will continue to function separately. (Para 12.11)

86. The head of the major laboratory should be treated at par with Deputy Collector or Additional Collector in independent charge and be given a limited separate budget for specific purposes. In essence the Head of the laboratory may be declared as head of office with all the powers that go with it. (Para 12.16)

87. The Joint Directors at Delhi and Bombay will write the confidential character rolls of all the senior scientific officers working in their zones. (Para 12.17)

88. The Director of Central Revenue Laboratories should be given sufficient Funds to distribute to the regional laboratories for purchase of sophisticated equipment. (Para 12.18)

89. The Committee recommends a new yardstick for chemist in the Customs and Excise Laboratories as 552 samples per year per chemist. (Para 13.6)

90 Testing work in the laboratories should be organised on the Divisional basis and each Division should specialise in a major commodity. (Para 13.7)

91. A system of refresher courses and visits to major outside laboratories should be devised and steps should be designed to encourage specialisation. Government should remove the impediments in

the way of Scientific Officers publishing scientific papers. The Divisional Heads of the Laboratories should be encouraged to attend symposia and seminars to read scientific papers. (Para 13.7)

Apparatus and Equipment

92. The list of instruments given in Board's letter issued in January, 1976 may be purchased if not already done; except X-ray diffraction apparatus, the purchase of which can be deferred for the time being. (Para 14.2)

93. Similarly the need to purchase Nuclear Magnetic Resonance by Neemuch factory be re-examined in the light of the Committee's observations. (Para 14.2)

94. The regional laboratories should be fully equipped with all necessary costly instruments, and the smaller laboratories in their zone can avail of these facilities. (Para 14.4)

95. The Refinery Laboratories should be adequately equipped for testing mineral products figuring in the Tariff. (Para 14.4)

96. It is necessary to recruit two instruments engineers at Junior Class-I level at Bombay and Delhi. (Para 14.6)

97. All laboratories should have qualified librarians. (Para 14.7)

98. The purchase of sophisticated apparatus by the Revenue laboratories should be coordinated by the Joint Director. (Para 14.8)

99. The Joint Director at Delhi will take complete stock of all the special apparatus in all the laboratories and will redistribute surplus or not constantly used apparatus to newly started Revenue laboratories or Departmental Refinery Laboratories. (Para 14.8)

Laboratory Accommodation and Infrastructure

100. The Committee has recommended several improvements to the infrastructural and other facilities in laboratories (i) two easily accessible exists, (ii) immovable fittings should be so fixed to provide adequate moving space, (iii) no fittings on the floor, (iv) the re-agent shelf should be easily accessible. (Para 15.1)

101. Adequate ventilation and efficient exhausts to be provided in the laboratory. (Para 15.2)

102. Should have ordinarily separate rooms for different purposes. (Para 15.3)

103. The laboratory should be provided with efficient fume cup-

board and relevant Indian Standards Institution specifications should be the guidelines. (Para 15.4)

104. There should be arrangement for cutting of the service connection from one point of the laboratory. (Para 15.5)

105. Sinks and drainage should be chemically resistant material.

106. There should be a well-lighted and ventilated room for stores and library. (Paras 15.9 and 15.10)

107. The space for the staff working in the laboratories should be determined by recognised norm. (Para 15.11)

108. There should be a separate room for receipt and despatch of samples. (Para 15.11)

109. In the Bombay Central Excise Laboratory the flooring should be improved and sufficient exhaust fans should be placed so as to make the place dust free. As a long term measure the Government can think of constructing new accommodation to locate the Central Excise Laboratory, Bombay which is now in a rented building in a suburb. (Para 15.15)

110. In the Refineries, the Departmental laboratory should be located preferably close to the Refinery's own control laboratory. (Para 15.16)

111. The Control Laboratory at Delhi should have separate accommodation for library, conference hall, common room for scientists, club room and better toilet facilities. (Para 15.19)

112. The Director, Joint Directors, Deputy Directors should have office accommodation facilities comparable to the officers of similar rank in the Customs House or Central Excise Offices. (Para 15.20)

113. As far as possible Government should have their own laboratory building and also make sufficient provisions for the expansion of laboratory for a period of not less than ten years. (Para 15.21)

114. The Committee does not favour a college type laboratory but instead recommends separate sections and rooms for different types of work. (Para 15.21)

115. In bigger laboratories similar facilities should be provided as suggested for Central Revenues Control Laboratory. (Para 15.22)

116. (i) Provision should be made for a guest-house at the Headquarters laboratory. (Para 15.23)

(ii) Control laboratories and the Regional Laboratories should be given intercom facilities. (Para 15.24)

(iii) Residential phone to be provided to senior officers of the laboratory. (Para 15.24)

Opium and Alkaloid Factories

117. Mechanical or electrical contrivance of mixer-cum-dryer should be extended to all the trays for drying process so as to avoid manual handling and to expedite drying. The mixer-cum-steam dryer as in use in Neemuch can be adopted in Ghazipur also. (Paras 15.6.4 and 16.20)

118. Experienced pharmaceutical technologists should examine all the processes in the Ghazipur factory with a view to minimise manual handling and to devise contrivances which can be operated upon mechanically or electrically. The possibility of extending mobile stirring contrivance to all the trays be taken up seriously. (Para 16.13)

119. The Industrial Toxicology Research Centre, Lucknow may be requested to examine the toxicology problem in the Opium and Alkaloid factory, Ghazipur and to suggest ways and means of avoiding contamination or health hazards. (Para 16.13)

120. A project for mechanisation of Alkaloid Works in Ghazipur should be entrusted to a competent body in consultation with Indian Drugs Pharmaceutical Limited in the light of experience gained at Neemuch. (Para 16.14)

121. The Research and Development Laboratory in Ghazipur should be modernised as soon as possible, in view of the Ghazipur's historic association with opium. (Para 16.17)

122. The observations of the Shib Naub Singh's Committee on improving storage and mixing facilities and structural improvements should be given effect to. (Para 16.18)

123. The procedure for drawal of samples at Ghazipur and Neemuch should be similar. (Para 16.18)

124. The design of the trays used in the Abkari Section can be improved greatly by lining them with think Aluminium metal. (Para 16.20)

125. Norms for determining permissible loss in storage should be worked out by weighments and tests at strictly controlled conditions. (Para 16.27)

126. The Committee is not satisfied with the effectiveness of Accounts Control on the various stages of transfers of raw opium for import sheds to Malkhana, Drying Trays, (Abkari) and finally to Export (Excise) stage as a counter-check on chemical control. The relation between consistency and morphine content is not scientifically established for effective accounts control. The necessity for numerous

weighments, sampling and tests and the effectiveness of production control may be examined by a body like the Central Drug Research Institute, Lucknow. (Para 16.35)

127. The additional storage facilities for opium should be provided immediately to avoid backlog. (Para 16.37)

128. The process control exercised must be properly related to the type of machinery in the use and technical advice should be sought on this. (Para 16.39)

129. Officers from Central Revenue Chemical Service should normally be selected if new posts are created at Neemuch or Ghazipur. If specialists are needed, Posts at appropriate levels in the service should be created instead of creating ex-cadre posts and appointing outsiders on special scales of pay. Outsiders appointed in ex-cadre posts should not claim posts in the regular Central Revenues Scientific/Technical Service. (Para 16.45)

130. The Science and Technology Ministry and the Scientists working in the Drugs Research Centre, Lucknow, may be asked to investigate whether a separate research unit for opium and alkaloid should be set-up in Ghazipur or Neemuch, or the work be entrusted to an outside specialised institution. (Para 16.52)

131. The yardstick of samples per chemist in the opium and Alkaloid works be taken as 2000 tests per year. (Para 16.54)

132. The yardsticks per chemist working on the finished and intermediate drugs in the Alkaloid plant laboratories be taken as 1750 tests per year. (Para 16.55)

133. There should be parity in the number of posts and pay scales in Neemuch and Ghazipur factories. (Para 16.56.1)

134. The Committee recommends for the opium factory, Neemuch, a Chemical Examiner Grade-I in lieu of Chemical Examiner, Grade-II. (Para 16.56)

135. For Government Opium and Alkaloid Works, Ghazipur the following reorganised set up is recommended:

(i)	Deputy Director, Grade I (Rs. 1800-2000)	1 Post
(ii)	Deputy Director, Grade II (Rs. 1500-1800) incharge of Alkaloid Works.	2 Post
(iii)	Assistant Director (Production) in the Scale Rs. 1100-1600.	1 Post
(iv)	Assistant Director for Research and Development and Quality Control	1 Post

	(Rs. 1100-1600)	
(v)	Scientific Officer (Research and Development (Rs. 700-1300)	1 Post
(vi)	Scientific Officer (Rs. 700-1300)	7 Posts
(vii)	Analyst (Rs. 550-900)	27 Posts
		(Para 16.56.1)

Staff Morale and Redressal

136. The frustration among the chemical service and the loss of incentive that results can be rectified only by improving their status and emoluments and working conditions. (Para 17.5)

137. An established Central Service, Class-I is recommended in lieu of several grades of chemists to be designed as Central Revenues Scientific/Technical Service. (Para 17.5)

138. Better methods of recruitment, training and service structuring are recommended. (Para 17.5)

139. The transfer of Analysts be done only within the region. (Para 17.6)

140. The Technical Assistants should be restricted to the laboratories to which they are recruited and may be transferred on request. (Para 17.6)

141. All India seniority list be kept for Analysts as well as for Technical Assistants. (Para 17.8)

142. Ghazipur and Neemuch must have their self-contained Colony. In other places technical service officers must be treated on par with officers of the executive branch in the matter of allotment of quarters. (Para 17.9)

143. In fixing the number of scientific officers and supervisory officers and Committee has based it on the fresh yardstick arrived at. (Para 17.21)

144. There should be one grade of chemical Assistant below the Class-I services and that grade should carry a scale of Rs. 550-900. (Para 17.23)

145. The present vacancies in the posts of laboratory attenders should not be filled up. A new class of laboratory assistants to be designated as technical assistants may be recruited instead on a better scale of pay. (Para 17.28)

Staff Structure, Recruitment etc.

146. The recruitment to Class-I posts in Central Revenues Scientific/Technical Services should be partly by competitive examination and partly by promotion. (Para 17.27)

147. The recruitment for chemical assistants (analysts) and technical assistants should be on a regional basis, and these officers should not be transferred ordinarily outside the region. The constitution of a recruitment Committee and the procedure for recruitment are suggested. (Para 17.28)

148. The Chief Chemist should be designated as Director of Central Revenues Laboratories and Scientific Adviser to Department of Revenue (Customs, Excise and Narcotics). The designations of the other posts recommended are Joint Director, Deputy Director Grade-I, Deputy Director Grade-II, Scientific Officers and Analysts. (Para 17.29.1)

149. The heads of the following five laboratories should be designated as Deputy Director, Grade-I:

1. Central Excise Laboratory, Bombay..
2. Customs Laboratory, Bombay.
3. Customs and Central Excise Laboratory, Madras.
4. Customs and Central Excise Laboratory, Calcutta.
5. Central Excise Laboratory, Delhi.
6. Opium and Alkaloid Laboratories, Ghazipur. (Para 17.29.2)

The heads of the three laboratories be designated as Deputy Director Grade-II:

(i) Central Excise Laboratory, Baroda;
(ii) Central Excise Laboratory, Kanpur;
(iii) Customs and Central Excise Laboratory, Cochin. (Para 17.29.3)

150. In the major laboratories, divisions (commodity-wise) are suggested and each division will be under an Assistant Director. (Para 17.29.4)

151. The bulk of testing work will be done by Junior time scale "scientific officers" and "analysts", assisted by technical assistants. (Para 17.29.5)

152. The services may be designated as the Central Revenues Scientific/Technical Service and this should be included in the list of established services along with Customs and Excise Services. (Para 18.1)

153. The following scales of pay are suggested:

(a)	Director and Scientific Adviser	Rs.2500-125/2-2750
(b)	Joint Director	Rs.2000-125/2-2500
(c)	Deputy Director Grade-I	Rs.1800-100-2000
	Deputy Director Grade-II	Rs.1500-1800
(d)	Assistant Director	Rs.1100-1600
(e)	Scientific Officer	Rs.700-1300
(f)	Analyst (Non-Gazetted)	Rs.550-900
(g)	Technical Assistant (Non-Gazetted)	Rs.425-700

(Para 18.1)

153. Each laboratory should have a librarian and he should be graduate with diploma or with certificate in library science and also a store-keeper. (Para 18.1)

154. The recruitment to the Class-I cadre should be on all India basis by Union Public Service Commission. (Para 18.3)

155. Educational and other qualifications and type of papers for the competitive examination are suggested. (Para 18.4)

156. The departmental promotion quota to Class-I cadre should be restricted to 50 per cent; except on initial formation. (Para 18.7)

157. Promotion should be decided by Departmental Promotion Committee in which there should be an outside scientist and a representative of the Union Public Service Commission. (Para 18.4)

158. For top posts of Director and Joint Directors, it should be advisable to follow generally the procedure adopted in all the National Laboratories, i.e., normally by promotion, and by open selection, if a suitable officer from inside the service is not available. (However this should be avoided as far as possible). (Para 18.9)

159. All existing Chemical Assistants who may be absorbed in Class-I service should be sent to the training school for an initial foundation course in Customs and Excise laws and procedures. For future direct recruits a regular training programme during the probationary period and a departmental examination are suggested. (Para 18.11.1)

160. Once in five years, both the officers in junior time scale and senior time scale should be sent for refresher courses in one of the Na-

tional Laboratories or specialised scientific institutions. (Para 18.11.4)

161. The Director should arrange for seminars periodically to encourage study and research. (Para 18.11.5)

162. Officers of the service with aptitude for research work may be encouraged to write 'papers'. (Para 18.11.5)

163. Laboratory attenders may be considered as semi-skilled workers. There is a case for giving them the scale of Rs. 260-350. (Para 18.12)

164. A pay scale of Rs. 260-430 without Efficiency Bar is suggested for laboratory Clerks. (Paras 18.14 and 18.6)

165. Officers of the Central Revenues Scientific/Technical Service may be sent on deputation to the various other Directorates, viz., Directorate of Training, Directorate of Drawback, Directorate of Tax Research, etc. (Para 18.21)

166. Officers of the Central Revenues Scientific/Technical Services can be sent on deputation to outside departments, viz. Ministry of Commerce and Industry (Director-General of Technical Development), State Trading Corporation, Indian Oil Company, Indian Petrochemicals Corporation Ltd., etc. (Para 18.22)

Expediting Test Reports

167. Various steps have been suggested for expediting test reports and re-test reports. (Paras 19.1 to 19.18)

9

THE COMMITTEE FOR TRAINING IN EVALUATION, 1979 — REPORT[1]

June 23, 1978 – October 10, 1979

Chairman S.S. Puri
(replaced Ajit Mazoomdar w.e.f. Ausust 1, 1979)

Members T.N. Chaturvedi; C.H. Hanumantha Rao; H.M. Mathur; S.P. Bagla; S.M. Shah; V. Venkatesan; Shri Prabhakar Ghate; U.K. Kohli; Shri G. Chidambaram; J.N. Mongia; Shri K.K. Singh; Prof. Nilkanth Rath; R.L. Pitale; D.C. Datta; Dr. S.K. Rau; Dr. V.R. Gaikwad; Dr. B.N. Sahay;

Convenor Dr. B.N. Sahay

Appoinments

In pursuance of the decision arrived at the Conference of the Heads of State Evaluation Organisations held in 14th and 15th November, 1977 it has been decided to Constitute a Committee on Training for Evaluation by the Government of India Programme Evaluation Organisation, Planning Commission vide its Office Memorandum No. PEO/10-6/77-TE, dated June 23, 1978.

Terms of Reference

1. To assess the training needs of the personnel for manning the State and National Evaluation Organisations;
2. To review the existing training arrangements in evaluation methodology;
3. To suggest various types of courses to be organised, their contents including the range of disciplines, frequency, and duration;

---

1. Programme Evaluation Organisation, Planning Commission, Government of India, New Delhi, 1979, 74 p.

4. To suggest methods and techniques of training in relation to the courses;
5. To identify suitable agencies for conducting various courses suggested under (3) above;
6. To suggest the terms of deputation for the trainees;
7. To suggest guidelines for the preparation of a Manual for Training; and
8. To recommend measures for strengthening the agencies suggested under (5) above so as to enable them to undertake effectively the training tasks.

Contents

Introduction; Training in Evaluation – A Historical Perspective; Existing Training Arrangements; Training Needs and Arrangements Proposed; Summary of Conclusions and Recommendations; Appendixes I to V.

Recommendations

1. The evaluation personnel have been broadly categorised, for the purpose of organising the training programme, into three levels – the Senior level (Director/Additional Director/Joint Director/ Deputy Adviser/Project Director), the Supervisory level (Deputy Director/Senior Research Officer/Assistant Director/ Research Officer/Evaluation Officer), and the Junior level (Investigator/ Technical/Research/Field/Statistical Assistant/Junior Statistical Supervisor/Analyst/Computer) (Paras 1.1 and 4.2).

2. The number of evaluation personnel engaged both in the Central Programme Evaluation Organisation and the State Evaluation Organisations comes to 868. This consists of Senior level (23), Supervisory level (211), and Junior level (634) (Para 4.4).

3. Training facilities for evaluation personnel are lacking in almost all the States/Union Territories. Whatever little training is there, it is by deputing their staff for training to Central Programme Evaluation Organisation and other research institutes. There is a need to organise systematic training for the evaluation personnel and to tailor the training programmes to suit the requirement of evaluation work (Paras 3.2 to 3.6).

4. There is scope for improving the quality, timeliness, and

follow-up action of the reports completed by the various State Evaluation Organisations. Training would go a long way in improving the quality of these evaluation reports (Paras 4.1 and 4.6).

5. The training of the Senior and the Supervisory level personnel should be the direct responsibility of the Central Programme Evaluation Organisation. For training the Junior level evaluation personnel also, the Central Programme Evaluation Organisation should take up the responsibility of coordinating the training activities with the State Evaluation Organisations. On the other hand, the State Evaluation Organisations may take the necessary guidance and support from the Central Programme Evaluation Organisation in organising and planning the courses (Paras 1.5 and 4.8).

6. The Regional Workshops on Evaluations should be a continuous feature to train Senior level personnel. The syllabus for this category of personnel should include conceptual/theoretical lectures besides discussion on the design, methodology, and findings of the selected evaluation reports of the Central Programme Evaluation Organisation and the participating State Evaluation Organisations. Emphasis should also be laid on the development of an evaluation design by each participant, on the topic likely to be taken up by him/his organisation for evaluation, in the second round of Workshop. Five such Regional Workshops per year should be organised, each for a duration of eight days. The participants of the Workshop should be treated as on tour and the non-official guest lecturers, if invited, should be paid an honorarium of Rs. 100 per lecture, besides TA/DA (Paras 4.10 to 4.12).

7. The syllabus for the Supervisory level evaluation personnel adopted by the Committee envisages the course contents of four weeks' duration. The course contents mainly include theoretical and conceptual lectures, designing of an evaluation study, data collection, and report writing. Three such courses should be organised per year with the help of the Training Division of the Department of Personnel and Administrative Reforms. The TA/DA of the participants should be paid as per the rules of their respective Governments. The honorarium for the guest Speaker/faculty should be paid as per the rules of the Department of Personnel and Administrative Reforms (Paras 4.13 to 4.18).

8. For the training of Junior level evaluation personnel, the Central Programme Evaluation Organisation should be responsible for coordinating the training activities with the State Evaluation Organisa-

tions. The State Evaluation Organisations, however, may take the necessary guidance and support from the Central Programme Evaluation Organisation. The course contents of four weeks duration has both theoretical and practical inputs. Five courses be organised per year to cover the entire number of Junior level personnel in the next five years. The TA/DA of the participants should be paid as per the rules of their respective Governments. The honorarium for the guest speakers/faculty should be paid as per the rules of the Department of Personnel and Administrative Reforms (Paras 4.19 to 4.23).

9. The idea of preparing a Manual for Training may be taken up at the appropriate time when the Central Programme Evaluation Organisation/State Evaluation Organisations have gained sufficient experience of conducting various training courses (Para 4.24).

10. In the light of the expectations from the Central Programme Evaluation Organisation regarding the Organisation of training programmes for various levels of evaluation personnel, documentation and editing of evaluation reports, assessment/reassessment of training needs, coordination with State Evaluation Organisations, etc., a pragmatic staff requirement has been recommended. This should include a Director, five Senior Training Specialists, five Training Specialists, ten Technical Assistants, and four other supporting staff. (Paras 4.25 to 4.29).

10

COMMITTEE ON LAND REFORMS, 1978 — REPORT[1]

Chairman	Prof. Raj Krishna
Members	Dr. A.M. Khusro; Dr. V.M. Dandekar; Shri Radha Krishna; Prof. G. Parthasarthy; Shri K. Balasubramaniam; Dr P.C. Joshi; Shri P.S. Appu; Dr. P.H. Prasad
M. Secy.	Shri R.K. Rath.

Appointment

The Committee on Land Reform appointed by the Government of India, Ministry of Agriculture and Irrigation, Department of Agriculture, in June 1978.

Terms of Reference

(i) The extension of the protection of the ninth Schedule of the Constitution to recent and future land reform enactments;

(ii) deletion of the Explanation under the Ninth Schedule of the Constitution; and

(iii) some measures to speed up the disposal of land reform cases by the revenue machinery.

Contents

Appointment; Terms of References; Recommendations.

Recommendations

(a) All land reform Acts passed by the States, assented to by the President, but not yet included in the Ninth Schedule, and all land

1. New Delhi, Ministry of Agriculture and Irrigation, Department of Agriculture, 1978, 10 p.

reform laws enacted in future and assented to by the President, should be automatically presented by the Central Government to Parliament for inclusion in the Ninth Schedule of the Constitution.

(b) The Central Government should immediately move the Parliament to delete the Explanation under the Ninth Schedule with retrospective effect.

(c) The State Governments should be moved to expand High Court Benches and request Chief Justices to name one or two or more judges to deal exclusively with and dispose of all pending land reform cases within a stipulated period.

(d) The number of Judges in High Courts where the pendency of land reform cases is heavy should be suitably increased.

(e) Land reform laws of the States should be immediately amended to provide that all land reform cases shall be dealt with by revenue functionaries alone below the High Court Level.

(f) The revenue machinery dealing with land reform Cases should be suitably expanded to clear all pending land reform cases by organizing camp courts.

(g) The revenue authorities of all States should establish a time bound programme for the disposal of land reform cases.

(h) Only one appeal and one revision should be allowed against the decision of the revenue authorities in land reform cases.

11

REVIEW COMMITTEE ON POST-GRADUATE EDUCATION AND RESEARCH IN ENGINEERING AND TECHNOLOGY, 1978 — REPORT[1]

Chairman Dr. Y. Nayudamma

Members Prof. C.S. Jha; Prof. B. Ramachandra Rao; Prof. M.M. Sharma; Shri Kan D. Mariwalla; S. Varadarajan; Shri F.C. Kohli; Shri J.H. Doshi; Prof. Jagadish Narain; Prof. A.K. De; Prof. Shankar Lal; V.S. Arunachalam; Prof. T.R. Anantharaman; Prof. G.S. Ladha; Shri J.A. Kalyanakrishnan; Shri B. Sinha, Prof. K. Koteshwara Rao; Prof. G.N. Garud; Shri A. S. Sekhon

M. Secy. Shri K. Gopalan.

Appointment

In any country scientists, engineers, and technologists are an important national asset. They provide instruction and training in the various fields of Science and Technology (S&T), conduct basic research to advance the understanding of nature and perform effective research and development (R&D) in a diversity of areas encompassing every human endeavour. In addition, persons trained in science, engineering and technology are employed throughout the economy – from industrial management to agricultural production – to provide the knowledge and skills which are essential in a technologically advancing society. The role of scientists, engineers and technologists in helping to meet the changing needs of the country, coupled with the extended time and high cost involved in their training, requires that continuous attention be given to trends and patterns in the production of such personnel.

---

1. New Delhi, Ministry of Education and Culture, Government of India, 1980, xiii, 164 p.

Reviews of post-graduate education and research in engineering and technology have been undertaken in the past and these are mentioned in this report. The present Review Committee was appointed on the basis of a suggestion made by the Expenditure Finance Committee (of the Government of India) and on the recommendation of the Board of Post-graduate Engineering Studies and Research (hereafter called Post Graduate Board) of the All India Council for Technical Education (AICTE). The Committee was constituted in consultation with the Department of Science and Technology (DST) and the University Grants Commission (UGC) in June 1978.

Terms of Reference

(1) To evaluate the progress made so far in the development of post-graduate courses and research in engineering and technology.

(2) To review the post-graduate programmes in university departments, Institutes of Technology (IITs) and other affiliated colleges and to recommend discontinuation of post-graduate courses which are not relevant to the national needs and to recommend areas of emerging interests for which post-graduate courses may be organised.

(3) To recommend the norms and pattern of assistance for post graduate courses in respect of University Departments, IITs and affiliated colleges.

(4) To examine advisability of concentrating post-graduate courses in selected institutions for better courses.

(5) To consider the manner of achieving close coordination of post-graduate training and research with the major developmental and engineering schemes of the country.

(6) To report on all other aspects of improvement and development of post-graduate courses.

Contents

Glossary of Abbreviations; Chairman's preface; Summary and Recommendations; Preamble; Earlier Reviews; Present Status of Post-Graduate Education and Research in Engineering and Technology; Major Issues, Problems and Suggestions; Findings and Recommendations; Annexures from I to XIII.

Recommendations

Previous Reviews, Need for Re-organisation

The role of scientists, engineers and technologists in helping to meet the changing needs of the country coupled with the extended time and high cost involved in their training requires that continuous attention be given to present and future trends and patterns in the production of each personnel.

This report is the latest in a series of official reports on post-graduate education and research in engineering and technology. All previous reports made many practical recommendations which are valid even today after many years since their issues. Unfortunately there have been short-comings in implementing them, which have resulted in the unsatisfactory state of affairs of post-graduate education and research today. Present status:

As at present, India produces about 350 doctorates, 2700 MEs/M Techs and 16500 graduate engineers (in the ratio of about 1:8:47) annually, whereas annual intake provisions are about 500,6000 and 26000 (1:12:52) respectively. About 70 per cent of the Ph.Ds. and 44 per cent of the MEs/M. Techs. are producted by the 5 IITs and IISc Bangalore.

Today the S&T content in the Indian society and the extent of India's involvement in R&D are very low. The number of scientific and technical personnel in India per thousand of population is only 3.8, whereas it is 12 in the United States, 19 in the FRG, 82 in the USSR and 185 in Japan. Scientists and engineers engaged in R&D in India per thousand population in only 0.09, this figure being 2.68, 2.97, 3.72 and 4.98 in the United States, FRG, USSR and Poland respectively. The Indian expenditure on R&D which was 0.23 per cent of GNP in 1958-59 has risen to 0.6 per cent of GNP in 1976-77. The expenditure on R&D as a percentage of GNP was 2.1 in UK (1972), 2.3 in FRG (1974), 2.3 in the United States (1975), 2.5 in Japan (1975) and 2.7 in Poland (1975).

The performance of a few institutions in the area of post-graduate education and research has been quite good mainly because of deliberate efforts and liberal investments in promoting them.

In spite of the considerably lower inputs, about 20 other institutions have also done creditably well. The performance of the remaining 50 or so institutions is poor, even though some of them have succeeded in developing some areas/disciplines well. The physical facilities such as faculty, accommodation/space, equipment and in library in many of these institutions are to be considerably improved.

The capacity for generating sustaining technological growth within the country has to be strengthened considerably and vigorous steps taken for the continual improvement of their capacity. Since the total stock of India's S&T manpower is quite small relevant to her population and corresponding national needs, this stock will have to grow at a faster rate – particularly in quality – during the coming decades. Therefore, the Indian national investment in scientific and technical educational and research should increase many fold to meet the growing needs of the changing social system.

Admission Policy, Scholarships

For a variety of reasons which include redundant and outdated courses, inadequate facilities, lack of motivation long duration of courses, lack of recognition and incentives, ineffective administration of the programmes, etc., it has not been possible to attract sufficiently large number of bright young people for post-graduate education. This is a serious matter which will have far reaching consequence on the future technological competence of this country.

Strong and firm measures as suggested in this report should be taken to ensure that only bright and motivated people are admitted to post-graduate programmes. Admission to post-graduate programmes should be restricted to only those who come through the GATE. The Government should consider imposing requirements on industry and Government departments to sponsor their engineers for post-graduate education and research in the respective areas of their interest. If necessary, upto 50 per cent seats should be reserved for sponsored candidates.

Post-graduate scholarships for ME/M. Tech should be enhanced from the present value of Rs. 400 per month to Rs. 600 per month and should be given to all those who are admitted through the GATE. However, sponsored candidates, who get paid, would be eligible to get only 75 per cent of the value of scholarship. Fellowships for doctoral aspirants should be raised from the present value of Rs. 500 p.m. to: 1st year Rs. 700 p.m., 2nd year Rs. 800 p.m. and 3rd year Rs. 900 p.m. The fellowship value should be enhanced by Rs. 50 after submission of the thesis and should be continued for 3 more months or till the viva is over, whichever is values of all scholarships/fellowships should be reviewed once in every three years.

Restructuring, Re-organisation, New Courses

The post-graduate diploma courses have not been found to be popular and successful in most institutions. It is felt that they need not be offered as regular programmes unless some of them are specifically asked for and paid for by the interested agencies.

All existing post-graduate degree programmes which are outdated stereotyped and unpopular should be wound up. Wherever possible, attempts should be made to redesign the existing courses to include relevant and emerging areas. Narrow and futile definitions of disciplines are dangerous. Care should be taken to see that inter-disciplinary areas encourage active cooperation among related departments and programmes of teaching and research are run jointly.

There are variations in the structure and requirements of existing post-graduate programmes, which have resulted in large differences in standards and quality of post-graduates produced. These have to be streamlined as suggested in this report.

All ME/M.Tech programmes should be of three semesters duration consisting of two semesters course work including core and elective subjects and one semester of dissertation work. The dissertation should offer an opportunity for the candidates to engage in a creative and self-learning experience. It should be either design oriented. The topic of the dissertation should be as far as possible trans-disciplinary in nature. The concept of joint guides for supervising project/dissertation work can have a very positive impact on the post-graduate education system and hence should be encouraged.

The ME/M.Tech programmes should be offered in suitable modules with credit system. This re-structuring of ME/M.Tech programmes should be undertaken as matter of urgency in close collaboration with people from industry, R&D organisation and others concerned. It is also necessary to set up post-graduate Curriculum Development Centres to revise, redesign and update the curricula of post-graduate programmes on a continuing basis as suggested in this report.

While restructuring the ME/M.Tech programmes, it should be clearly remembered that they are to prepare persons of high quality and calibre for all engineering functions including design, development, technology assessment and transfer, management, research, etc. An individual department/institution may wish to emphasise one or more of these functions depending upon the kinds of faculty students and facilities it has.

Doctoral work should be regarded as preparation for the highest levels of creative leadership in all areas of engineering practice including teaching and research. The minimum duration for doctorate after ME/M.Tech should be two years. In exceptional cases, when B.Techs are allowed to register for doctorate, the minimum duration for doctorate should be three years; in either case, fellowship would not be paid for more than four years. All aspirants for doctorate should invariably go through some advanced courses relevant to the thesis. "Candidate-based" Doctoral Committee should assess the candidate's competence and identify his deficiencies. The course work for doctoral programmes should be revised and updated every year.

A critical aspect of the doctoral requirements has to be the thesis, which should provide an important creative experience to the candidates. The successful completion of this creative experience should make the doctoral programme a valuable career preparation. Innovation, originality and practical/social relevance should be the hall-marks of doctoral work.

The policies for recognising supervisors for guiding doctoral candidates should be made uniform. There are wide disparities at present.

Post-graduate courses in 'applied sciences' now being offered in most places are not of good standard. They should be critically reviewed.

In view of the changes taking place in the pattern of education system, efforts may be made to re-structure the science courses so that the science degrees are comparable to the corresponding degrees in engineering/technology. In many of the emerging areas, which are science-based but heavily technology oriented, there is need to train scientist-technologists who can handle the twin responsibilities of scientific research and innovative application. The traditional framework of engineering programmes is inappropriate for this purpose and a separate stream of post-graduate courses of 3 semesters duration after M.Sc. in science has to be developed on the pattern of the ME/M.Tech programmes suggested in this report. These countries should be introduced only in selected engineering/technological institutions/university departments having adequate infrastructural facilities.

In view of the limited resources available and also the need to maintain high standards, sanctioning of post-graduate courses has to be done with utmost care on the basis of the criteria mentioned in this report. Under no circumstances should further proliferation of existing programmes in conventional or irrelevant areas be permitted. Empire building within institutions and between institutions should be discouraged. Neighbouring institutions including national laboratories and others should be encouraged not only to conduct post-graduate programmes jointly, but also to share facilities such as faculty, library, equipment, etc., jointly.

Part-time Courses Containing Education Programmes

There is increasing demand for part-time (evening) post-graduate programmes especially in industrialised areas in the country. It is recommended that introduction of part-time post-graduate programmes on the basis of the guide-lines mentioned in this report should be encouraged. There is a real opportunity for innovation to facilitate high quality off-campus instruction in India. It is suggested that new techniques and arrangements be devised for extending high quality post-graduate education to engineers/technologists employed at locations remote from established campuses.

Institutions like the IITs should play a leading role in organising part-time and off-campus post-graduate programmes. Needless to say that matters of academic standards in part-time programmes especially at off-campus locations warrant special attention.

Engineering profession and academic institutions should look forward to a growing activity in continuing education programmes as a distinct educational function outside regular post-graduate programmes. The Government and industry should work together within a major national programme of training and re-training of engineers and technologists to develop the skills and support needed to implement and sustain new technologies. It is recommended that a Dean (Industrial Liaison) be appointed in each post-graduate institution to take care of these programmes.

While assessing staff requirements of institutions, full account should be taken of the importance of allowing adequate senior staff time for building up their activities in continuing education programmes.

Employment Potential, Manpower Planning, Manpower Utilisation

It is necessary to recognise publicly and to publicise more widely that in today's world post-graduate studies of master's degree level are a normal part of basis engineering education. The unreasonably restrictive conception that a bachelor's degree is sufficient preparation for most engineering work should not be perpetuated. It is a sad situation that today of the total S&T manpower employed in the public sector R&D organisations in the country, only 2 per cent are Ph.Ds. and 12 per cent MEs/M.Techs. in engineering. In the private sector these figures are one per cent and nine per cent respectively.

A sustained national programme should be launched to stipulate more widespread understanding among employers of the nature and importance of the engineering dimension and of the potential benefits to them from employing post-graduate engineers in a wide range of activities. Employing organisations should review their salary and career structures for engineers to ensure that they adequately reflect a value for post-graduate engineers' contributions.

It should be made mandatory to prescribe post-graduate degree as the minimum qualification for recruitment to many positions in the engineering profession in industry, R&D organisations, Electricity Boards, PWDs, P&T Railways, etc.

It is high time to do away with the present policy and practice of regulating graduate engineers at the lowest levels (single point entry) to many services. As an incentive and mark of recognition, it should be mandatory to give not less than two extra increments whenever post-graduate degree holders are recruited. A suitable number of advance increments should also be given to doctorate degree holders.

The proposed National Authority – suitably strengthened and reorganised with statutory powers as indicated in 5.48 should play a vital role in linking post-graduate training and research with major developmental and engineering schemes by liaison effectively with national agencies such as the NCST, Planning Commission, Department of Economic Affairs, UPSC, etc.

The Government should take every possible measure to link up all developmental projects and industrial expansion with the requirement of induction of competent post-graduate engineers and technologists into the respective projects. Both public and private sector undertakings should be asked to institute regular engineering manpower audits' building upon the best employment practices in this country and overseas to ensure that they are making the best use of post-graduate engineers as their key assets within the engineering dimension. Proper utilisation and deployment of scientific and technical manpower is most important.

It is recommended that a reliable national information system for the storage, updating, retrieval and analysis of manpower information should be established to assist technical educational planning. It is also suggested that future official census surveys should be suitably structured to collect the information necessary for the maintenance of a continuing national inventory on engineering manpower.

It would be worthwhile to study the employment pattern of post-graduate in industry, government, education, etc., and also to make inter-comparisons regarding their characteristics, attitudes and performance information on the relevant numbers of engineers, technologists engaged in various functions such as design, operations, production, research development, management, teaching, etc., would be a useful guide to engineering educators and planners. They industry, educators, government and others concerned should join hands and together undertake this survey as a matter of urgency.

Faculty Improvements

Next to the student body, the faculty is the most important factor in assuring success of any engineering education programme. The Committee received numerous complaints relating to indifference and incompetence, incorrect attitudes and inadequate aptitudes, etc., on the part of teaching faculty. It was also pointed out that a tendency to inbreeding even in our national institutions has brought down the calibre of teachers and the levels of post-graduate education. Mobility and exchange of faculty between academic institutions, R&D organisations and industrial establishments should be encouraged to prevent inbreeding. Industrial experience should be prescribed as an essential qualification for teaching positions at post-graduate level. Technical competence, scientific understanding creative ability and humanistic wisdom should be the requirements for teachers particularly at post-graduate level.

Possession of a doctorate degree or equivalent qualification representing an advanced level of intellectual attainment and creative endeavour should be made a pre-requisite for post-graduate teaching. Educational institutions, engineering profession, industry and Government should jointly develop a variety of programmes designed to enhance the development of engineering faculty members as practising engineers through the effective use of study leave, summer training, consulting and research opportunities.

The recruitment to teaching positions at all levels should be made only on an all-India basis after close scrutiny of the competence and qualifications of the candidates vis-a-vis the prescribed job requirements. TA/DA should be given to all those who are called for interview. A rigorous staff appraisal scheme to assess the teacher annually in the area of teaching, laboratory work, research and publications should be introduced in every post-graduate institution. Staff appraisal records (these are different from confidential reports) should be looked into at every stage of promotion. Suitable merit promotion schemes should be introduced in engineering colleges/institutions.

Equipment Maintenance, Training in Instrumentation

In almost all post-graduate institutions, including institutions of national importance, many items of costly and sophisticated equipment are neither maintained nor utilised properly. A specialist cadre of maintenance technicians engineers with proper status and attractive scales of pay should be built up at least on a regional basis. Meanwhile a small team of competent instrument mechanics experts should be asked to examine the sophisticated equipment now lying idle in the various post-graduate institutions with a view to set them right.

It is necessary to create in some of the institutions an infrastructure for training in the instrumentation area with particular reference to repairs and maintenance of sophisticated equipment. Institutions like the IITs should ensure that they are capable of maintaining and repairing their own equipment and those of others in that region. Instrumentation is becoming more and more complicated and sophisticated incorporating latest technologies. Huge and costly facilities are indispensable to carry out research in many new emerging areas. In view of the limited resources and to facilitate proper maintenance, it is advisable to create some more centralised facilities at a few more centres of Excellence identified for advance research in these emerging areas.

Institution-Industry Collaboration

The Government should consider imposing requirements on industry as well as on post-graduate institutions to collaborate with each other on the basis of the various suggestions made in this report. Legislative action should be taken, if necessary.

Every effort should be made to further increase and expand the two-way exchange of staff between industry and teaching establishments including the introduction of systems of recognition and incentives.

Industrial establishments should examine how to strengthen their access directly and indirectly to teaching/research institutions with a view to make better use of the consultancy and research services offered by the teaching/research institutions. Higher technological institutions and industrial establishments should prepare corporate plans for working together for social development and mutual benefit. The tendency on the part of the industry to look at the West for technical know-how should be discouraged. It is recommended that a tax be levied on any know-how imported.

A research cess should be levied on each industry for research in the areas of industry's interest. This fund should be kept and operated separately with the active participation and involvement of industry. Regular long-term post-graduate programmes suggested by industry jointly or otherwise should be financed by industry at least on a 50 per cent basis. Short-term courses suggested by industry should be financed by them on a 100 per cent basis. A 133 per cent tax deduction should be allowed on all payments/contributions/investments made by industry in post-graduate education and research. Polite persuasion and concealed compulsion are called for to legitimise industry's involvement in post-graduate education and research.

Research, Socio-economy Relevance

Post-graduate programmes can survive only on a strong R&D base. Unfortunately a good amount of research work going on in the country is without review and accountability. Most of the work is done under western perspectives and on borrowed ideas and relate to fashion-oriented problems which are totally out of Indian context. There is urgent need to take deliberate action to prevent enormous wastage of resources on repetitive and irrelevant research projects. Academic research should emphasise work done in the context of socio-economic development.

Some institutions have done well in undertaking sponsored research projects and consultancy projects. This culture should be developed without detriment of course to the academic and training duties/commitments of the institution.

The institutions should be allowed to charge sponsored research projects and consultancy projects. This culture should be developed without detriment of course to the academic and training duties/commitments of the institution:

The institutions should be allowed to charge sponsored research projects. Consultancy should be encouraged and should, as far as possible be only institutional, but individual consultancy especially when institutional facilities are not used should also be allowed. In either case, consultancy should be regulated on the basis of predetermined norms. The money earned from sponsored and consultancy projects should be utilised for developing the research capability of the institutions. Industrial consultancy should not be confused with routine testing and analysis, which should be discouraged.

Multi-disciplinary, Trans-disciplinary

Transorganisational research with emphasis on design and development should be encouraged at all levels. The post-graduate projects should, as far as possible be sponsored and/or techno-economic oriented. Problems of industry should be documented and distributed to post-graduate institutions on a continuing basis. It is recommended that a national level R&D Newsletter (like the *Employment News*) should be published regularly giving information on research projects at master's doctoral and post-graduate institutions, R&D organisations and industry. It is recommended that all-India conferences on post-graduate projects may be organised once in two years and these projects documented area/discipline-wise.

These institutions which have the competence to undertake on a large scale research projects sponsored by outside agencies should be permitted to recruit and maintain a core of competent scientific staff in the area of their expertise on permanent basis with all service benefits. The expenditure in this regard should of course be a change on the cost of the various projects and should be collected from the sponsoring agencies including Government departments.

Funding Pattern, Elimination of Imbalances

One of the main reasons for the degeneration of post-graduate programmes in engineering and technology in India has been the poor norms of funding these programmes.

Consequently post-graduate activities have remained under-nourished and ineffective in most of the institutions. The courses have remained simple academic exercises unable to generate adequate R&D activities, which are absolutely necessary to train competent engineers in areas of design, development and innovations.

Immediate action should be taken to revise the norms of funding the post-graduate programmes on the basis of the guidelines suggested in this report.

Recommendations of grants for any new post-graduate programme should be based on the overall post-graduate activities of the departments concerned and not on a narrow truncated basis of specific post-graduate course/courses proposed by an institution.

While it is necessary to undertake in a phased manner the need-based consolidation of all institutions (running approved post-graduate programmes) including modernisation of laboratories and replacement obsolete equipment, it is strongly recommended that such need-based consolidation be undertaken on a priority basis in selected institutions/departments, which, despite poor funding, have proved their merit by their past performance. These institutions/ departments should be subject to close scrutiny by competent Visiting Committees with a view not only to consolidate, but also to identify expertise they have by now achieved in emerging areas of national relevance and to promote them as Centres of Excellence/Advanced Studies. They should serve as nuclei for technological development in their respective regions. A provision of about Rs. 20 crores may have to be made for the purpose during the Sixth Five-Year Plan (1980-85).

The disparities in the pattern of funding post-graduate programmes have created lost of problems particularly in the university departments under the control of the UGC. The portion of post-graduate grants released to the university departments of State Universities through the UGC (with the complicated condition that the concerned State Governments should take over the responsibility of funding after 5 years) is a small fraction of the total expenditure incurred by the Central Government on post-graduate education and research in engineering and technology. It is recommended that funding post-graduate education and research in engineering and technology in all engineering institutions including university departments should be a 100 per cent Central Government responsibility and the existing dichotomies/disparities in funding should be eliminated.

In the case of institutions of national importance, which are to be maintained and further developed as peace-setters, funding should be based on integrated infrastructural development as at present. However, even in these cases, assistance to the various departments should be performance-based.

Since non-Plan provisions have been approved with effect from 1979-80 for meeting for recurring liability in respect of the on-going post-graduate programmes, the Central Government should advise State Governments to extend retirement and other service benefits to post-graduate staff in institutions which are governed by the State Government grant-in-aid rules.

Information Services, Data Banks

One of the biggest stumbling blocks in the path of scientific and technological research and development in India has been – and is – the lack of proper data banks, information services. There is immediate need to educate and train information users by introducing user education/training programmes in the post-graduate institutions and research centres. A suitable national agency should undertake this responsibility in collaboration with INSDOC, NISSAT, etc.

India has started importing bibliographic data bases alongwith the appropriate software to develop a computerised information retrieval system in the country. It is not only necessary for India to absorb this imported 'information technology', but also to develop her own to suit local needs.

One very important approach to information is computerised information retrieval. It is recommended that there should be a couple of National Data Centres in India which should get all the major data bases of science and technology in the form of computer readable magnetic tapes and act as data banks.

Administration and Control, Evaluation and Accreditation

The main factor which has been primarily responsible for almost all the ills of post-graduate education and research in engineering and technology in India today has been the failures of the administration – the AICTE/Post-graduate Board – to implement the recommendations not only of the Committees appointed by it, but also of its own. This

Committee's most important single recommendation linked to very many other proposals in various sections of this report is that the Government should make the AICTE/Post-graduate Board a new statutory organisation – a National Authority – with powers granted to it by Parliament to advance and promote the technological development of this country by maintaining high standards of engineering and technological education and research. This is only a reiteration of the recommendation made two years ago by the Estimates Committee of Parliament.

It is essential to optimise the utilisation of available resources and provide impetus to all the centres engaged in post-graduate programmes and research. The planning, organisation and prescription of standards for post-graduate education and research programmes conducted at universities, IITs, Indian Institutes of Management and affiliated colleges should be effectively coordinated by the proposed National Authority, which should have a separate full-time secretariat with suitable administrative, executive and financial powers.

Evaluation and accreditation of post-graduate courses should done at least once in five years. For this purpose, a National Evaluation and Accreditation Agency should be established.

Methods should be developed for the performance audit of institutions engaged in post-graduate education and research to facilitate comprehensive reviews of the various programmes. The general practice of financial expenditure audit should be done away with.

TCDC, Policy for Training Overseas Students

India has a leading role to play in the new concept of TCDC. In her own interest India should formulate a coherent 'country training policy' for training overseas students in emerging areas of engineering and technology.

12

REVIEW COMMITTEE ON FOREIGN TECHNICAL ASSISTANCE RECEIVED BY THE INDIAN INSTITUTES OF TECHNOLOGY AND OTHER ACADEMIC INSTITUTIONS, 1978 — REPORT[1]

Chairman Prof. Y. Nayudamma (replaced Dr. Ramachandran in October 1978)

Members Prof. C.S. Jha, Shri J.A. Kalyanakrishnan, Shri K.R. Sivaramakrishnan

M. Secy. Dr. K. Gopalan

Appointment

Early in 1978, while considering certain proposals for foreign technical assistance submitted by some IITs, the Planning Commission suggested that the Ministry of Education should undertake a review of the foreign technical assistance so far received by the IITs, the capabilities developed in IITs with such assistance, and the areas that need to be further developed and supported through foreign technical assistance programmes. Accordingly, the Review Committee on Foreign Technical Assistance received by the Indian Institutes of Technology and other Academic Institutions was constituted by the Government of India, Ministry of Education and Culture in June 1978.

Terms of Reference

1. to review and evaluate the foreign technical assistance/aid so far received by the IITs.

2. to assess the capabilities developed in IITs with such assistance/aid, and

1. New Delhi, Ministry of Education and Culture, Government of India, 1980, 51 p.

3. to identify areas that need to be further developed and supported through foreign technical assistance/aid *vis-a-vis* the emerging areas and national perspectives.

It was subsequently suggested that the Committee could perhaps also have a look at the foreign technical assistance/aid received by other academic institutions and also make recommendations on the procedure and principles to be followed for processing proposals for foreign technical assistance received from academic (engineering and technological) institutions. It was further desired that the Committee should examine how the IITs could offer technical assistance to academic institutions of lower formations such as engineering colleges.

Contents

Brief Summary of Findings and Recommendations; Preamble; Quantum of Aid Received by the IITs; Impact of Foreign Collaboration/ Technical Assistance/Aid; Foreign Technical Assistance received by Academic Institutions other than the IITs; Problems of Foreign Technical Assistance/Collaboration/Aid; Model for Future Technical Assistance Programmes; Areas Identified for further Foreign Technical Assistance/Collaboration/Aid; Some Aspects and Corollaries; Findings and Recommendations; Annexures I to XIII.

Recommendations

The amount of foreign technical assistance/aid so far received by the 5 IITs (as on 1-1-1979) may be quantified as equal to about Rs. 24 crores worth of equipment, 5202 man-months of Indian faculty training abroad and 8166 man-months of foreign experts in the IITs. The figures in respect of 17 non-IIT institutions are roughly Rs. 5.5 crores. 1781 man-months and 2836 man-months respectively. The non-recurring Indian capital input into the 5 IITs has been of the order of Rs. 58 crores. (Paras 2.1, 2.2, 4.0)

Foreign technical assistance has had a significant impact on the IITs and in turn on the technical education system in the country. It has helped the IITs to develop expertise at international levels and to build up competent R&D infrastructure in a wide variety of scientific and technological fields. The IITs have also been able to produce about 35,000 engineers, scientists and technologists of high calibre. (Paras

3.1, 3.2, 3.3, 3.4, 3.6)

Fifteen (15) areas have been identified (3 for each IIT) for possible further foreign technical assistance. These areas which are relevant to the national needs may be developed into "Centres of Excellence". In these areas, the IITs should inter-act with their counterparts in foreign countries on a continuing basis to reduce the temporal phase-lag in developing these areas in our country. (Paras 7.1, 8.1)

Twenty-five (25) other areas have been identified (5 for each IIT) which may be considered for foreign collaboration on equal partnership basis. These are all emerging areas and have national perspectives. Foreign collaboration is considered necessary to maintain the levels of research and development in these areas at international levels. (Paras 7.2, 8.1)

The IITs will need foreign capital aid (as distinct from foreign technical assistance of collaboration) by way of budgetary support to replace old obsolete equipment and to consolidate and further develop areas in which they have already acquired expertise of high standards in case adequate internal resources (including necessary foreign exchange component) are not available for these purposes. (Paras 3.3, 5.1, 7.0, 7.3)

The so-called obsolete equipment in good working condition should be transferred from the IITs to the other needy institutions.

A small team of competent instrument mechanics/experts should be asked to examine the sophisticated equipment now lying idle in the various IITs with a view to setting them right. If it is necessary to import spares, this should be done as a matter of urgency.

It is necessary to create in the IITs an infrastructure for training in the instrumentation area with particular reference to repairs and maintenance of sophisticated instruments. (Paras 5.1, 5.2, 8.4)

It is unrealistic and unproductive to use foreign technical assistance/collaboration/aid programmes indiscriminately and in an uncoordinated manner. These programmes should be used only on a selective basis for new and emerging areas, for inter-action in areas of excellence and for procuring sophisticated equipment not available indigenously. In all these cases, the proposals should be based on overall national priorities and commitments. (Paras 6.0, 7.1, 7.2, 7.3, 8.5.2, 8.5.11)

No foreign technical assistance programme should be such that it would perpetuate our dependence in the area concerned on foreign expertise and support. The objective should always be to develop indigenous capabilities and self-reliance. In all programmes, formulation and management of the projects, decision-taking, evaluation, etc., should be our responsibility. Mechanisms other than, "expert-equipment-training" should be sought. (Paras 8.5.3, 8.5.4)

Foreign technical assistance/collaboration/aid programmes should not be aimed at replacing existing indigenous endeavours; they should be directed to strengthening and upgrading them. (Paras 8.5.2, 8.5.3, 8.5.5, 8.5.11)

Proposals for foreign technical assistance/collaboration/aid received from the IITs and other academic institutions should not be considered in isolation. They should be considered on the basis of overall national perspectives and in relation to what is happening in other departments (such as Electronics, Science and Technology, Space, etc.) and agencies (such CSIR, ICAR, ICMR, etc.). It is, therefore, suggested that all proposals for foreign technical assistance should be considered by a National Screening Committee in the Ministry of Education and with representatives from the Ministry of Education, Planning Commission, Department of Science and Technology and Department of Economic Affairs. This Committee could invite for its meetings representatives from other departments and agencies depending upon the subject areas of the proposals under consideration. (Paras 8.5.1, 8.5.2)

In all foreign technical assistance/collaboration programmes, the flow of funds from foreign agencies should be with the full knowledge of and/or through the national authorities. (Paras 8.5.1, 8.5.6, 8.5.11)

It is necessary to review the foreign training programmes of various agencies including Government departments. Even today, a large number of people are being unnecessarily sent abroad for training in areas for which ample facilities are available in India. Even in emerging areas, it is possible to give major part of the training in India; such preparatory training in India would greatly enhance the benefits from foreign training inputs. (Paras 3.2, 5.4, 8.5.2, 8.5.7)

Foreign experts/consultants should be obtained only for absolutely essential areas of gaps in technology and that too only for short periods. But at the same time there should be a free flow of experts between India and other countries on equal partnership basis. Only sophisticated equipment/instruments which are not available indigenously should be included for import under foreign technical assistance programmes. Efforts should always be to develop such equipment/instruments in India. (Paras 5.2, 5.3, 8.5.2, 8.5.8, 8.5.9)

Institutions of the same category like the IITs should consult each other and submit to the National Screening Committee coordinated and agreed proposals for foreign technical assistance/collaboration aid preferably in August every year. Institutions like the Indian Institutes of Management and Regional Engineering Colleges could also do the same. (Paras 8.5.2, 8.5.10, 8.5.11)

There is a remarkable increase in the number of sponsored research projects undertaken by the IITs. These projects are done on a no-loss-no-profit basis. It is suggested that the IIts may be allowed to generate funds from sponsored research programmes on the basis of norms of charges to be laid down by the appropriate authorities.

The IITs should not undertake routine testing jobs in the name of consultancy. (Para 3.4)

The IITs should not work in isolation. They should build up and increase formal linkages with other academic institutions, R&D organisations and national laboratories. (Paras 3.5, 8.2, 8.5.11)

The IITs are competent and willing to give assistance—sans financial support—to institutions of lower formations in a variety of ways. Concrete steps should be taken to promote the flow of such technical assistance from the IITs to engineering colleges, etc. The expertise available in the IITs to offer consultancy services should be fully utilised by the Educational Consultancy Company proposed to be set up under the auspices of the Government of India. (Paras 3.2, 3.3, 3.4, 8.2)

There is need to establish in the IITs Centres for Assessment and Transfer of Technology. (Para 8.13)

RAILWAY ACCIDENT INVESTIGATION REPORT ON OCCURRENCE OF CASUALTIES AMONG PASSENGERS OF No. 40-UP AHMEDABAD-BOMBAY PASSENGER TRAIN AT Km. 199/7-9 ON THE UP MAIN LINE AT VALSAD STATION ON THE SURAT-BOMBAY CENTRAL BROAD GAUGE DOUBLE LINE ROUTE OF WESTERN RAILWAY AT ABOUT 09.31 HOURS ON SEPTEMBER 18, 1978[1]

One Man Commission Shri P.M.N. Murthy

Appointment

The Commission was constituted under Ministry of Tourism and Civil Aviation (Commission of Railway Safety) in accordance with Rule 4 of the Statutory Investigations Rules 1973 vide Notification No. RS. 13-T(8)/71 dated April 19, 1973 on September 18, 1978.

Terms of Reference

To enquire into the occurrence of casualties among passengers of No. 40-Up Ahmedabad-Bombay Passenger Train at Km. 199/7-9 on the Up Main Line at Valsad Station on the Surat-Bombay Central Broad Gauge double line route of Western Railway at about 09.31 hours on September 18, 1978.

Contents

Summary; Inspection and Inquiry; Summary of Evidence; Observa-

1. Delhi, Controller of Publications, 1982, p. 20

tions and Tests; Discussions; Conclusions; Remarks and Recommendations; Annexures; Copy of Railway Board, New Delhi's letter No. TC-R/1057/18/69 dated August 21, 1969 addressed to All Indian Railways.

Conclusions

39. On full consideration of the factual material, and circumstantial evidence, I have reached the following conclusions:

(a) *Cause of Accident*: Casualties amongst passenger of No. 40-Up Ahmedabad-Bombay Passenger train at Km. 199/7-9 on the Up Main line at Valsad Station on the Surat-Bombay Central Broad Gauge double line electrified section of the Western Railway at about 09.31 hours on 8th September 1978, resulted from their getting struck by the infringing steel rods of the consignment loaded in an open bogie-wagon which was being shunted on the dead end siding alongside.

The consignment had not been packed in accordance with the stipulations in P/37 of the I.R.C.A. Goods Tariff at Ghaziabad whence it originated and the steel rods which, in the absence of the required complement of chain lashings and hooks/couplings had been inadequately secured on a make shift basis, got dislodged in the course of shunting, leading to some in the top layers protruding out and forming an obstruction in the path of the incoming passenger train.

(b) *Responsibility*: The following officials may be considered culpable in this case:

(i) The Train Examiner at Ghaziabad, Northern Railway, who certified the fitness of BFR No. SE 19059 loaded with ribbed steel rods (bent double) for haulage, despite its deficiency in chain lashings and securing device which had been sought to be made good with 3mm/5mm dia wire links and secured at 4 locations (instead of the intended 5) in a manner inadequate for the type of consignment carried therein;

(ii) Shri R. Shiv Narain, Officiating Train Examiner, Gangapur City, who conducted an intensive examination of Train No. 1 BRC which included BFR No. SE 19059 and allowed the BFR to pass despite the deficiencies and with its consignment insufficiently secured for safe travel over a long stretch;

(iii) Shri D. Aswin Kumar, Basic Yard Fitter, Vadodara Marshalling

Yard, who supervised the load adjustment in the BFR and certified its soundness for further transit on behalf of the Wagon Foreman;

(iv) Shri V.M. Parab, Head Train Examiner, Vadodara Marshalling Yard, for permitting running of the BFR after load adjustment apparently without exercising sufficient judgement, particularly in the context of his earlier knowledge of the state in which the BFR had arrived at Vadodara from Gangapur City 6 weeks or so earlier with the consignment displaced and had been rightly held back under his orders for setting it right; and

(v) Shri N. Navnitrai, Train Examiner, Valsad, who, noticing the condition of the shifted consignment in this wagon marked it sick, but failed to advise the Yard Master to bestow special care in the movement of this wagon in the yard so as to ensure against further shifting of the load in the shunting process.

40. *Relief Measures*: Although the evidence adduced did not disclose anything wanting in relief measures, my attention was drawn to a grievance recorded in the 'Complaint Book' at Valsad station by some passengers, alleging delay in the arrival of Doctors at site inspite of approach to the nearest 'Railway Station Officer on duty' and the Medical Van coming to site without the key so much so that the lock had eventually to be dismantled after 15 minutes. On examination of the relevant evidence I find that 4 Railway Doctors reached the site within 25 minutes of the occurrence and made immediate arrangements to take those who were in need of urgent attention straightway to the Railway Hospital at Valsad by Ambulance Van; hospitalisation was completed by 10.30 hours. None of the complainants appeared at the Inquiry. Both the injured passengers whom I met in the Jagjivan Ram Hospital, Bombay Central on 20-9-1978, as well as relatives of the one (who was then still in an unconscious state) in the Kasturba Hospital, Valsad, expressed their satisfaction at the assistance given to them after the mishap. Also, the non-availability of the key of the Medical Van was not significant as the slight delay in opening it did not materially affect the rendering of medical attention to those who needed it most. Apropos Section II of the Report, the relief measures were reasonably prompt and adequate. The said complaint appears to have arisen out of some misapprehension.

Recommendations

41. It was recommended in my Report on the occurrence of Casualties among passengers of 5 Down Punjab Mail at Jakhaura station, Central Railway on 6th October 1968, that 'extend instructions on proper securing of consignments particularly those which are liable to shift in transit the need for strictly adhering to the stipulated packing conditions, and the deficiencies meriting rejection of goods stock during train examination, may be re-emphasized to staff'. This recommendation was endorsed by the Railway Board vide their letter No. TC-R 1057/18/69 dated 21-8-1969 to all Railways, in which it was desired that suitable instructions should be issued to the staff on the need for proper securing on consignments particularly those which are liable to shift in transit to avoid accidents being caused on this account [Copy reproduced at Annexure-VI]. Apparently, these instructions have not gone home. There was also an accident near Vadodara on the Western Railway on 9th May 1978, when some travellers on No. 50 Up Passenger train came into contact with a block section limit board which had been hit by a protrusion on an earlier Up train and twisted towards the Up Main line, resulting in four of them getting killed and one sustaining grievous hurt. The precedent errant train, which must have been a freight train, could not be identified by the Railway Administration. These occurrences under-score the need for a special drive in the matter, including effective supervisory checks at various points on the existence of the prescribed complement of chain lashings and couplings on BFRs and the securing of consignments liable to displacement on the run.

42. The length of each lot of steel rods which had been bent in U form loaded in BFR No. SE 19059 was only of the order of 5.7 metres or so. Such a short length consignment need not have been loaded in a BFR. I had also drawn attention to this aspect in my Report on the Accident referred to in Para 41 and had suggested that "As far as possible, short length consignments should not be loaded in open bogie wagons of the BFR type. Where unavoidable, such consignments should be specially secured by tying and lashing". The Railway Board had expressed the following views on this suggestion vide their O.M. No. 68/Safety/1/19 dated 10-10-1969: "A study of midsection derailments caused by defective loading was made in the Board's office. The R.D.S.O. has been advised to evolve suitable methods for loading/stacking/securing of commodities which are liable to shift in

transit. They have also been adviced to bring out pamphlets similar to the booklets produced by the American Association of Railroads for securing consignments in order that they do not shift on the run". Pursuant thereto, the R.D.S.O. issued a set of instructions together with loading arrangement drawings for sheets, plates, coils and tubes/pipes, vide letter No. MW/ACT/BG dated 11-3-1975. These instructions do not cover steel rods and are also not included in the Goods Tariff. Steel rods, particularly of the ribbed variety used for structural reinforcement, which are normally transported in bent form, need, special care in securement as they have a tendency to open out and pose a safety hazard. RDSO may be directed to develop suitable guidelines to cover other consignments like ribbed steel rods, urgently and issue to Railways for strict compliance. The pamphlets referred to in Railway Board's O.M. of 10-10-1969 may also be brought out expeditiously in handy form for reference by the Commercial and Train Examining staff.

43. (a) Many of the packing conditions in contained in the Goods Tariff are not compulsory, although, they have a vital bearing on public safety, e.g., P/37, P/38, P/41, etc. Apart from amplifying some of the extent packing conditions in the light of the guidelines framed already for some and to be framed for others by the RDSO, those which have a bearing on safety should be made compulsory.

(b) Train Examiners are at present not made aware of the Packing conditions laid down in the Goods Tariff which are deemed purely as a commercial requirement. It appears essential that the compulsory external packing conditions should form a part of the Train Examiners' Manuals to enable them to verify their compliance during their examinations. These should also be included in the curriculum of Training Establishments where Train Examiners undergo initial and refresher courses.

44. Instructions may be issued that whenever wagons or other stock marked 'sick' or 'damage labelled' are to be shunted on yard lines which are situated immediately alongside the passenger running lines, this should be done only when 'block' conditions are ensured on the passenger lines. It may also be enjoined that such stock should be worked into the sidings where it is proposed to be attended to with minimum shunt movements.

45. The weight of steel rods loaded in BFR No. SE 19059 was 46.4 tonnes — 3.1 tonnes more than the marked carrying capacity. A loading tolerance of 2.5 tonnes over the marked carrying capacity is

permitted for steel consignments carried in BFRs vide Railway Board's letter No. TCR/1394/76/48 dated 27-7-1978. While the object of allowing for a loading tolerance is 'purely for any error in loading' [vide clause 3.9.3.1 of Conference Rules' Part III], it appears that the tolerance is being adopted as a normal expedient even for consignments which are susceptible to a reasonably accurate assessment of load – e.g., steel rods. Overloading of wagons was referred to the Railway Board by the Commissioner of Railway Safety vide his letter No. RS 25-T(53)76 dated 19-3-1977, wherein it was pointed out that overloading beyond the design capacity had serious implications affecting safety. It is desired that the Railway Board may go into all the cognate aspects of this issue and review their extent orders.

Railway Board's Comments on Various Paras of the Report

Para 41: Board's instructions contained in their letter No. TCR/1057/18/69 dated 21-8-67 were duly circulated by the Railway Administration to all the Divisions for compliance. After the occurrence of the subject accident, instructions have been issued afresh by the Railway, drawing attention to the provisions contained in the Conference Rules Part-III regarding securing of loads which are likely to shift in transit particularly on open trucks. It has also been emphasised that special checks should be held at frequent intervals to pinpoint and correct irregular working and also make good the deficiencies particularly in regard to the prescribed complements of chain lashings and couplings on BFRs and ensure securing of consignments liable to displacement on the run.

Para 42: R.D.S.O., who have examined the relevant packing conditions, namely, P/37 of the Goods Tariff, have stated that these conditions for packing and securing of steel consignments such as steel rods of the ribbed variety are adequate. The Ministry of Railways agree with the findings of the R.D.S.O. Efforts will be made for stricter enforcement of these packing conditions.

Para 43(a): Issue of suitable guidelines for loading and securing of consignments likely to shift during transit, has already been taken up by the Railway Board with RDSO. Considering the number of items as well as the types of wagon in which these will be transported, there will be a large variety of consignment-wagon combinations for which these guidelines will have to be laid down. It is proposed to set up a team of officers of Mechanical and Commercial disciplines to examine and make suitable recommendations in this regard.

Para 43(b): The advantages of educating the TXRs on the relevant packing conditions which have a bearing on safe running of trains, are appreciated. At present, the responsibility for ensuring the compliance with appropriate packing conditions is with the commercial staff and this should continue to be so. If this also is made a responsibility of TXRs, by including such packing conditions as Part of Train Examiners' Manual and asking TXRs to verify their compliance during their examinations, it will result in dual responsibility or dilution of the responsibility, which is not desirable. CRS's recommendation for inclusion of the compulsory external packing conditions in the curriculum of TXR training institutions where TXRs undergo training, refresher courses, etc., is accepted. IRCA will be directed to identify such of the conditions which should be made fully known to the TXRs during their training. Suitable instructions will be issued to the railways for arranging inclusion of these in the training syllabus after the relevant packing conditions are indentified.

Para 44: As explained by the Railway Administration, it would not be feasible to impose a firm restriction on the movement of 'sick' and 'damage' labelled wagons on adjacent lines during passenger train movements in view of the nature and tempo of yard operations. Instructions have however, been issued by the Railway to all concerned to exercise utmost caution while performing shunting of such stock and to regulate movements as far as possible in the intervals between passenger train movements on the adjacent lines.

Suitable instructions on the subject have been issued to other Railways also.

Para 45: It may be clarified that in respect of a number of commodities, the revision of minimum weight condition to carrying capacity plus 2 tonnes was undertaken during 1975 after detailed examination of all the implications. The prime consideration behind the revision orders of 1975 was to prevent loss to the railway revenues amounting to crores of rupees and to augment the earnings without jeopardising safety. Experience prior to the revision showed that the railways were in fact carrying the extra weight above the carrying capacity for years due to consignors utilising the loading tolerance of 2 tonnes above carrying capacity more or less regularly. All that the Ministry of Railways did in 1975 was, therefore, to permit the railways to charge for the overloading up to 2 tonnes, which was till then being carried free by them as a loading tolerance. Simultaneously with these orders, no loading tolerance over and above the carrying capacity plus 2 tonnes has been given. Such being the case, these orders did not permit the consignors to overshoot the limit of carrying capacity plus 2 tonnes which also the position prior to the issue of these orders.

Adequate safeguard has been provided to Rule 163 of Goods Tariff under which the minimum weight conditions of carrying capacity plus 2 tonnes automatically gets reduced to the limit of loading due to restrictions warranted by local and other conditions. Added to this are the penal provisions of Rule 161 of the Goods Tariff laying down charges at double the highest class rate being recovered for the distance such over weight is carried in case of over-loading of a 4-wheeler in excess of 1 tonne or a Box wagon in excess of 2 tonnes.

In the above background Ministry of Railways find it difficult to view the revised minimum weight condition of 1975 as an infringement of safety rules.

The entire issue is, however, being studied again in depth in consultation with RDSO and the Commission of Railway Safety would be advised further after a decision is taken.

14

RAILWAY ACCIDENT INVESTIGATION REPORT ON COLLISION BETWEEN No. 316 UP 'MIRAJ-PUNE PASSENGER' AND M-32 LNN DOWN DIESEL GOODS BETWEEN BHAVANINAGAR AND TAKARI STATIONS OF THE MIRAJ-PUNE B.G. SINGLE LINE SECTIONS OF SOUTH CENTRAL RAILWAY ON OCTOBER 11, 1978 — REPORT[1]

One Man Commission Shri A.V. Jacob

Appointment

The Commission was constituted under Ministry of Tourism and Civil Aviation in accordance with Rule 4 of the Statutory Investigation into Railway Accidents Rules 1973 Vide Notification No. RS-13-T(8)/71 dated April 19, 1973 on October 11, 1978.

Terms of Reference

To enquire into the Collision between No. 316 UP 'Miraj-Pune Passenger' and M-32 LNN Down Diesel Goods between Bhavaninagar and Takari Stations of the Miraj-Pune B.G. Single line sections of the South Central Railway on October 11, 1978.

Contents

Summary; Inspection and Inquiry; The Trains Local Features; Damage; Summary of Evidence; Tests and Observations; Discussion; Conclusions; Remarks and Recommendations; Views of Railway Board on Various Paras of Report.

---

1. Delhi, Controller of Publications, 1987, 19 p

Conclusions

33. *Cause of Accident*

On full consideration of the factual and circumstantial evidence, I have come to the conclusion that the collision between No. 316 Up "Miraj-Pune Passenger" train and M-32 LNN Down Diesel Goods train at about 07-44 hrs. On 11-10-1978 at Km. 227/12-13 between Bhavaninagar and Takari stations of the Miraj-Pune B.G. section of the Hubli Division of South Central Railway was due to the Driver of the Goods train having passed the Down Main line Starter and Advanced Starter at Danger and going into the Block section Bhavaninagar-Takari without proper authority. He, therefore, contravened G.R. 76 and G.R. 79.

The deficiency of brake power of the Goods train also is a contributory factor.

34. *Responsibility*

Driver Shri Anthony Jeevarathanam must be held responsible for the accident. No individual can be held responsible for the weak brake power as the train was not subjected to examination at Lonand where it originated.

35. *Bio-Data of Drivers Shri Anthony Jeevarathnam of Goods Train*

Driver, Shri Anthony Jeevarathnam, aged 54 years, was originally appointed as a Shed Khalasi in 1945 and has put in 35 years of service. He has been working as Steam Goods Driver from 1960, though he was permanently posted as 'C' Grade Driver only from 23-1-1974. He had his Diesel training at Kazipet from 16-8-1977 to 6-12-1977. He has worked as Diesel Driver from January 1978 to October 1978, doing 83 trips on Diesel and 39 on Steam during this period. He has a long list of punishments since 1962.

Recommendations

36. (a) M-32 Lonand Special Goods was formed at Lonand from empty wagons supplied piecemeal from various directions and on various dates and sent out on its journey to Miraj a distance of 187

kms. without a train examination and issue of a brake power certificate by competent staff. It should normally have been treated as an originating train and provisions of para 3.2 of Conference Rules—Part III complied with. According to South Central Railway, however, the train, is to be examined by Guard in terms of G.R. 113/S.R. 113(i) and General Manager (T), South Central Railway, Secunderabad's letter No.T. 157/P/20 of 16-1-1971. It is no doubt true that G.R. 113(b) states that the Guard should satisfy himself that the train is provided with prescribed brake power but the manner of ensuring this has not been clarified. The Guard not being a trained carriage and wagon hand cannot be expected to check brake power without assistance from train examining staff. In my view, therefore, when a full train load or a substantial number of wagons (say above 10) have to be attached at a way-side station without train examination facilities, special arrangements must be made for examination by a trained TXR or Carriage and wagon Fitter who should issue the necessary brake power certificate as per rules. This will ensure that Goods trains are not run with insufficient brake power. The South Central Railway may make suitable amendments to their letter referred to above.

(b) In this connection, attention is also invited to the recommendation contained in Para 38 of my Report of Inquiry into "Derailment of No. 23-A Down Mixed Train between Furkating and Golaghat stations of Northeast Frontier Railway on 14-7-1976". The Railway Board's Orders on this recommendation are still to be received. However, the need for training Operating staff like Driver, Guard, Station Master and Goods Clerk in the examination of wagons is reiterated.

37. According to the Railway Board's extent orders 85 per cent of the vacuum cylinders must be operative before a Goods train is started from a train examining station. However, it is quite common for a number of additional cylinders to go out of order on the run resulting in a reduction of brake power available to the Driver. Since there can be no question of a different level of brake power being safe when the train is in the initial stage of journey and at later stages, it is clear that 85 per cent should be treated as minimum and if more cylinders are found in operative en-route, the maximum speed of the train should be reduced till the percentage of effective cylinders is again brought back to 85 per cent.

Apart from the above, as stated in Para 3.2 of my Report on the Collision between No. 9 Up "Barauni-Kanpur Express" (M.G.) and Down (B.G.) Garhara Goods Special on 24-2-1977 at Bachwara station on the North Eastern Railway, the travel of the piston of the vacuum cylinder has a vital bearing on the actual brake pressure exerted on an axle and, therefore, instructions may be issued for checking this during brake power examination and treating all pistons whose travel falls outside the minimum and maximum prescribed as in operative.

38. The number of punishments imposed on the Driver of the Goods train Shri Anthony Jeevarathnam since 1962 clearly go to show that his record was unsatisfactory. His accident index worked out by the Division also comes to 882 whereas the Railway Board in their letter No. 69/PSYCL/14 of 15-10-1969 had considered an accident index of 300 as requiring special watch. It is also clear that no special machinery exists for watching such Drivers on Railways.

I would, therefore, repeat here the recommendations I made in the collision at Bachwara already referred to above.

38.1 "An attempt to study the accident proneness of individual Drivers was made by the Board as a result of which instruction about classifying Drivers, their counselling and Training was issued vide Railway Board's letter No. 69/PSYCH/14 of 15-10-1969. This was a step in the right direction but there does not appear to have been much follow up on these, as was revealed in this inquiry. The Railway Board may like to take steps to see that the orders contained in this letter are implemented. It may perhaps be desirable to make this the responsibility of the Safety rather than that of the Mechanical Department".

38.2 "Incidentally, the list of irregularities to be taken into consideration as listed in Para 2 of the above letter do not include acts of indiscipline such as "not turning on duty", "careless working", "Obstructive working", etc. It is considered, that these also should be included in this list as these Offences are those of one who is not duty conscious and, therefore, likely to be cause accidents."

38.3 "Again the present formulae is:

$$\text{Accident Index} = \frac{\text{No. of Accidents} \times \text{Severity}}{\text{Total length of service as Fireman onwards}} \times 100$$

This allows for calculation of the Index at one particular point of time but does not convey any information about change for better or worse in the Driver's accident proneness over the years. It is, therefore, suggested that both numerator and denominator in the above formulae be limited to a specified period say 5 or 10 years as considered by the

RDSO to be suitable. The exercise of checking on Loco running staff's accident proneness at these intervals must then be made a regular work of the Safety Departments on the Railway who should also be responsible to see that the Mechanical Department follow up with counselling and refresher in case of individuals whose accident index exceeds the desirable maximum. The Railway Board may like to consult the Psycho—Technical Wing of RDSO on the suggested changes in the procedure and issue orders."

The Railway Board's orders on these paras are still to be received.

39.1 I would also recommend for consideration that a Driver having an accident Index higher than 500 be not considered for Diesel working and one reaching 750 be taken off running duties and be restricted to shunting.

40. At present with Upper Quadrant Signalling a Green or 90° aspect at the Distant merely indicates to the Driver that the train is being received on the Main line but does not give him an indication whether the train is being stopped or allowed to run through. This information he gets only when he notes the aspect of the Home Signal. While with the cautious Driver the non-availability of this distinction leads to his being over-cautious and nullifies the operating advantage of Upper Quadrant Signalling, with a rash Driver the danger of his over-shooting the Starter at 'ON' is always there. I, therefore, recommend that an effective means of enabling the Driver to differentiate when sighting the Distant itself whether he is to run through or stop on the Main line be evolved, without obliterating the present distinction in the aspects of the Distant when the train is being received on the Main line or on the loop. A suggested method is the provision of two fish tail arms to be taken off to 90° for run through trains by day and double green at night.

41. As has been stated by the Diesel Assistant Shri Anthony Joachim, he has absolutely no knowledge of the working of a Diesel engine having had no Diesel training. Since a Diesel Assistant is required to take over and work the train to the next station in case the Driver becomes incapacitated en-route, the position revealed by this admission is disquieting. In fact, according to him, since he joined as a Shed Khalasi and subsequently promoted as 'C' Grade 'B' Grade Fireman, he has had no training at all. In answer to a question he has stated that "I have had no training in any school during my service". The Railway Board's and Railway Administration's special attention is drawn to the need for proper training of train working staff at every

stage of promotion not only in their Technical duties but also in rules and regulations. In case of Diesel Assistants, before being put to work as such, they should undergo a full course in operation of Diesel engines. A sufficient reserve of such trained staff should be maintained from amongst Steam Firemen to meet all contingencies.

42. Attention is invited to the different timing for the same event given by Station staff, Guards, Controllers, etc. Though rules provide for Guards checking of their watches and SMs their clocks with Control, this is not being regularly done. The importance of synchronisation of time in a highly complex operating system like Railway cannot be over emphasised. The Railway Administration should pay greater attention to compliance by all staff to the extant orders on the subject.

Views of Railway Board on Various Paras of the Report

Findings

The findings of the Commissioner of Railway Safety with regard to the cause of the accident and responsibility therefore as given in Paras 33 and 34 of the report are, *prima facie*, acceptable.

Regarding Commissioner of Railway Safety's finding that deficiency of brake power of the goods train was a contributory factor to the accident, attention is invited to the observations made by the Commissioner of Railway Safety himself in para 29.7 of the report which reads as under:

> "The electrical systems for the working of the Dynamic Brakes were checked for continuity and found functioning satisfactorily. It appeared, therefore, that the Dynamic Brake system was also functioning normally before the accident and no condition which would have made the Dynamic Break to trip when applied as alleged by the Driver could be discovered. In fact the concerned switches were found in the operated position immediately after the accident."

The Commissioner of Railway Safety's conclusion is that the dynamic brakes were in normal working order. Further, as the load of the train was not high (1675.4 tonnes including the weight of the locomotive), the dynamic brakes by itself would have been adequate to decelerate the train at 1/1000, level, and 1/400 gradients within a distance of about 2.5 kilometres between 224/2-3 and 226/11-12 km. Even on the falling gradient of 1.100 for a stretch of about 4 kms. prior to this, the dynamic brakes would have been adequate to hold the train at a speed of about 30 km/h.

As regards the train brakes, these were also working quite satisfactorily. Evidence of the HTXR, Miraj and Junior Fuel Inspector, Ghorpuri, vide Paras 25 and 26 of the report, clearly indicates that the brakes of the individual wagons on the train, not damaged in the accident, were mostly operative. The tests conducted by Commissioner of Railway Safety, vide Para 29.1 also indicate that there would have been no difficulty in controlling the train with train brakes.

Thus the available evidence and the tests conducted clearly show that both the dynamic brakes and the train breaks were functioning satisfactorily prior to the accident. In view of this, the conclusions of the Commissioner of Railway Safety about deficient brakes of the goods train being a contributory factor for the accident is not consistent with his own conclusions and tests and observations made in the report.

Since both the dynamic and train brakes were functioning satisfactorily, the driver by judicious application of these could have controlled the train. Normally both the brakes are used in combination, the vacuum and train brakes being applied to a limited extent, after which the dynamic brake is used to get smooth braking effect. The dynamic brakes will trip when emergency brake application is done on the train. Possibly, the driver was not vigilant and he applied emergency brakes first resulting in tripping of dynamic brakes. Because of the number of vacuum cylinders with excessive piston stroke, there would have been a time delay before full brake application had its effect. Apparently, the driver had panicked in the meanwhile and, therefore, did not adopt the practice of taking the A.9 handle to vacuum reduction and going in for full dynamic brake application. The accident is, therefore, attributable not only to the failure of the driver to be vigilant and cautious and control the train short of the stop signals at the station, but also due to his lack of enginemanship.

In view of the position set out above, the conclusions of Commissioner of Railway Safety that deficiency of brake power of the goods train was a contributory factor, do not appear to be sustainable.

Comments on Various Paras of the Report

Para 36(a): Instructions being issued to the Railways to sec that whenever any change in the composition of the train, to the extent of 15 per cent subject to a minimum of 10 wagons, is made as a result of attachment/detachment of vehicles at a station, a fresh brake power certificate should be issued, at the next train examining station.

Para 36(b): This matter was raised by the Commission of Railway Safety in Para 38 of the report on the derailment of No. 234 Down Mixed train between Furkating and Golaghat stations of the Northeast Frontier Railway on 14-7-76. As already explained in this Ministry's O.M. No. 76/Safety (A&R)/1/16 dated 11-4-79, the wagons which are made available or are sent for loading at way-side stations are those whose road-worthiness is already checked up by a competent TXR. The road-worthiness of such wagons is again checked when they pass through a station where TXR facilities are available. It was also explained therein as to why it was not possible for train operating staff like Station Master/Goods Clerk Assistants to examine the wagons.

Para 37: It may be clarified that stipulation of 85 per cent effective brake power for a Goods train is necessarily with reference to the originating stations and cannot be deemed to be mandatory for the entire journey of the train. If at any intermediate point after attachment/detachment of wagons vacuum level is found to be lower, the driver is required to suitably regulated the speed of his train to keep it under control and have the vacuum examined and rectified at the next train examining station. Attention in this connection is invited to this Ministry's endorsement No. 77/Safety (A&R)/1/5 dated 18-5-79.

Para 38.1: As already advised in this Ministry's O.M. No. 77/Safety (A&R)/1/5, dated 18-5-79, in terms of Board's circular letter No. 69/PSYCH/14/1 dated 15-10-69 a driver with an accident index of 300 is treated as a potential safety risk, and special steps are required to be taken to correct and counsel such accident prone staff. Safety Counsellor/Loco Inspector have to maintain a close watch on their method of working and counsel them. The Divisional officers (PME/DSO) are also required to informally interview some cases for corrective counselling. Also highest priority is to be given for sending such staff to refresher courses and safety camps. Drivers with accident index of 1000 are called for special safety counselling by the Chief Superintendent the South Central Railway.

Para 33.2 & 38.3: The formula for calculating the accident index has been subjected to review in respect of steam drivers by the RDSO, and the same is under trial on the Western Railway. It may be mentioned that the RDSO is also working on the revised formula for calculating the accident index in respect of diesel/electric drivers and motormen.

Para 39: The recommendations of the Commissioner of Railway safety is accepted in principle. Suitable instruction on the subject would be issued to the Railways.

Para 40: In view of the Chief Commissioner's remarks that this matter appears to be receiving the attention of RAEC-78, we may await their views on the subject.

Para 41: Instructions have been issued to the Railways, vide Board's letter No 79/M (M&P)/7/2/SC-2 dated 17-4-79, to ensure that only regularly qualified running staff should work on diesel locomotives.

Para 42: Instructions on the subject have been reiterated by the railway administration. Chief Commissioner of Railway Safety has noted the action taken by the railway administration.

THE REVIEW COMMITTEE ON UGC PROGRAMMES, 1978 — REPORT[1]

Chairman Prof. Satish Chandra

Members Prof. B. Ramachandra Rao; Shri P. Sabanayagam; Prof. B.M. Udgaonkar; Prof. R.P. Bambah; Dr. Malcolm S. Adiseshiah; Prof. G. Rama Reddy; Dr. Ramaranjan Mukherji; Prof. (Miss) A.J. Dastur; Prof. Ram Lal Parikh; Dr. C.S. Jha; Dr. S.N. Saraf.

M. Secy. Dr. S.C. Goel

Appointment

In exercise of the powers Conferred under Section 20 of the UGC Act, 1956, the Central Government in the Ministry of Education and Social Welfare (Department of Education) directed the University Grants Commission Vide its letter No. 10-14/78.U-1 dated the 18th October 1978 to undertake a comprehensive review of the various programmes being implemented by it and the impact that these have made on the fulfilment of the statutory responsibilities of the Commission namely, determination and maintenance of standards of teaching, examinations and research in universities. The Commission was also asked to identify schemes which are considered peripheral or which have not registered any impact on the maintenance and improvement of standards of university education and to discontinue them.

The University Grants Commission at its meeting held on the 14th November, 1978 noted the contents of the above letter and observed that it had already taken steps to review the existing schemes being implemented by it to determine the schemes that may be continued in the next plan. In this context, the Commission desired that only those quality programmes be reviewed at this stage which have been in

1. New Delhi, University Grants Commission, 1981, 208 p.

operation for about three years or so, in order that their full impact may be assessed.

Terms of Reference

"To undertake a comprehensive review of the various programmes being implemented by it and impact that these have made on the fulfilment of the statutory responsibilities of the Commission, namely, determination and maintenance of standards of teaching examinations are research in Universities. The Commission was also asked to identify schemes which are considered peripheral or which have not registered any impact on the maintenance and improvement of standards of university education and to discontinue them."

Contents

Foreword; Introduction; Commission's Programmes and Schemes — A Review; Impact of Commissions Programmes on Universities and Colleges; Centres of Advanced Study/Departments of Special Assistance; College Science Improvement Programme/College Humanities and Social Science Improvement Programmes; Financial Assistance to Teachers for Research Work; General Observations and Recommendations; Summary of Observations and Recommendations; Annexures from I to XXXIV.

Recommendations

Appointment of the Committee

8.01 The Review Committee was appointed in terms of the directive of the Central Government in the Ministry of Education (a) to undertake a comprehensive review of the various programmes being implemented by the UGC and the impact of these programmes on the determination and maintenance of standards of teaching research and examinations in the universities, and (b) to identify schemes which are considered peripheral or which have not registered any impact on standards and to discontinue these.

8.02 Sub-committees, consisting of experts in the humanities, social sciences and science subjects were constituted to visit selected universities and colleges in order to assess the impact of UGC grants.

Three universities and three colleges were selected in each of the four zones in a manner that the selected institutions represented different levels of development.

8.03 A sub-committee was also appointed to suggest schemes that may be taken up for an indepth study, keeping in view the financial inputs and the importance of the scheme. The sub-committee suggested a detailed study of the following schemes: (a) centres of advanced study/departments of special assistance, (b) college science improvement programme/college humanities and social sciences improvement programme, (c) financial assistance to teachers for research, and (d) scholarships and fellowships.*

Objectives and Functions of the Commission

8.04 In view of the ground covered by the UGC Review Committee appointed by the Government of India, it was not considered necessary by the present committee to go into the structure of the UGC. Nevertheless, the Committee has dealt with the objectives and functions of the UGC in order that its report and recommendations are understood in a broad perspective.

8.05 The significance of the establishment of the UGC as an autonomous and statutory body (since 1956) lies in the fact that it interacts closely with a large number of scholars and scientists in the universities and colleges and formulates its programmes and policies keeping in view the national priorities as well as the need for the maintenance and coordination of standards.

8.06 The Jha Review Committee has already reviewed critically the functioning of the Commission during the period August, 1956 to March, 1975. Developments in the Commission since April, 1975 have been reviewed by the present committee (Paras 1.26 to 1.31).

8.07 The Committee particularly endorses the formulations in (i) *Policy Frame for the development of Higher Education in India* over the next 10-15 years and (ii) *Approach to Development* during the sixth plan period, with particular reference to the development of universities and colleges as detailed in Paras 1.33 and 1.34.

8.08 The programmes implemented by the Commission during the period may be put under the following broad heads: (a) develop-

2. * The scheme of scholarships and fellowships is being reviewed separately by the Commission.

ment of universities (b) development of colleges (c) faculty improvement programmes (d) support for research work (e) student welfare programmes, and (f) academic and cultural programmes. The objectives of these programmes and the Commission's *modus operandi* in this regard are discussed in Paras 2.02 to 2.25 of the report.

Review of Commission's Programmes and Schemes — Additional Staff Positions

8.09 These are sanctioned by the Commission on the recommendations of the plan and other visiting committees with a view to enabling the university departments to introduced new courses or areas of specialisation or to enable them to become fully viable. Evidence shows that utilisation of additional staff positions approved by the Commission has not been adequate. The main difficulty in filling the posts is that some of the state governments are hesitant to commit themselves to undertake concurrent or subsequent responsibility for funding. Selection procedures in some universities are also cumbersome.

8.10 It is of the utmost importance that remedial steps are taken to ensure that plan positions approved by the UGC are filled as expeditiously as possible. In order to ensure that non-plan posts are not kept vacant by the universities and the plan posts are utilised for the purpose for which these are created. The universities should be asked to supply annual statements regarding teachers in position, including information regarding the number of non-plan posts lying vacant, the duration for which these posts remained vacant and justification for the same. The gaps in each case should be identified and the matter discussed with the state government/university concerned. The sanction of additional staff positions should invariably be linked with the utilisation of plan and non-plan posts already available to the university concerned.

8.11 In order to attract teachers of a high calibre and to retain their services, it may be necessary to make adequate provision for faculty housing. Attention will also have to be paid to provision of quarters for essential administrative staff. While in the sixth plan, the Commission may continue to give priority to academic building, in universities where the provision for academic buildings has reached a reasonable level, assistance may be provided for faculty housing and quarters for essential (administrative) staff. This is an important activity and as such the Central and State Governments should be approached to grant low-interest loans for the purpose either through the UGC or the state governments, as the UGC may not be able to find sufficient resources for the purpose.

Buildings

8.12 Buildings form an integral part of development as effective utilisation of grants for additional staff, equipment, books and journals cannot be ensured unless these are linked with the minimum building requirements. Buildings are also necessary in order to ensure the mobility of students and teachers. It may also be noted that, generally speaking, the infrastructure provided by a state at the time of establishment of a new university is rather inadequate.

8.13 The utilisation of grants placed at the disposal of universities for the construction of buildings went down from 83.2 per cent in the fourth plan to 52.4 per cent during the period 1974-75 to 1978-79. It would, therefore, be necessary to (a) further simplify the procedures regarding certification of rates and estimates, (b) coordinate building requirements on a faculty basis rather than a departmental basis, (c) link further grants for construction with the optimum utilisation of existing buildings, and, (d) consider how far the needs in priority areas like faculty housing can be met through low-interest loans by the Central and State Governments.

Books and Journals

8.14 The present level of expenditure on books and journals is far below the norms suggested by the Education Commission. The main problem concerning library resources is that the additional inputs provided by the Commission are not supplemented by other sources.

8.15 It would be desirable for the Commission to suggest to the states to treat expenditure on additional journals subscribed to during a plan period and text books or book prescribed as necessary reading as part of maintenance during the next plan period.

8.16 Steps should also be taken to avoid unnecessary duplication in the acquisition of books and costly journals and particularly foreign journals.

8.17 The Commission may also consider the need for making specific provision for support towards the appointment of technical staff in the university libraries.

8.18 More working hours and working days, easy accessibility to books, designing of library as a centre of community education and cultural activities, multiple copies of text-books which may be loaned to needy students, a better display of new reading material, organisation of book-clubs, exhibitions, paintings, tape-records of classical music, separate rooms for periodicals, reference books and research works, are some of the measures that should be taken in order to raise the standard of library service and utilisation of available resources.

Equipment

8.19 It is a matter of serious concern that even costly and sophisticated equipment are lying idle in some universities. There is a need for some central agency to oversee that equipment are serviced properly and remain functional over a long period of time.

8.20 The Commission should give high priority in the sixth plan to the provision of support for the appointment and training of laboratory technicians. State Governments, which have primary responsibility in this regard should also pay adequate attention to these aspects which are vital for the proper functioning of laboratories.

8.21 A lump sum grant should also be placed at the disposal of each university for (a) maintenance of equipment, and (b) training programme for technicians. In non-plan also adequate provision should be made for repair and maintenance of equipment.

University Service and Instrumentation Centres (USICs)

8.22 The Commission has so far approved proposals of 50 universities for setting up university service and instrumentation centres with the objective of assisting universities to maintain and repair equipment and also in pool together sophisticated equipment. Two regional instrumentation centres have also been established, one at the Bombay University and the other at the Indian Institute of Science, Bangalore.

8.23 User committees with representatives from all other user departments should be constituted by the universities concerned in order that the common facility and equipment pooled in USICs are utilised to the maximum advantage.

Computer Development

8.24 The Commission has so far accepted 28 proposals recommended by the Computer Development Committee for the installation of computers in the universities. While it is too early to assess the impact of Commission's assistance for this purpose, it is suggested that guidelines should be formulated for the initial choice of the computer system, space requirements and ancillary services, off-line equipment facilities for users from other institutions, provision of staff, computer library needs and security and insurance of the computer centre and consultancy work by the technical staff.

8.25 The university should also assume responsibility for meeting the current demand for properly trained personnel for various computer centres at different levels.

8.26 It is also necessary to develop staffing patterns so that adequately qualified technical staff in the computer centres receives due recognition and status.

8.27 Suitable methods should be devised to monitor performance of the computer centres as also the grants provided for purchase of computer time by those universities which do not have in-house computers or those which have computers, but require access to large computers in the neighbourhood for scientific research.

Seminars, Summer Institutes and Workshops

8.28 The Commission has been giving high priority to faculty improvement programmes and consequently the number of seminars, summer institutes and workshops has gone up considerably during the period under review.

8.29 It is suggested that summer institutes, seminars, etc., should be organised after adequate preparation is made and well-documented papers become available. The programme may also be linked with restructuring of courses, curricular reform and other innovations.

8.30 There should also be a time-bound programme for college teachers so that all the teachers in a college are covered under this programme over a period of time.

Teacher Fellowships

8.31 The Commission has been implementing the teacher fellowship scheme since 1975-76. So far more than 5,000 fellowships have been awarded of whom 3,000 teachers are in position. The Commission has recently decentralised the implementation of the scheme.

8.32 The scheme has made good impact and during the short period of its existence it has succeeded in generating a climate of research even in colleges in remote and backward areas. It is, therefore, recommended that efforts be made to meet the growing demand by increasing the number of identified departments so that teachers from all parts of the country can take advantage of the scheme in a big way.

Scholarships and Fellowships

8.33 Scholarships and fellowships are awarded to enable academically bright students to carry their research as an independent and full-time activity.

8.34 The scheme has been taken up for an indepth study. In the meanwhile it is suggested that there should be (a) better correspondence between the total number of research fellowships and facilities for supervision, care being taken that no research supervisor should ordinarily have more than five research scholars working under his guidance, (b) some provision for typing and binding of these out of unassigned grants in respect of research scholars not getting any scholarship or fellowship, (c) reduction in the time lag between the submission of theses and the declaration of results through better monitoring, and (d) fixation of a ceiling on the number of research scholars by each department on the basis of well-defined criteria.

Publication Programme

8.35 The Commission has laid down comprehensive guidelines for the publication of learned research works and doctoral theses. It has also agreed to provide assistance for the publication of quality journals identified by the subject panels concerned.

8.36 It seems that the objectives of this scheme have not been achieved fully and a number of learned works remain unpublished although adequate funds have been placed at the disposal of the universities. It would, therefore, be desirable for the Commission to allocate grants, keeping in view the extent of utilisation by the different universities.

Student Welfare Programmes

8.37 It is our understanding that the various student welfare programmes, viz., students aid fund, non-resident student centre, student home and book banks have not made a uniform impact in all the universities and colleges and there are certain gaps in implementation. However, there is an obvious need to continue these programmes as they are meant to help the needy and poor students.

Correspondence Courses

8.38 Twenty-one universities and one institution deemed to be university are presently offering correspondence courses for B.A., B.Com. and M.A. level courses. The total enrolment is 1,15,000.

8.39 The reports of the review committees on schools of correspondence courses indicate problems regarding the quality of lessons, evaluation of response sheets and conduct of contact programme. It is suggested that these problems may be examined in depth by the UGC Standing Committee on Part-Time and Own-Time Education.

Examination Reforms

8.40 The Commission has been emphasising the implementation of various measures of examination reforms, viz., continuous seasonal evaluation, development of question banks, introduction of grade system and semesterization with a view to improving the reliability, validity and objectivity of examinations and bringing about a closer integration of teaching, learning and evaluation.

8.41 High priority should continue to be given to the programme. It is also suggested that the UGC Implementation Committee on examination reforms may go into the reasons for the setback during the last two years and indicate steps that may be taken to accelerate the programme. It would also be useful to call a series of regional or state meetings of vice-chancellors, teachers and students of universities that have gone back on some of the reforms so that remedial steps may be taken in the light of their experience.

Adult Education and Extension Programmes

8.42 While noting that the scheme of adult education and extension is being implemented by the Commission in accordance with the guidelines formulated by a working group and the Commission has already given high priority to this programme, no comments have been offered by the committee as the scheme is under review by the Government of India.

Cultural Exchange Programme

8.43 The Commission's emphasis in implementing the cultural exchange programme has shifted to development of bilateral academic links in identified fields instead of general exchange of visit by academics from both sides. This shift in emphasis and approach is commended.

Area Studies

8.44 In view of the well-defined objectives and positive impact of the programme of area studies, it is hoped that in years to come the Commission would make the programme broad-based and extend its scope to cover other important areas as well.

Unassigned Grants

8.45 Unassigned grants are allocated to the universities every year for meeting the expenditure on (a) travel grants to teachers and scientific technical staff for participation in international conferences, (b) travel grants to teachers, research scholars and technicians for visiting centres of research or to participate in academic conferences within the country, and (c) for exchange of teachers.

8.46 It is suggested that states should also assume some responsibility in regard to the items for which unassigned grants are provided by the Commission. The Commission should also fix unassigned grants to the universities in the same manner as the ceiling for a plan period, i.e., for the entire plan period instead of being made every year.

Impact of UGC Programmes on Universities and Colleges

8.47 Although it is not easy to define standards or to measure them with the help of objective tools, the committee has with the help of certain parameters made an attempt to assess the impact of UGC programmes on universities and colleges with particular reference to the impact of developmental assistance provided by the Commission during a ten-year period: 1969-70 to 1978-79.

8.48 The picture that emerges from the assessment made by the committee is one of light and shade; of achievements as well as failures. The general impression is that the best students are as good as ever, if not better and that the contents of courses are generally of a high level. It is also a fact that outstanding work is being done by some of the university departments and a number of teachers have been receiving recognition from well-known centres of learning. The out-turn of Ph.Ds has gone up significantly and so has research output by way of publications. It is equally noteworthy that various schemes of national development have been implemented by personnel trained in our universities. On the other hand, instruction in some universities has not kept pace with modern developments. There is a resistance to change and innovations on the part of teachers and an atmosphere of growing violence and intimation on the part of students, teachers and in some cases even employees. There is also a lack of trust between the students and teachers. It is not surprising that under the present conditions, the potentialities of the students are not fully utilised and developed by our universities and colleges. The prevailing situation is also considered unsatisfactory from the point of view of the growing expectations, the demand on the system being far greater as compared to the inputs and availability of resources.

8.49 In so far as performance in terms of the parameters evolved by the committee is concerned, one of the sub-committees, viz., the Western Zone sub-committee has attempted quantification of targets in relation to the impact of UGC development programmes. The sub-committee has come to the conclusion that the overall performance is around 60 per cent of the expected target. This is essentially a subjective valuation and other sub-committees have not made a similar exercise. However, it would be fair enough to state that the position regarding the maintenance of standards and overall performance is uneven and, broadly speaking, less progress has been made by the state universities in the Eastern and Northern Zones, as compared to those in the Western and Southern Zones. This would require an indepth study.

8.50 The analysis of the percentage utilisation of developmental assistance by the 12 selected universities on books, equipment and buildings and percentage of staff positions filled during the fourth plan and 1974-75 to 1978-79 (Annexure XXI-A) does not suggest that there is any perceptible distinction between the developed and developing universities in their capacity to absorb the developmental support provided by the Commission during the period under reference. It, however, does indicate that a part of the university system suffers from a certain degree of disability in absorbing the inputs provided to it.

8.51 There is an obvious need to rationalise the methods for providing developmental support to the universities. Data similar to those collected from selected universities for study in our report should form an integral part of the development proposals of the universities. This data should be analysed and specific issues identified for close examination by visiting committees. Specific guidelines in the form of a checklist should also be formulated for the guidance of the visiting committees. The universities should be asked to furnish a detailed note on their present status in terms of physical facilities, their utilisation, and additional requirements in terms of precise objectives and critical needs. Universities should also prepare a flow chart of year-wise utilisation of facilities approved by the Commission during a plan period in order that the programmes may be mentioned and evaluated regularly.

8.52 If all the universities are grouped together, it is seen that the best performance has been achieved by the oldest of the universities which is located in a centre with a tradition of learning, and the poorest by a university in a comparatively backward part of an under-developed state. Performance is also better in universities which provide for participation by teachers and students in the process of academic decision-making at all levels. It is also observed that universities which have been relatively free from student agitations and politicalisation of teachers have performed better than those which had polarisation in one form or another. Similarly, universities with an effective planning machinery and mechanism for joint consultations have also been able to bring about necessary changes in their courses, syllabi, methods of examinations, etc., and thus maintain standards at a reasonably good level.

8.53 A comparison of the total expenditure during the period 1969-70 to 1973-74 and 1974-75 to 1978-79 show that the expenditure in equipment increased by 2.2 times and the expenditure on books and journals by 2.5 times. However, there was a decline in the expenditure on staff, buildings, and infrastructural facilities. The reasons for this are given in the report. The analysis of expenditure over the ten-year period shows that the order of priority has substantially changed in favour of equipment, books and journals during the year 1974-75 to

1978-79 as compared to the period 1969-70 to 1973-74 as part of the development strategy proposed by the planning group in the beginning of the fifth plan period.

8.54 The Commission's policy in regard to the development of colleges is governed mainly by the twin objectives of removal of disparities and regional imbalances and the improvement of standards. This is sought to be achieved by a system of liberalised grant-in-aid for colleges located in rural or backward areas on the one hand and selecting colleges noted for their high standards as essential growth points, on the other. It is not easy to reach these challenging goals and the task becomes more difficult when account is taken of the limited resources available for the development of colleges.

8.55 While the support provided by the state governments towards the development of colleges is well-acknowledged, it is a matter of regret that some of the state governments do not accept the development of colleges as their primary responsibility. But for UGC assistance no worthwhile development would have taken place in the college sector in these regions in the last two decades or so. If the Commission has provided support to the colleges (even though marginal), inspite of its funds being severely limited, it is because it has rightly taken the stand that it is not possible to delink the development needs of post-graduate and under-graduate education.

8.56 It is not easy to measure the impact of UGC grants on the college system, partly because in so far as the colleges are concerned, UGC is one of the partners and that too with a very limited share, and partly because the colleges (except those which have been granted autonomous status) do not have the necessary degree of freedom and flexibility to restructure their courses or to bring about improvements in methods of teaching, evaluation, etc. Nevertheless, some positive achievements have been accomplished by the colleges visited by the sub-committees (Annexure XXVI).

8.57 The Committee has made the following suggestions for the development of colleges keeping in view the likely allocation of resources for the purpose during the current plan period: (a) The system of matching contribution may be reviewed and the share of the state government increased keeping in view the existing division of resources between the centre and the states; (b) The Commission may concentrate its efforts and available resources on the development of about 750 well-established colleges on the one hand and about 250 colleges in rural or backward or tribal areas on the other; (c) Bearing in mind the infrastructural facilities already created and the existence of a large number of colleges with inadequate enrolments and the decline in the rate of growth of enrolment during the past few years, *there should be a moratorium on the establishment of colleges during the current plan period:* (d) The UGC should make a detailed study of the terms and conditions for the affiliation of colleges and formulate suitable guidelines for implementation by universities and state governments on a uniform basis; (e) The Commission may examine the feasibility of linking its developmental assistance to the colleges with the results of districtwise surveys regarding the need for expansion at different levels, specially in relation to the development of postgraduate studies in the colleges.

Centres of Advanced Study/Departments of Special Assistance

8.58 The scheme of recognising certain departments as centres of advanced study was initiated by the Commission in 1963-64 with the object of strengthening postgraduate teaching and research and channelling available resources effectively for the purpose. The scheme is intended to encourage the pursuit of 'excellence' and team work in study and research and to accelerate the realisation of 'international standards' in specific fields. With this end in view, the Commission decided to give active support and substantial assistance to promising departments in the universities so that efforts and resources are concentrated on certain growth points instead of being scattered thinly over a wide area.

8.59 The scheme of providing special assistance to a limited number of selected departments (DSA) was initiated in 1972-73 with the object of enabling these departments to develop their existing potentialities and become active centres of teaching and research in selected areas and also attain the level of centres of advanced study in course of time.

8.60 Twenty-three centres of advanced study (14 in science and 9 in the humanities and social sciences) and 53 departments of special assistance (33 in science and 20 in the humanities and social sciences) are functioning at present.

8.61 The scheme has made the maximum impact and its importance has been recognised not only in India but also by several foreign scientists and scholars and international organisations like the UNESCO. Grants to the centres for improving their library facilities and laboratories and for academic and non-academic staff have enabled the centres to make important contribution to the advancement of knowledge and influence to a large extent the standards of research and teaching at the postgraduate and undergraduate level in other universities. The additional teaching staff has helped the centres to strengthen their teaching and research activities and to initiate new programmes of training and research. Scholarships and fellowships have encouraged students and teachers from other universities to receive advanced training and research in the centres. The provision of funds for visiting fellows has been utilised by the centres to invite scientists and scholars of repute from India and abroad. A number of publications have resulted from the research activities, seminars and symposia, etc., organised by the centres.

8.62 While expressing general agreement with the basic philosophy of the scheme of centres of advanced study/departments of special assistance (which is to concentrate the available resources and expertise on building peaks of excellence on a selective basis) the committee has suggested a careful analysis of the problems that have stood in the way of realisation of these objectives.

8.63 It is sometimes felt that owing to difficulties at the university level or at the level of leadership in the centre/department concerned, some centres have not been functioning as national centres. This is reflected in the recruitment of teachers and in the selection of students from generally within the region. The UGC has already made a provision that at least 50 per cent of the fellowships available to a centre should be awarded to candidates outside the university. It is hoped that this would bring about greater mobility. In so far as the teaching staff is concerned, it is suggested that the UGC should, through the Standing Committee on Centres of Advanced Study, lay down the necessary guidelines in the matter. The Commission should also provide adequate support to the centres/departments to enable them to have interaction with each other on discipline to discipline basis either at the national or regional level.

8.64 It would be useful if the head of the CAS and DSA programmes is identified. This has become essential in view of the new development of rotating headship of departments in many universities. It is also necessary that the programme is assigned to an active and viable group in one or more specified fields of specialisation. This would ensure that the programme does not receive a setback in case the head of the centre goes away from the university. The head of CAS/DSA may be designated as 'Programme Coordination' or just 'Coordinator'. It would be appropriate for the university to have prior consultation with the Commission in case it becomes necessary to change the coordinator of the programme.

8.65 It must be ensured that a department being considered under DSA has an active group of research workers and teachers who could continue the approved programme even if the coordinator retires or leaves the university. In this connection advantage could be taken of the departmental profiles being prepared by various subject panels. While considering a department for recognition as DSA, the export committee should also examine whether the department has any active programme of collaboration with allied departments in an outside the country and if so, in which field and with what results.

8.66 While identifying a department for recognition as DSA, thrust areas may be clearly indicated and proper balance kept between various regions and disciplines, as well as, between humanities and social sciences on the one hand and science subjects on the other.

8.67 The work of a centre of advanced study or department of special assistance should be evaluated carefully and thoroughly after every five years with a view to ascertaining whether the objectives are being met and if so, to what extent. This should be done objectively by visiting committees of specialists in the subject fields taking into consideration the various factors mentioned in Para 4.31 of the report.

8.68 Seven centres were taken out from the scheme of centres of advanced study with effect from the 1st of April, 1974 as the performance of these centres was not found to be of the highest standard to deserve continuing support from the Commission. This was a step in the right direction and an instance in which the Commission took a bold stands for the maintenance of standards and the realisation of objectives. It is, however, suggested that in future the basis for deleting a centre or a department from the scheme should be suitably defined so that the Commission can take a decision in the matter in as authentic a manner as possible.

8.69 The role of the advisory committees as envisaged for each centre/department needs to be clearly formulated. The work of these committees also needs to be activised. They should meet regularly to evaluate the work being done at the centres and tender advice for improving the functioning of various programmes at the centres.

8.70 For the programmes of CAS, DSA and departmental support, there is an upper limit of Rs. 20, 15 and 10 lakhs respectively by way of assistance from the Commission. It is suggested that the limits in monetary terms should be kept flexible enough, keeping in view the nature of the programme and the assessment of likely needs and requirements.

8.71 The period of UGC assistance for these quality programmes should also be kept flexible. There need not be any rigidity regarding assistance to a department/centre for a maximum period of 15 years. It would be more appropriate if, instead of this upper limit, optimum level of assistance specially in terms of staff to a particular department/centre is determined up to which it may be assisted depending upon its performance and programmes. It would be difficult to lay down any common optimum level for all the disciplines/specialisations. This will have to be determined by the expert groups keeping in view the needs of the area/specialisation in which the centre/department has been recognised.

8.72 In the UGC Act, provision has been made to enable the UGC to fund certain programmes even in state universities on a recurring basis under non-plan projects. The Commission may explore the possibility of including the recurring expenditure of the CAS/DSA as part of the non-plan expenditure by approaching the Government of India for allocation of funds for the purpose.

College Science Improvement Programme (COSIP) College Humanities and Social Sciences Improvement Programme (COHSSIP)

8.73 The college science improvement programme was initiated by the Commission in 1970-71 in order to bring about qualitative improvements in the teaching of science at the undergraduate level. The purpose of the programme is to accelerate the development of the science capabilities of undergraduate students and to initiate a process of continuous self-renewal. This is brought about through an integrated approach and simultaneous improvements in the subject-matter, methods of instruction, syllabi, curricula, laboratory exercises, workshop, library and teaching material.

8.74 Encouraged by the success of COSIP, the Commission in 1974-75, decided to extend the programme to the humanities and social sciences. The college humanities and social science improvement programme (COHSSIP) aims at bringing about improvements in the teaching of humanities and social sciences at the undergraduate level with particular reference to (a) adoption of new teaching methods, e.g preparation of synopsis, use of audio-visual and other teaching aids, tutorials and seminars, etc., (b) extension of library services, (c) introduction of special courses, (d) inter-disciplinary programmes, (e) adoption of various measures of examination reforms, (f) remedial teaching and (g) field/project work, etc.

8.75 The college science improvement programme and the college humanities and social sciences improvement programme were taken up at two levels (a) in selected colleges to include the entire faculty, and (b) in one subject in all the colleges affiliated to a university (university leadership project).

8.76 Presently 177 colleges and 40 departments are being assisted under COSIP and 126 colleges and 15 departments under COHSSIP.

8.77 The committee has tried to assess the impact of the programme on the basis of the reports of the sub-committees that visited ULP departments and COSIP/COHSSIP colleges as also the report of the Western Region Committee which visited a few colleges in Bombay, Poona and other places to assess the first phase of the programme, as also their own knowledge and experience.

8.78 The general impression of the committees that visited universities and discussed the impact of the programmes with the vice-chancellors is that these have made a meaningful and important contribution to the improvement of standards of undergraduate teaching. Accordingly, it has been suggested that COSIP and COHSSIP should be continued and further strengthened in the current plan period, taking into account the suggestions for improvement made in the following paragraphs.

8.79 There should be the fullest coordination between COSIP and COHSSIP activities within each college. It is necessary that in the UGC Office itself adequate steps are taken to coordinate the COSIP and COHSSIP by drawing upon the programmes of one for improving the other and maintaining an integrated view of a college having both COSIP and COHSSIP.

8.80 Proper feedback and interaction among different colleges is important not only for sharing a experience but also for ensuring that changes in curriculum, methods of teaching, evaluation, etc., are introduced simultaneously in all the colleges affiliated to a university for ensuring a spread effect. The state level advisory committees should play an important role in establishing an effective network of communication, which is vital for the success of the programme.

8.81 Steps should be taken to encourage the participation of teachers in COSIP and COHSSIP activities on a much wider scale to remove the present indifference on the part of a large number of college teachers towards COSIP and COHSSIP.

8.82 The interaction between the colleges and ULPs is not as wide as envisaged under the scheme nor is there enough consultation with the colleges by some of the university departments regarding planning the programmes and activities. The UGC should organise regular meetings between ULP departments and COSIP/COHSSIP colleges on a regional basis in order to work out the details of the programmes to be implemented and steps necessary to achieve better coordination between the ULP departments and the colleges.

8.83 It would be useful for ULP departments to take initiative in imparting training to laboratory technicians in the colleges in order that the proper upkeep of equipment, instruments and audio-visual aids is ensured.

8.84 It would be useful to involve the state governments in COSIP/COHSSIP from the very inception, i.e., when a department or college is included in the programme.

8.85 The teaching aids developed under COSIP/COHSSIP and the equipment designed and fabricated by ULPs should be made available to all colleges including even those colleges which are not presently participating under COSIP and COHSSIP.

8.86 The UGC office should carry out a more thorough analysis and evaluation of the reports received from COSIP/COHSSIP colleges and ULP departments, to provide guidance to them and to serve as an effective clearing house of information.

Financial Assistance to Teachers for Research Work

8.87 The scheme of financial assistance to university/college teachers for undertaking short-term/minor research projects in humanities, social sciences and science subjects was initiated by the Commission in 1963-64 with a view to enabling individual teachers and more specifically college lecturers and young lecturers in the universities to engage themselves in research work. The scheme is also intended to provide facilities which would help teachers in launching a research project and provide minimal support by way of books, equipment, field work, etc., to those members of the teaching community in the universities and colleges who have an aptitude or research but do not have the resources to pursue it. Thus the main objective of the scheme is to promote a climate of research in the universities and colleges and thereby strengthen teaching as well.

8.88 It is seen from the annual reports received from teachers participating in this scheme and the resulting publications that the objectives of the scheme have been adequately realised. The average expenditure per teacher under the scheme during the last three years comes to Rs. 4,069 in science and Rs. 2,737 in the humanities and social sciences, which shows that the scheme has been operating at the minimum cost. The scheme should be continued and strengthened in the light of the following suggestions.

8.89 Some guidance should be available to junior teachers from established research workers in their subject; along with opportunities to visit other institutions, laboratories and libraries for short periods by using the contingent grant in the project. Support should also be provided through regional centres with specialised facilities of library and sophisticated equipment, and there should be an inbuilt device for monitoring and evaluation through proper infrastructure at the central level.

8.90 The UGC should bring out a directory of research facilities available in the country giving information about services, specialised equipment, source materials, etc., so that the teachers can use such information in their research work.

8.91 A catalogue of current periodicals and journals subscribed to by different libraries should be prepared on a zonal basis.

9.92 The various schemes envisaged by the UGC such as computer centres, regional instrumentation centres, zonal libraries with facilities for reprography and xerox could be made more functional with the help of user committees which should have fairly wide representation.

8.93 There should be better cooperation between the national laboratories and the universities in the use of equipment, library and research facilities for the promotion of research activities and exchange of knowledge and experience. This matter should be pursued at the highest level.

8.94 Specific provision should be made in the scheme for travel and field work to enable the awardees to seek guidance from eminent scholars and scientists in their fields and to visit other institutions, laboratories, libraries, museums, archives, etc., for short periods during the tenure of the award. The application form may also be revised accordingly.

8.95 The possibility of bringing together awardees in a subject during summer or long holidays may be explored to facilitate exchange of views and discussions on the results of their study and investigation and guidance from subject experts and resource persons.

8.96 The committees which initially select the projects should be asked to evaluate the final reports at the end so that a comparative evaluation of the results achieved is available.

General Observations and Recommendations

8.97 Attempts will have to be made, on the basis of the highest priority, to improve the standards of teaching, research and examinations, which is a statutory responsibility of the Commission. However, the various measures for improving standards will need considerable investment in men, materials and money. But more importantly, they need motivation on the part of students and involvement on the part of teachers.

8.98 The improvement of curricula and restructuring of courses should also receive high priority during the current plan period. The Commission has already initiated steps in this regard through the reports of regional workshops, subject panels and expert committees but there has been some tardiness in giving effects to the various recommendations. Revision and updating of courses.

8.94 The principle of flexibility is also important in order to enable students to break away from the traditional combinations of subjects and to offer new combinations, thus bringing a new approach to study and learning. This is possible if courses are divided into smaller units, care being taken to ensure that only those course units are taught for which there is a sufficient demand. The courses should also be diversified, especially to include newly emergent and interdisciplinary areas and borderline subjects.

8.100 It is also suggested that the courses at the first degree level be made more relevant to the rural or urban environment and to the development needs of the community.

8.101 There is an imperative need to look at the structure, management and staffing pattern in the universities.

8.102 Efforts should be made to bring about a substantial amount of decentralisation as well as diversification of educational programmes, so that individual universities, their departments and the colleges may experiment with new ideas rather than follow a stereotyped pattern.

8.103 The above implies considerable autonomy and academic freedom to be given to the constituent departments of a university. Vigorous efforts have also to be made to grant autonomous status to as many colleges as possible during the current plan period to enable them to restructure their courses and to try out new methods of teaching and evaluation.

8.104 Facilities should be provided for the expansion of higher education through non-formal method such as correspondence courses, evening colleges, and private appearance at university examinations, but in the regular full-time courses universities and colleges should resist the pressures that are exercised from time to time. Steps should be taken for the maintenance of high standards in correspondence courses and to make such courses as challenging as possible. It should also be ensured that the unplanned proliferation of institutions which has been going on the consolidation and strengthening of facilities in the existing institutions.

8.105 There seems to be a lack of planning consciousness as well as adequate machinery at the university level with a few notable exceptions. The universities need a new vision of perspective planning spread over 15 to 20 years with well-defined goals and objectives. The planning process should also have the fullest participation of teachers, students, administrators and citizens of the area.

8.106 At the university level, there is often a lack of inter-departmental cooperation and inter-disciplinary programmes. There is some evidence of common discussion on the development schemes of the UGC amongst the staff in a department, departmental heads and university authorities but not to the extent of this being a regular feature or a continuing activity. The university system has also not become fully responsive to the needs of the community around it. There is also a need to strengthen the process of monitoring, review and evaluation within the university system itself.

8.107 There should be a strong planning machinery at the state level supported by investigations into the needs of higher education in the region in order to bring about coordinated development of universities, colleges, etc., and to help the policy regarding the establishment of new institutions or the starting of new courses and the development of areas of specialisation.

8.108 Similarly, there should be a strong planning machinery in the colleges. It has been reported that in formulating proposals for development, the members of the faculty in the colleges are not consulted. It is of the utmost importance that students, teachers and the college authorities become fully involved in the processes of planning within each college. The colleges should also formulated plans of development keeping in view the objectives of academic excellence and social relevance.

8.109 The very size and complexity of the system of higher education in India indicates that improvements can be brought about only with the active collaboration of the universities and the state governments concerned. Such a collaborative effort is crucial for the implementation of various developmental activities and maintenance of standards. It is suggested that each state government may set up a coordination committee consisting of vice-chancellors of all the universities in the state and one or two representatives of colleges and a representative of the UGC.

Plan Visiting Committees

8.110 The suggestions of the committee for streamlining the procedures of sending plan visiting committees to the universities are given in para 7.18 of the report. It has been suggested, *inter alia,* that the financial ceiling for a university should also be indicated with some suggested limit for (i) humanities and social sciences, (ii) science subjects, and (iii) general development.

Distribution of Grants

8.111 A major weakness in the implementation of the programmes is the somewhat uneven pattern of distribution of grants between the central and state universities on the one hand and universities and colleges on the other. The historical developments which have brought about this imbalance are given in Para 7.20 of this report.

8.112 The scope of maintenance grants needs to be redefined so that instead of bringing about disparities, they help in maintaining proper regional balance.

8.113 Bringing more items within the ambit of non-plan, particularly those which ensure high standards of teaching and research, would help to reduce the existing disparities between central and state universities and also help central agencies to bring about a better coordination between plan and non-plan expenditure. There is also an urgent need to look at plan and non-plan expenditure in the universities, in the central as well as state sector, in an integrated manner.

Periodical Review

8.114 It was for the first time that a comprehensive review had been attempted by the UGC through the present Review Committee. It is but proper that such a review is carried out periodically, say after every five years.

8.115 More time should be spent in each institution taken up for review at a future date to enable the committees to make real indepth students. A common form should also be evolved for submission of reports.

Peripheral Schemes

8.116 Although the committee has come to the conclusion that in the ongoing programmes of the Commission, there are no peripheral schemes as such, it has suggested regrouping or re-orientation of some of the existing schemes for proper administration and closer attention.

8.117 In view of the fact that the over the years, greater emphasis has been laid on contribution to research, under the scheme of retired teachers, it is suggested that the scheme be discontinued in its present form. The proposals may be considered under the scheme of support for research or book-writing or for undertaking educational innovations. However, in view of the value of contact with students, retired teachers selected under any of the above schemes should be required to devote some time to teaching. The modalities of the proposed scheme may be worked out by a committee.

8.118 The Commission has been awarding twenty scholarships for postgraduate studies in Sanskrit/Pali/Prakriti/Ardhmagadhi and twenty scholarships in Arabic/Persian of the value of Rs. 250 per month. It is suggested that these scholarships be transferred to the Ministry of Education and Culture in order that the Ministry may implement the scheme as part of its overall programme for the promotion of these languages.

8.119 The Commission has been providing assistance for improvement-development of play fields in order to encourage participation in games and sports of as large a number of students as possible. Without detracting from the value of the scheme, it is suggested that this may be kept in abeyance until a clear picture emerges regarding the availability of funds during the current plan period.

8.120 It would be desirable to lay down comprehensive guidelines for the schemes of (a) planning forums, and (b) national integration samitis. A suggestion that may be kept in view while formulating the guidelines is that the level of assistance should be raised to make the programmes meaningful. Assistance should also be linked with detailed and comprehensive programmes and plans formulated by the universities and colleges.

Annexure XX-A

Percentage Utilisation of Development Assistance on Books, Equipment and Building and Percentage of Staff Positions Filled During Fourth Plan and 1974-75 to 1978-79 (University Position)

Sl. No.	Name of the University	Books		Equipment		Buildings		Staff		Average	
		IV Plan	1974-75 to 1978-79	IV Plan	1974-75 to 1978-79	IV Plan	1974-75 to 1978-79	IV Plan	1974-75 to 1978-79	IV Plan	1974-75 to 1978-79
1	2	3	4	5	6	7	8	9	10	11	12
1.	Sardar Patel	57	100	68	88	68	69	100	94	73	95
2.	Poona	87	100	97	100	89	16	93	81	91	74
3.	Jabalpur	100	100	99	83	100	100	78	41	94	81
4.	Calicut	100	100	100	91	100	100	100	69	100	90
5.	Sri Venkateswara	100	99	100	97	100	100	75	95	94	98
6.	Madras	91	76	83	81	100	100	77	89	88	86
7.	Panjab	99	97	100	84	92	34	74	69	91	71
8.	Gorakhpur	100	69	85	47	94	35	95	53	93	51
9.	Delhi	100	87	88	46	90	47	98	81	94	65
10.	Gauhati	45	62	38	63	34	48	95	32	53	51
11.	Calcutta	98	96	99	64	77	47	88	60	90	67
12.	Ranchi	96	100	81	100	100	52	100	56	94	77
	*Average	90	89	87	76	83	52	90	69		

* The average has been calculated on the basis of the actual figures of utilisation and not the percentages indicated above.

Annexure XXVI

Evaluation of Colleges Visited by the Sub-committees

Western Zone

Sophia College, Bombay, has taken up several projects for improvement of curriculum, integration of science department, study of environment and building up of social awareness. The Internal assessment system has existed in the colleges for about eight years. The colleges has also tried out unsupervised examinations, annual evaluation of teachers by students and self-evalution by the teaching staff. The polytechnic on the campus of the college officers various diploma and certificate courses. This has helped the University of Bombay to introduce new subjects with applied components as part of the restructing of undergraduate education. The new courses are of a job-oriented nature such as secretarial practice, Business communication, communication skills, etc. There is also a school on the campus for the mentally retarded and a nursery teacher training programme which give the students of the psychology department contact with child psychology and abnormal psychology in real life situations. The college also collaborates with a number of institutions at both the undergraduate and postgraduate levels. The Kasturba Gram Rural Institute, Indore, has taken up extension work, community development, investigations into the health and other problems of the local village. The Government College, Ajmer, has courses in English, Sanskrit and Mathematics. At least two to three teachers in each discipline are doing research without financial support from any agency. About a dozen faculty members have been selected for the award of teacher fellowships. Students and teachers participate actively in such programmes as youth against famine and flood, hospital services and agricultural extension projects.

Southern Zone

American College, Madurai, has introduced projects by students in their fields of specialisation as cocurricular work. Courses and curricula have been designed in keeping with the objectives of the college for achieving an autonomous status. Besides the regular courses under each major, time is set apart for inter-disciplinary, need-based and job-oriented courses, promotion of ethical and moral values and a compulsory course in science for the humanities and social science students and *vice-versa.* Chemistry has a course in Industrial Chemistry taught entirely by persons drawn from a few local industries. Physics has courses in practical electronics and photography. Botany has a course in economic botany. Tamil and English have introduced courses in Tourism and Journalism. The Department of Applied Science, a non-teaching department of this College is engaged in servicing the equipments of the Agricultural University and of the soil Testing Laboratories in the state. The college supported as many as 25 research projects in 1977 and 21 projects in 1978 from its own funds. The staff and students of the colleges also participate in extension and community service work in some village and in the Karunmalai slum. Mount Carmel College, Bangalore, offers a course in journalism under the supervision of the department of English. The college also organised a programme of adult education for attendants working in the college. The college carried out a survey of the economic conditions of domestic workers living in Begner. Students have also been trained in the extraction of plant products and analysis of minerals and ores of iron and copper found in Karnataka. The New Science College, Hyderabad introduced a two-year M.Sc. course in Applied Electronics in June, 1973 and M.Sc. course in Biological Sciences (including new areas) in June, 1974. The undergraduate science courses have also been restructured and the students are now exposed to practical application in major areas, e.g., industrial electronics, computer science, linear programming, biochemistry, groundwater and mineral prospecting, industrial microbiology, general microbiology, fisheries, etc. Students of M.Sc. (Applied Electronics) have compulsorily to take one-and-a-half months or practical training in different division of the EGIL. Further, they also visit Signal and Telecommunications Department of South General Railway besides various smaller establishments. Students of M.Sc. (Biological Sciences) attend training course in Fisheries Training Institute managed by the Government of India. They also visit the Fisheries Institute at Karinada. Students of Physics, Major who have Electronics and Industrial Electronics as their subjects, are allotted annually, simple projects, and visits to local industrial centres are also arranged. Students of Chemistry Major who have Biochemistry as well as Industrial Biochemistry as their subjects have so far not been linked up with any industrial centres for practical training. However, they maintain closest contacts with the Biochemistry department of

Osmania University, National Institute of Nutrition Laboratories. Students of Zoology Major who also do Biochemistry, Limnology and Fisheries as given an opportunity to visit Fisheries Institute and also undertake project work on the material collected by them during the field work. Students of Geology Major go for field work regularly. Students of Botany Major also undertake field work and projects.

Eastern Zone

B.N. College Patna undertook a project under the auspices of the department of sociology for surveying the local community. Students and teachers of J.B. College, Jorhat have, over the years, participated in constructive work in the rural areas by constructing and repairing bridges, roads and schools. Special camps are organised during the summer vacations in the rural areas for the organization of rural youth, improvement of sanitation and health and eradication of illiteracy.

Northern Zone

Agra College, Agra, is an outstanding college and although it has received meagre grants from the Commission during the past ten years, its contribution to teaching and research has been noteworthy. D.A.V. College, Jullundur has taken up several projects like hospital services, adult education and adoption of villages. G.M. College, Srinagar has formulated a proposal under the scheme of restructuring of courses for the introduction of applied and relevant aspects of courses at the undergraduate level.

COMMITTEE ON INDUSTRIAL LICENSING, 1978 — REPORT[1]

Convenor Shri H.P. Nanda

Members Shri M.V. Arunachalam; Shri P. Anubhai; Shri C. Amin; Shri R. Bajaj; Shri J.H. Doshi; Shri S. Jalan; Dr. F.A. Mehta; Shri I.L. Mirchandani; Shri P.K. Nanda; Shri R.J. Shahaney; Shri L.M. Thapar; Shri T. Thomas; Shri H.C. Bhaya (resigned on December 1, 1978)

Appointment

The Hon. Minister of Industry, Shri George Fernandes in the wake of a earlier Ramakrishna Study Group report on the subject of Industrial Licensing which was submitted only as late as February 1978 brought fit to invite the views and recommendations of the representatives of Industry by appointing a Committee on Industrial Licensing in October 1978.

Terms of Reference

(a) To review the existing procedure relating to grant of letters of intent/industrial licenses, approvals for foreign collaboration, import of capital good registration with DGTD, etc.; and

(b) To suggest ways and means of improving procedures to eliminate avoidable delays and to make recommendations in this regard.

Contents

Summary of Principal Conclusions and Recommendations; Industrial

1. New Delhi, Ministry of Industry, 1979.

Licensing as an Instrument of India's Industrial Growth — An Evaluation; Basic Reasons behind the Primacy of Regulation over Development; Re-defining the "Cut-off Points"; Industrial Licensing Policy (general observations and specific recommendations); Foreign Collaboration; Industrial Licensing Procedure (general observations); Industrial Licensing Procedures (specific proposals); Amendment to the MRTP (Classification of Goods) Rules, 1971; Industrial Licensing and the Financial Institutions; Industrial Licensing as a positive Instrument of Balanced Growth.

Recommendations

The Committee wishes to express its sincerest appreciation of the opportunity offered to it by the Ministry of Industry to express its views on both the procedures and the policies which have direct or indirect bearing on the system of Industrial Licensing.

1. The Committee, after a historical review of the evolution of the industrial licensing system since the enactment of the Industries (Development & Regulation) Act (IDR Act), has come to the conclusion that sincere efforts have been made on specific occasions to effect liberalisation, but these efforts being basically of an *ad-hoc* nature, have failed to stem the tide of increasing regulatory powers vested in the system of Industrial Licensing.

2. The economy in general, and industry in particular, has therefore, paid the penalty of scarcities and rigidities, and while industrial licensing cannot be said to be the only factor inhibiting the rapid growth of production and investment in industry, it is certainly one of the most important factors, since without an industrial licence industrial investment cannot fructify at all.

3. It is the unanimous opinion of the Committee that circumstances have now placed the Indian economy in an ideal position to step up both the production and the investment in the industrial sector. On the one hand, the rate of savings as tended to exceed the rate of investment, clearly implying that the shortage today is not so much of investible resources but of projects, which are unable to get off the grounds due largely to delays in the licensing system. On the other hand, the foreign exchange constraint which has been another important ingredient in the rigidity of industrial licensing, has also virtually disappeared. The Committee cannot stress too emphatically, therefore,

that the time is now opportune to seek a massive increase in industrial production and investment. But for this to happen, it will be necessary to take bold and pragmatic steps in the field of industrial licensing, since without such steps the ability and agility of the economy to respond to these opportunities is stifled.

4. The Committee, therefore, expresses its belief that Government, in appointing it, has, in fact, recognised *the immense contribution that liberalisation in industrial licensing can make towards rapid economic growth consistent with the claims of social justice and the demands of fuller employment.* The Committee believes that its recommendations are in harmony with this overall approach of the Government.

5. The Committee cannot escape the conclusion that the marked deceleration in the annual growth rates of industrial production and in real capital formation which has taken place during the decade (1966-67 to 1976-77, is, to a major extent, the outcome of the increasing regulations that have come to be imposed in this decade of regulation and stagnation. There have been periodic attempts at liberalisation, no doubt, but these have been too few, and in a number of cases, what has been conceded in principle has been defeated in the details of implementation.

6. The Committee believes that no effective and lasting changes can be brought about either in our policy framework or in our industrial licensing procedures so long as certain attitudes continue to prevail in ever major segment of Indian industry both in the public and the private sectors as also in the attitudes of scientists, of the bureaucracy and of government in general, at the Central as well as State levels.

(i) It is imperative for this intellectual breakthrough that the nation be not saddled with the simultaneous achievement with equal degree of emphasis on a number of socio-economic goals, some of which are in direct conflict with each and one another;

(ii) It is even more imperative that the system of industrial licensing must not be used as a multi-purpose mechanism for achieving these goals in a simultaneous manner. The fundamental cause of the delays in the industrial licensing system stems from this fact of usage of the industrial licence to secure simultaneously all the socio-economic goals;

(iii) Therefore, re-orientation is required, on the one hand to convince the policy-makers in the country not to seek to achieve all goals simultaneously and to rotate such goals over different time periods, as is done in different countries; and simultaneously innovative policy must be demonstrated in the use of fiscal and financial incentives to achieve the socio-economic goals instead of loading the industrial licensing system with the burden of achieving such goals. The Committee, therefore, suggests that a fundamental attitudinal re-orientation is an essential prerequisite for an effective and lasting simplification of the industrial licensing system in India;

(iv) The Committee would also invite the attention of Government to what the Ramakrishna Study Group has already noted, namely, that whereas by law and by logic, the innumerable regulatory legislation and the institutions that have come into existence after the enactment of the IDR Act in 1951, should have lessened the regulatory powers implicit in this Act, tragically "these innumerable powers" of legislation and institutions have in fact reinforced the regulatory powers. The time has, therefore, come to "unshackle" industrial licensing from as many regulatory aspects as possible, since these regulatory mechanisms have already been planted into the economy through a number of other channels; and

(v) The Committee is also convinced that the belief, so assiduously cultivated during the last two decades, that industrial growth requires a system of industrial licensing which divides industries into "boxes" has to be discarded. The truth is that, barring a few very special cases, the growth of the large and the medium sectors of industry — both in the public and the private sectors — tends to bring an even sharper growth in the small scale industrial sector. The Committee enjoins the economic policy-makers to recognise that the dynamics of modern economic growth involves the complementary relationships between the large and the small scale sectors of Indian industry. There is no surer recipe of throttling the growth of the small scale sector than by placing an embargo on the rapid development of the large-scale sector. Empirical studies substantiate and economic theories support this central contention, which is overlooked in current policy formulations.

7. The Committee would, therefore, earnestly call upon Government for reconsideration of the basic promise of the current system of

industrial licensing. It must be reconsidered whether the socio-economic goals can be, without prejudice to the claims of social justice, "rotated" over different time periods; it must be examined how far other economy policy instruments, instead of being in addition to, can act as substitutes for industrial licensing. Indeed, with some boldness, the Committee ventures to suggest that the time has come to ask whether industrial licensing in its present form is at all the real answer to the demands of Indian economic development.

8. The Committee recognises that the issues it raises may be easily misrepresented as a retreat into a *laissez-faire* economy. What can to be challenged, however, is the necessity of inducting into the Indian industrial licensing system, a mechanism for continuously up-dating over every 3 or 5 years the "cut-off points" into which the various "boxes" of Indian industries are currently divided by the present system of industrial licensing policy. This would be justified not only by the demands of continuous inflation, but by the dynamics of rapid economic growth. The Committee, therefore, calls upon those in charge of administering the industrial licensing system to continuously review the demands made by both inflation and economic growth in respect of these 'cut-off points'.

9. The Committee recommends 3 central areas in which the cut-off points' must now be redefined so as to (a) considerably reduce the workload of the licensing authorities; (b) take into account the erosion caused in the real value of investment; and (c) spur economic growth without jeopardizing goals of creating new entrepreneurship or new sources of employment.

10. After a most careful examination, the Committee feels that the time has now come to delicense the core sector of the economy for a variety of reasons which are economically justifiable.

11. Till such time that the above recommendation can come to be implemented, the Committee would recommend that subject to certain limitations such as the reservation of industries for the small-scale sector, the time has come for new "cut-off points" to be established. These are indicated below.

12. Industrial licensing should be exempt for all units for projects with value of assets upto Rs. 15 crores provided they satisfy certain conditions outlined in the Committee's report. In other words, only projects above Rs. 15 crores should require industrial licences.

13. Again, subject to specific limitations mentioned in the report, the limit of Rs. 20 crores for MRTP Companies should be raised to

Rs. 45 crores for MRTP companies. Only where a company is a "dominant undertaking" or if the value of its assets exceed Rs. 45 crores, should it be covered by the MRTP Act.

14. The Committee notes that the definitions of both "the market" and "value of assets" need to be brought into line with economic rationalities. Once this is done, dominant undertakings will, henceforth, be defined as undertakings with more than 1/3 of the market share and with value of assets of Rs. 3 crores or more (redefined by the Committee).

15. The Committee emphasises that if a multi-product company is dominant in one product, then it should be considered dominant only in respect of that particular product and not in all other products. Similarly, if a company, with its elaborate R&D work, brings out a new product into a market, such a company is considered dominant in this product. The Committee would request that considering the importance of R&D and the product, the dominance of the said Company deserves to be condoned and should be condoned in the public interest.

16. The Committee would like to compliment the Secretariat for Industrial Approval (SIA) for bringing about — considerable improvement in the expeditious disposal of industrial licence applications. The Committee feels, however, that the system of industrial licensing has, in fact, ceased to be a system; it has become a web of perennial entanglements. It has, therefore, come as no great surprise to the Committee that as many as 28 per cent of the original industrial licence applications have had to be returned to the prospective entrepreneurs because of their failure to understand the complexities of this web. The Committee, therefore, recommends that the 'Entrepreneurial Assistance Unit', which currently functions only in Delhi, should now have its counter-parts under the auspices of SIA in the principal cities of India.

17. Another major finding of the Committee has been that considerable delays occur in the case of several industrial licence applications covering major industrial projects, due to the lack of concrete policies having been evolved by Government. Hence, such licences continue to remain in the domain of uncertainty and ambiguity as Government itself is not clear about the various aspects related to the growth of such major industries. The Committee, therefore, strongly recommends that at least in the case of the major 25 to 30 industries, even at the expense of spending time in the initial stages in preparing the ground rules and the guidelines for such industries, such an exer-

cise must be made so that at the time of the industrial licence applications, all the parties connected with this industry are aware of these ground rules and guidelines. Every hour spent in getting a clear picture of what the Government would want a particular industry to achieve (and how) will reduce the disposal of the industrial licences, and, therefore, the Committee recommends that every major industry must be supplied the necessary "policy inputs".

18. The Committee strongly recommends that in the preparation of such basic 'Policy inputs' for major industries, the Development Councils must be intimately associated with the drawing-up of the major industry plans.

19. The Committee also recommends as a general principle of industrial licensing that the policies in existence at the time when an entrepreneur applies for a licence, should normally be policies that should govern the conditions of such a licence application, and the induction of totally new factors must be kept to the barest minimum.

20. The Committee agrees with the Ramakrishna Study Group that the time has now come to reactive the Development Councils. The Committee feels, however, that the role of the Development Councils is so central to the effective functioning and growth of an industry, that it should not be merely an official body. The Committee, therefore, has indicated at great length, the composition of the newly activated Development Councils and the manner in which it can play an effective role.

21. The Committee would like to make it clear that the activities it contemplates for the newly activated Development Councils would not in any way conflict with those of the Working Groups appointed by the Planning Commission.

22. The Committee strongly believes that the principles of automatic growth must be accepted for a variety of economically compelling reasons. The Committee, therefore, recommends that an automatic annual growth of 5 per cent compound rate, or 30 per cent for a 5-year period in the registered/licensed capacity should be permitted to all the industries including dominant undertakings without any conditions attached.

23. The Committee must express its apprehensions in respect of the thesis, now sought to be advanced in certain quarters, that Industrial Licensing, particularly in so far as it pertains to MRTP companies, should permit "vertical expansion", but discourage and, indeed, forbid "horizontal proliferation". The Committee, on the basis of

several economic grounds, strongly feels that "horizontal proliferation" by companies, irrespective of whether they are MRTP companies or not, is, in fact, a powerful instrument for the diffusion of economic power and far from being forbidden, should in fact, be encouraged if the goals of promoting competition and reducing the market share of the large companies are to be achieved.

24. The Committee is also perturbed about the time-consuming and indeed economically injurious effects of the proposed Urban Land Ceiling Act, and has, therefore, made specific recommendations as to how, without in any way subtracting from the goals set for this Act, it can be made flexible enough to accommodate the requirements of industrial growth and mobility.

25. The Committee feels that though it has no mandate to make any recommendations in the areas of the small-scale sector it would only plead that the principle of continuously reassessing the 'cut-off points' be also applied to this sector, so that success in growth is not converted into a penalty for the small scale sector. The Committee has rejected outright the thesis that 'once small is always small'.

26. The Committee recognises that the subject of import of foreign technology is a complex one which defies easy solution. Nevertheless, the Committee does feel that, once the demarcations have been made of the areas in which technology can and should be promoted, all impediments in terms of time and the rates of royalties and technological fees should be removed or reduced. In developing this argument, the Committee would also invite the possibilities opened up by the new system of "Buy-back Arrangements", which are emerging in international trade and investment. The Committee would also like the country, within permissible limits, to avail itself of the opportunities of importing second hand machinery, which due to various reasons, are now cheaply and easily available. The Committee recognises that there are dangers in this area. But this can be no excuse for missing out opportunities provided by the current world economic situation, for India to import such second-hand machinery will help to bring down the cost of capital equipment, which have escalated by several times during the last 8 years.

27. The Committee has made a number of observations regarding the causes of delay in the current system of industrial licensing. It cannot, however, accept the plea that the SIA should be dismantled and that each administrative ministry should henceforth be entrusted with the task of industrial licensing. The Committee, however, does believe

that some degree of decentralisation is both inevitable and desirable in the shape of setting up Screening Committees within each administrative Ministry so that the prospective entrepreneur making an industrial licence application is made aware at the earliest of what, in the judgement of the different governmental ministries/agencies, are the weaknesses or deficiencies in his proposals. The Committee, therefore, strongly recommends setting up of such Screening Committees in the manner suggested in its report. The Committee recommends that after Licensing Committee meeting, the decision reached should be communicated to the applicant within 30 days.

28. The Committee notes that in certain cases, inspite of the existence of the Licensing-cum-MRTP Committee, an applicant has once again to await a whole chain of clearances. This duplication needs to be avoided. The Committee recommends that once a Letter of Intent has been issued, no new conditions should be set by any agency either associated with the relevant Licensing Committee, or for that matter by any other agency except the financial institutions.

29. The Committee fails to understand why in several areas pertaining to an industrial project, one and the same aspect comes within the scrutiny of different governmental agencies. Such 'commonalities' in the areas of technology, of finance, of monopoly legislation, etc., should not exist. If the different governmental agencies must be consulted, they must arrive at a common set of conclusions and conditions to be imposed in a concurrent and not sequential manner. In this connection, interconnected help would be secured in the case of major industries by implementing our recommendation of having major industry plans worked out in advance.

30. While the Committee is convinced that only projects with a value of assets of over Rs. 15 crores must henceforth, go to the licensing committee, it is equally convinced that even so the SIA needs to be strengthened in terms of both its staff and its powers. The Committee, however, cannot accept a view-point placed before it that the SIA should be endowed with executive powers. The SIA must remain a servicing organisation, but must be made a strong and effective servicing organisation. The Committee has, therefore, suggested ways and means of implementing this recommendation.

31. The Committee hopes that its appeal for securing "a deadline project" is not used for the negative purpose of quick disposals but for the positive purpose of early acceptance. The Committee greatly appreciates the painstaking work of the Sachar Committee but fears that

its recommendations in several areas will add substantial delays in securing the early fructification of industrial investments and industrial projects. Indeed, the Committee is convinced that the entire task it has been entrusted with, namely of expediting the decisions under the present system of industrial licensing and monopoly legislation will be rendered null and void if the recommendations of the Sachar Committee in this respect are accepted. A number of recommendations of the Sachar Committee will retard whatever little liberalisation the Indian Industry has secured during the last few years, and its insistence on "compulsory reference to the MRTP Commission" is only one of the several objectionable recommendations made by the Sachar Committee. Our Committee has, therefore, dealt with at great length on the irrationality of such recommendations.

32. The Committee suggests that a Licences Reviewing Committee be set up so as to serve as a sustaining mechanism ensuring continuous interactions between Government and industry in the vital areas pertaining to the early fructification of an industrial project.

33. The Committee recognises the extremely useful work undertaken by the DGTD but believes that it will not be capable of living up to the deadlines set for it so long as its present staff remains what it is and so long as its relationship with the Development Commissioner of Small Scale Industries is not properly defined.

34. The Committee has made specific recommendations in a large number of areas covering industrial licensing, import of goods, import of foreign technology, etc., and these recommendations are spelt out at considerable length in its chapter on 'Specific Proposals to Expedite Industrial Licensing'.

35. In the scheme suggested by the Committee, only such projects which have a far-reaching qualitative and quantitative significance in the Indian economy, would be put up for clearance from the angles of both Industrial Licensing and Monopoly Legislation. The Committee, therefore, feels that it may be deemed more expeditious that one centralised body should deal with the issues raised by such major projects instead of the present three Licensing Committees whose composition is more or less identical.

36. The Committee views with apprehension, the suggested amendment to the Monopolies and Restrictive Trade Practices (Classification of Goods) Rules 1971. In the opinion of the Committee the principles by which this amendment is sought to be made are so open to challenge on both logical and statistical grounds, that such an

amendment should not be effected unless a more careful examination is made. As the Committee has laid great stress on the creation of Development Councils for each major industry, it feels that the task of classifying products should be entrusted to such Development Councils. The Committee, however, does not reject the idea that a reclassification of products and goods has to be made every 5 to 7 years on the same principle which it has advocated before, namely, that the dynamics of the economy creates new products and new technology, which must be taken care of through reclassification of goods.

37. The Committee feels that there is some justification in the continuous complaint made before it regarding the delays in fructification of an industrial project caused by what has been called the 'detailed scrutiny' by the public sector financial institutions. The Committee, however, cannot accept the suggestion that the grant of an industrial licence must automatically carry with it the right of an assured supply of finance. The Committee would also not like the financial institutions to be associated with the licensing authorities right from the outset. However, the financial institutions should be given representation on the Development Councils set up for each major industry.

38. The Committee strongly feels that the principle of convertibility is not only a major impediment to industrial investment but also the cause of considerable delays, involving as it does, a great deal of negotiations. If the objective of the convertibility clause is not a political one, it would not be difficult to institute devices, whereby, the growing prosperity of a concern, initially assisted by the financial institutions, can be shared in an increasing manner by such institutions.

39. The Committee would recommend considerable caution about the manner in which the linking of Letter of Intent with the financial institutions has been recommended by the Narasimhan and Ramakrishna Study Groups. Apart from the fact that clarity is lacking in this area, the practical difficulties of linking financial assistance with the system of industrial licensing are immense.

40. The Committee would like to take this opportunity of stating that one of its central recommendations of using fiscal and financial incentives as a means of taming the regulatory impact of industrial licensing can be achieved through the instrument of the financial institutions. The Committee would, therefore, assign a special liberalising influence to this role instead of having the present liberalising influence to this role instead of having the present system of "banned areas". The guidelines given to the financial institutions could provide

for positive incentives to new entrepreneurs, as part of the overall industrial policy to strengthen the weak instead of the current system of weakening the strong.

41. The Committee believes that a novel approach can be tried out with the system of the industrial licensing. The present system has been associated with a negative code of vetoes and prohibitions. But there are district possibilities of using the industrial licensing system as a means of rewarding entrepreneurs who achieve certain socio-economic goals. Thus, in the vital areas of promoting Research and Development, of exports, of anti-pollution schemes and, last but not the least, of "ancillarization", rewards could be given to industries in terms of automatic expansion of the capacity of existing projects or by way of easy entry into new projects where socio-economic goals would be successfully served and achieved by such entrepreneurs. The very system of industrial licensing which today hinders economic growth, can, indeed, be used as a powerful instrument for promoting industrial growth provided certain socio-economic objectives are achieved.

42. The Committee recommends that in any major industry if the figures of production show a stagnancy for a period of more than three years, the system of industrial licensing must be made so operative as to immediately bring into existence new additional capacities. In other words, a monitoring mechanism must be established within the present system of industrial licensing not only to continually update the 'cut-off points' but also to give the early warning signals of stagnancy in investment and production in major industries.

43. The Committee recommends that henceforth, while the Ministry of Industry will continue to be the co-ordinating Ministry for all the economic ministries involved in securing the desired rates of growth in industrial production (for which incidentally the Ministry of Industry is currently held responsible), it is necessary at the inauguration of every financial year that each Economic Ministry, under which specific industries are entrusted, must declare to the nation its targets of growth. If such a target is too ambitious, it will be found out to be hollow; if it is too modest, it will hardly reflect well on the Economic Ministry concerned. In working out such targets, proclaiming them and then seeking to achieve them, the different economic Ministries will come to acquire a vested interest in chasing-up the industrial licence applications and in expediting their early fructification. Hence in our scheme, while the SIA will remain as an important arm of the Ministry of Industry to pursue the deadlines set for the early sanctioning of the Letter of intent

and, subsequently, the industrial licence, it will also give incentive to the economic Ministries to actively engage themselves in trying to ensure that the licences, which come within its purview, are granted at the earliest so that the targets of growth and investment for the specific industries, which come within its purview are achieved.

44. The Committee is firmly of the view that the Ministry of Industry has a vital role to play in the promotion of industrial development within the country. The Committee desires that the Ministry of Industry must become a powerful engine of industrial development in a manner ideally set by the example of MITI in Japan. The Committee, therefore, would suggest that the Ministry of Industry carefully studies the operation of MITI in Japan and adopt suitable and desirable features for Indian industry. The Committee would like to think that the Ministry of Industry should come to be looked upon by the various segments of Indian industry, not so much as a regulative body, but as a positive instrument of industrial growth, harmonising the conflicts between the different segments of Indian industry and establishing incentives to achieve higher production along socio-economic goals of the country. We are sure that this is the role of the Ministry already sees for itself, and we can only hope that our recommendations will help the Ministry to achieve its goal of being a powerful promotional agency of India's industrial development.

17

RAILWAY ACCIDENT INVESTIGATION REPORT ON DERAILMENT OF 1 UP HOWRAH-DELHI-KALKA MAIL AT KM 27/11-13 BETWEEN BARUIPARA AND KAMARKUNDU JN. STATIONS ON THE HOWRAH-BURDWAN CHORD (ELECTRIFIED DOUBLE LINE BROAD GAUGE SECTION), IN HOWRAH DIVISION OF EASTERN RAILWAY AT ABOUT 21.17 HOURS ON 4TH NOVEMBER, 1978

November 4, 1978 – February 14, 1979[1]

One Man Commission	Shri B.J.J. Rao, Ex-Additional Commissioner of Railway Safety, Eastern Circle, Calcutta
Officers Present	Shri A.C. Sen Sarma; Shri V.C.V. Chenulu; Shri S.K. Gupta; Shri S.S. Kapoor; Shri S. Chatterjee; Shri B. Singh; Shri S.R. Sengupta; Shri G.S. Biswas

Appointment

The Commission was constituted under Ministry of Tourism and Civil Aviation (Commission of Railway Safety) in accordance with Rule 4 of the Statutory Investigation into Railway Accident Rules, 1973 Vide Notification No. RS.13-T(8)/71, dated April 19, 1973 on November 4, 1978.

Terms of Reference

To inquire into the Derailment of 1 Up Howrah-Delhi-Kalka Mail at Km. 27/11-13 between Baruipara and Kamarkundu Jn. Stations on the

1. Ministry of Tourism and Civil Aviation (Commission of Railway Safety), Government of India, New Delhi, 1981, ii + 22 p.

Howrah-Burdwan Chord (Electrified Double Line Broad Gauge Section), in Howrah Division of Eastern Railway, at about 21.17 hours on 4th November, 1978.

Contents

Summary; Inspection and Inquiry; The Accident, Casualties; Relief Measures; The Train; Local Conditions; Observation and Tests; Conclusions; Remarks and Recommendations; Annexure from I to III.

Conclusions

41. *Cause*

(a) On full consideration of the factual, material and circumstantial evidence, I have reached the conclusion that the Derailment of No. 1 Up Howrah-Delhi-Kalka Mail at Km 27/11-13 between Baruipara and Kamarkundu Jn. Stations on the Howrah-Burdwan Jn. Chord (Electrified Double line Broad Gauge Section), in Howrah Division of Eastern Railway, at about 21.17 hrs. on 4-11-78 was the result of unauthorised interference with the track by some persons yet unknown.

(b) A full length rail (12.4 metres long) on the left of the track, ahead of Electric Mast 27/11, was disjointed by unfastening the fish plates at a joint 30 metres in advance of the Up Advanced Starter of Baruipara station and laterally displaced after disengaging the same from the two-key type A.C. bearing plates after removal of the keys.

42. *Responsibility*

Detection of such discontinuity in the track in time being impossible, no responsibility rests with the Driving Crew.

43. *Relief Measures*

I am satisfied that the relief measures were generally satisfactory.

Recommendations

44. The cases of sabotage and attempted sabotage have been on the increase on the Indian Railways in the recent past. Thefts of per-

manent way fittings are also quite common. Security patrolling cannot be an answer to these anti-social acts, since the same is not only expensive but also ineffective because of the long time interval between two successive patrols apart from dislocation that would be caused to maintenance of track on account of diverting gangmen for patrolling duties. Hence other methods will have to be thought of to counter this menace.

(a) Apropos my note on anti-creep bearing plates in Annexure II, there is a definite case to review the position in regard to selection of single key/two-key type anti-creep bearing plates, selective use of non-removable keys with two-key type anti-creep bearing plates and provision of reversed jaw single key anti-creep bearing plates along with ordinary single key anti-creep bearing plates. The need for the provision of reversed jaw anti-creep bearing plates and use of non-removable keys was also stressed by the Additional Commissioner of Railway Safety, Bangalore, who inquired into the case of Derailment of No. 47 Up 'Trivandrum Central-Cannanore Express' train between Kuruppantara and Piravam Road stations of Southern Railway, on 1.8.1978.

(b) Apropos my note on anti-theft and anti-sabotage measures in Annexure III, there is a case for a review of the existing anti-theft/anti-sabotage measures and suggest comprehensive measures to combat this twin evil. While it is true that the ultimate and best solution to the problems of theft and sabotage is the improvement in law and order situation, the efficacy of anti-theft and anti-sabotage measures should not be under-estimated.

(c) It is, therefore, recommended that the Track Standards Committee may take up the subjects mentioned in sub-paras (a) and (b) supra for their consideration.

45. (a) The Chief Engineer, South Eastern Railway, had reported sometime back that WAM-4 locomotives were developing excessive lateral and vertical oscillations. The Research Designs and Standards Organisation (RDSO) also conducted certain detailed tests subsequently in this connection which did show that excessive vertical and lateral accelerations, as well as lateral forces, were being developed by these locomotives. But they could not come to any definite conclusion regarding the cause of such behaviour. It was, however, considered by the RDSO that elimination of the lateral links of the traction motors, by carrying out suitable alterations, served to improve the riding characteristics and, as such, considerable relief to track was likely to be obtained by using WAM-4 locomotives without the lateral links on the

Mail and Express services on the Howrah-Durg route. With this in view, the RDSO had requested Railway Board in July 1978 to arrange for transfer of 9 WAM-4 locomotives without the links from Northern and Central Railways to South Eastern Railway and, in addition, to supply the next 20 WAM-4 locomotives to be manufactured by C.L.W. without links, to be supplied to South Eastern Railway. It would thus be evident that WAM-4 locomotives with lateral links have been under a cloud for some time.

(b) I am, therefore, surprised that WAM-4 locomotive No. 20678, which hauled the ill-fated high speed train, should have been a locomotive with lateral links and that this should belong to Northern Railway possessing a number of locomotives without lateral links. The Board may issue instructions to all Railways regarding the restrictions to be placed on the use of WAM-4 locomotives with lateral links and also take steps to ensure that no more such locomotives are turned out from Chittaranjan Locomotive Works. Severe speed restrictions should be imposed in the case of WAM-4 locomotives in service with broken lateral links.

46. This accident occurred at a place about 27 kilometres from Calcutta where Police dogs are available. But no attempt has been made to deploy them immediately after the accident. The Inspector-in-charge of Government Railway Police, Howrah explained that there was no Alamath (articles left behind by the culprits) at site and the scent on the fish plates would have disappeared on account of mist and dew and that he, therefore, felt that there was no point in bringing the Police dogs to the site of the accident. This issue did not appear to have received consideration at higher levels. It is considered desirable to deploy Police/RPF dogs in such cases, since tracing of even a few culprits by such deployment will act as a deterrent to the future commitment of similar crimes. This matter may be got examined at an expert level and a policy decision taken.

47. Welding of rail joints, no doubt, eliminates one of the vulnerable points of track from the point of view of sabotage. Hence when welding is undertaken on a length, the joints should be welded to the maximum extent technically permissible. In this particular case, joint L_0-L_1 , i.e., the tampered joint, could have been welded and this would made the task of miscreants more difficult. The Railways may be impressed that when welding of rail joints is undertaken on a length, all redundant joints technically amendable to welding, such as those on track circuited portions, should be welded.

48. 1/2 Kalka Mails are high-speed trains running at maximum permissible speed of 110 km/h. There is, however, a speed restrictions of 100 km/h. from km 10/0 to 40/0 on Howrah-Burdwan Chord Section on account of bad bank. There are also a number of local restrictions between km 0/0 to 10/0. Thus the maximum speed permissible from km 0/0 to 40/0 is virtually 100 km/h. The Railway treated the same as a speed restriction and booked Kalka Mails at 100 km/h., i.e., the same as the maximum permissible speed. I am afraid that this is not correct. In case, a speed restriction exists covering a complete Block Section/Sections, the same should be treated as the maximum permissible speed and the booked speed should be limited to 10 per cent less than that speed so that reasonable make-up time is available for Drivers to cover unforeseen losses on the run without exceeding the maximum permissible speeds. Necessary instructions may be issued by the Board on this issue.

49. It is regretted to note that the speed recorder on a high-speed train like the ill-fated train should have been found out of order in spite of importance attached to such gadgets from the point of view of safety. Responsibility for failure should be fixed and disciplinary action taken on the person (s) concerned.

50. The accident message was received in the Control office at Howrah at 21.30 hours. But the Medical Van departed from Howrah Loco Shed only at 22.28 hours, i.e., 58 minutes after the receipt of the accident message against 30 minutes permitted. The train arrived at Baruipara at 23.12 hours and took 44 minutes to cover a distance of about 25 kms. No damage was done in this case on account of late arrival of Medical Van at site because of simple injuries sustained by passengers. It is, however, needless to point out that the Railway should take steps for quick dispatch of Medical Vans in the case of serious or suspected serious accidents.

Railway Board's Views on Various Paras of the Report

Para 44

The recommendations of the Commissioner of Railway Safety contained in this para regarding use of reverse jaw single key CI bearing plates and development of non-removable anti-sabotage fittings have been considered by the Board. According to the experience gained so far on the Indian Railways, the use of anti-far on the Indian Railways, the use of anti-sabotage fittings does not serve any useful purpose except making the normal maintenance of track very difficult and costlier. It is on this consideration that such anti-sabotage measures as burring of fish bolt threads after tightening the nuts, use of non-removable two way keys and use of earless dog spikes, tries on the Railways in the past have been given up. Therefore, the Board do not consider it necessary that any work should be done on the development of anti-sabotage or non-removable track fittings. As a matter of fact no track fittings can be made non-removable because renewal of track fittings is frequently required in connection with various rack maintenance and replacement operations. The use of reverse jaw single key CI bearing plates has already been considered by the Track Standards Committee and after due deliberation, it has been decided not to use such bearing plates as it was not considered necessary. The Board do not propose to reopen this issue.

The Board also do not agree with the view of Commissioner of Railway Safety that welding of rails is not an effective anti-sabotage measure. The Commissioner of Railway Safety has based his view on the assumption that welded rail may not be maintained properly. For that matter any track whether laid with welded rails or not or even track provided with most effective anti-sabotage devices, if not maintained properly, could be a potential safety hazard. It is a widely acknowledge fact that welding of rails is an effective anti-sabotage measure.

Regarding the suggestion of the Commissioner of Railway Safety about development of a fit and forget type sleeper fastening, it is stated that this subject is already receiving the attention of the RDSO in connection with developing such a fastening for use on concrete sleepers. However, a fit and forget type fastening need not necessarily be a non-removable or anti-sabotage fastening. In this connection Board's decision communicated to the Chief Commissioner of Railway Safety against para 43(a) of the Commissioner of Railway Safety's report about the derailment of No. 17 Up Sawai Madhopur-Loharu Express train between Jhunjhunu and Ratanshahr stations vide Board's letter No. 78/ Safety (A&R)/1/21, dated 22-9-79 also please be referred to.

Para 45

RDSO have issued instructions to Railways to delete the lateral link arrangement on all existing WAM 4 and WCAM 1 locomotives and also from the future CLW built locomotives of these two types. RDSO have circulated special modification instructions to enable the railways to initiate a phased and planned programme of implementing the requisite modification which would be carried out in POH shops, or during major schedules of locos in sheds with the assistance of POH shops and could be synchronised with the re-discing of wheels.

Para 46

This Ministry agree with Commissioner of Railway Safety that in a case where sabotage is suspected, the Railways should themselves take initiative and suggest the deployment of Police/R.P.F. dogs to the investigating Police Officers. The Railways are being advised suitably.

Para 47

The Railway Administration have taken necessary action in compliance with Commissioner of Railway Safety's recommendation.

Instructions on the subject are also being issued to other Railways.

Para 48

Instructions are being issued to the Railways that whenever there are long stretches of speed restrictions, the booked speed should be 10 per cent less than the permanent speed restriction on a long stretch.

Para 49

It has been decided that indigenous development of reliable speed recording and Indicating Equipment for application to Diesel Electric and Electric locomotives should be pursued further. Also, till such time a service for continuous supply of reliable speed recording and indicating equipment for locomotive application is established in the country, import of Hasler Speed Recorders by the Railways for fitment on Electric locomotives has been approved by the Board and Railways have been instructed accordingly.

Para 50

The Commissioner of Railway Safety's observations regarding delayed start of the Medical Van from Howrah loco shed have been taken note of by the railway administration with a view to avoiding such a lapse in future. In the subject case, however, this delay did not matter because the injuries were only trivial and first aid was rendered by the Guard immediately after the accident.

18

NATIONAL COMMITTEE ON THE DEVELOPMENT OF BACKWARD AREAS, 1978 — REPORT ON DEVELOPMENT OF COASTAL AREA AFFECTED BY SALINITY

November 30, 1978 – November 12, 1981[1]

Chairman Shri B. Sivaraman, Member, Planning Commission

Members Shri Som Dutt; Prof. Marinal Datta Chaudhary (ceased to be member w.e.f. November 30, 1978), Shri S.S. Marathe (ceased to be member w.e.f. November 30, 1978), Shri Ranchor Prasad; Shri Ramakrishanayya; Shri K.P.A. Menon; Shri R.M. Honavar (ceased to be member w.e.f. January 31, 1981); Shri S.A. Dave; Dr. Y. Nayudamma; Shri Anand Sarup; Dr. B.D. Sharma; Shri Suresh Mathur; Dr. D.M. Nanjundappa; Shri S.M. Ghosh.

M. Secy. Shri Nitin Desai

Appointment

The Government have been pursuing certain policies and programmes in regard to the development of backward areas since the Fourth Five Year Plan. It is now necessary to review the working of these various programmes and to set out a suitable startegy or strategies for the development of the Backward Areas in the context of the priorities and objectives set out in the draft 1979-83 plan. The Planning Commission have therefore, decided to set up a High Level Committee to formulate appropriate strategy or strategies for effectively tackling the problems of Backward Area Vide its Resolution No. PC(P)17/NCDBA/78-MLP dated November 30, 1978.

---

1. Planning Commission, Government of India, New Delhi, 1981, xiii + 113p

Terms of Reference

(i) To examine the validity of the various concepts of backwardness underlying the definitions in use for present policy purpose and recommend the criteria by which backward areas should be identified.

(ii) To review the working of:

(a) The existing plans for dealing with the general development problems of backward areas like Tribal Sub-Plans, Plans for Hill Areas, etc., and
(b) The existing schemes for stimulating industrial development in backward areas such as the schemes for concessional finance, investment subsidy, transport subsidy, sales tax concessions, etc., similar schemes in the agricultural and allied fields like DPAP, and general measures for tackling the problems of poverty and unemployment with a view to find out their efficacy in the removal of backwardness; and

(iii) To recommend an appropriate strategy for strategies for effectively tackling the problems of backward areas, classified, it necessary, according to areas, causes of or prescribed remedies.

Contents

Introduction; Strategy of Development; Brackish Water Fish Culture; Marine Fisheries; Crop Planning and Allied Programmes; Irrigation, Drainage and Salinity Control; Development of Saurashtra and Kutch Areas of Gujarat; Development of Sunderban area in West Bengal; Annexures – Chapter I–1 to 1.8; Chapter 3–3.1 to 3.7; Chapter 4–4.1; Chapter 5–5.1 to 5.2; Chapter 7–7.1 to 7.3; Chapter 8–8.1.

Recommendations

Introduction

1. The National Committee on the Development of Backward Areas has identified different types of fundamental backwardness and is seeking remedies for rectifying the same. The coastal areas affected by salinity constitute one such category. (Para 1.1)

2. The problem of salinity in coastal areas is a national problem and requires detailed studies in all the coastal states. The development of such areas requires special attention because they have remained neglected since long and the developmental efforts of the post-independence plan era have also not generally reached there for want of proper strategy, infrastructure and impediments due to backwardness. (Para 1.6)

Strategy of Development

3. The Committee is of the view that for special treatment as saline areas, coastal saline areas need to be identified as:-

(a) Soil salinity areas where the top soil is saline;
(b) Water salinity areas where either the water strata for great depths is saline, or even if top 30 ft. has fresh water where fresh water is entirely by rainfall alone. (Para 2.2)

4. With a view to providing the right type of development technology suiting of different conditions such areas may then be classified into:

(a) Saline soils;
(b) Saline alkali soils;
(c) Non-saline alkali soils; and
(d) Degraded saline alkali soils. (Para 2.5)

5. The entire area of Sunderban faces the problem of salinity, water logging and drainage. In the absence of upland water supply the area is exposed to tidal action making the water highly brackish. For the development of the Sundarban an integrated programme simultaneously covering crop production, fisheries, animal husbandry and forestry and providing for improvement in infrastructural facilities including communication and supply of potable water will be necessary. For the protection and development of land and for increasing availability of fresh water for agricultural and drinking purposes, engineering and other measures as envisaged both in the Interim plan of development of the Sundarban and in the Sundarban Delta Project should be undertaken. Industrial development should be restricted to such agro-based industries as do not aggravate the

problem of fresh water in view of its limited availability. As an integral part of the overall development of the region, river road and rail transport facilities should be considerably improved. Electrification should be extended to the area to support development. (Para 2.8)

6. On the east coast the principle of developing existing skill will lead to the obvious strategy of developing fisheries. The next important part of the economy will be agriculture in which some beginning of development can already be seen in these areas wherever fresh water is available. Development of village industries and tertiary sector growth will have to follow the primary growth in both fisheries and agriculture. (Para 2.9)

7. In the West coast the entire economy will be based on fisheries except where agriculture be developed on the lines of Kuttanand. It will be found that such development on the West coast today would be a high cost development and may not give a competitive agricultural economy to the population. (Para 2.9)

8. The Committee has generally been informed that there is no arrangement for any systematic soil surveys in most States particularly in the coastal areas. The Committee would urge that if a solution is to be found for the problem of the coastal areas affected by salinity, these areas can only be identified on the basis of a systematic soil survey. It is only then that it would be possible for the State Governments to identify areas of high, medium and low saline conditions and seek remedial measures. (Para 2.10)

9. It is important to undertake evaluation of the various measures taken by the State Governments to reduce the problem of salinity and how far these have been successful. (Para 2.10)

10. The fishermen class in the coastal saline areas subsist mainly on marine fisheries. Optimal utilisation of the potential needs to be aimed at. (Para 2.11)

11. The current controversy on the serious competition between traditional boats and mechanised boats needs to be resolved. Demarcation can be based on cost-benefit analysis and suitable rehabilitation of the displaced fishermen, if any, should be done. Possibilities of processing and marketing including export of frozen fish has to be worked out rationally and optimally. (Para 2.11)

12. Brackish water fishery provides a sizeable potential for development. On account of large areas of brackish water, the reservation of the pursuits for the smaller people would help improve substantially the economics of these persons. Individuals farms of

smaller size are desirable but these need to be supported through areas development approach and also through the provision of appropriate supporting services including technical consultancy services. (Para 2.12)

13. The transfer for technical knowledge to the fishermen is very vital and this responsibility should be shouldered by the State Governments by providing the technical consultancy free of charge. The systematic development of the fishermen class should be the focus of attention and would have to be intensified. (Para 2.12)

14. Hectare for hectare brackish water fisheries which can develop prawns in addition to brackish water fish, give much greater income than the composite fish culture followed in inland fresh water fisheries. Fresh water being the most difficult ingredient in the coastal saline areas, its utilisation for culture fisheries whilst a more remunerative technology in brackish water is available, will not be warranted. The Committee, therefore, recommends that culture fisheries in the coastal saline areas should invariably be brackish water fisheries. (Para 2.13)

15. With the higher rainfall on the east coast it should be possible to bring drainage waters from the land mass through controlled channels to teach the top soil in the saline areas and also impregnate the sub-soil with fresh water pushing down the saline accuifer. Proper fresh water use is, therefore, the main strategy for agriculture in these areas. Further, as fresh water will be scarce inspite of these attempts, the cropping system that will be developed has to be based on suitable cash crops whose water requirements will be low. (Para 2.14)

16. Very little work has so far been done on finding suitable horticulture cultivators of various fruit trees suited to the area. The Agricultural Universities will have to rapidly survey available information about suitability of fruit trees for their coastal saline areas and in due course undertake development of the necessary cultivers for better production. Any how, coconut production would prime facie appear to be the most remunerative horticultural strategy. (Para 2.15)

17. For the appropriate development of horticulture, etc., and also for the protection of habitation, the shelter belt approach is very desirable. The Committee would like to commend the strategy of complete shelter belt for habitations. (Para 2.16)

18. Animal husbandry will have to take a back seat for the time being, until the Agricultural Universities check on the type of fodder that can be grown in the coastal areas and which will be suitable for

animal rearing. (Para 2.17)

19. Sundarban has developed a cheap road system which allows for utilising pedal trays to move the goods to be collecting markets. The strategy of road development will have to take note of these innovations. (Para 2.18)

Brackish Water Fish Culture

20. A project profile for brackish water culture development by the West Bengal expects distinguishes three types of areas suitable for brackish water culture and they are:-

(i) Zones of low saline and low tidal amplitude;
(ii) Zone of moderately saline and moderate tidal amplitude; and
(iii) Zone of high salinity and high tidal amplitude;

If the brackish water areas in the other coastal states are investigated, it will be found that these three types will be replicated all along the coat. Each of these zones, require a different type of brackish water culture (Para 3.2)

21. The areas most favourably situated in the zone of high salinity and high tidal amplitude should be selected in each of the coastal saline states for brackish water culture during these two plans. (Para 3.3)

22. For the low salinity and low tidal areas the bheri culture appears to be the most economic approach. It does not interfere with the paddy culture and, at the same time, gives a subsidiary income in fish culture. Such areas will have to be identified in all the coastal states and a programme of action developed. (Para 3.5)

23. Large areas have to be embanked for culture fisheries. In agriculture, already there are very substantial land reforms laws which fix the rights of various parties on the land for agriculture. For culture fisheries at present there is no such law. It is suggested that the laws should provide compulsorily for common operations and for arbitration by governmental machinery. It should also define the rights of the owners of the land to the produce on a fair and equitable basis. The Committee recommends that the Fisheries Division in the Ministry of Agriculture should take up the development of a model law. (Para 3.6)

24. In the zone of moderately saline and moderate tidal amplitude, where the designs can be suitably developed on the model applicable to the high salinity, it is desirable to follow a culture fisheries approach.

In other areas where capital cost on culture fisheries is very substantial, immediate introduction of bheri culture of the controlled variety would benefit the people to a very large extent. The Committee would advise the classification of such lands in the coastal saline States and developing a suitably phased programmes. (Para 3.7)

25. In areas where paddy-cum-prawn culture is now prevalent and in new areas where the technique can be introduced, it is necessary to improve the method. Introduction of water carrying mixed fry, both desirable and undesirable varieties, will have to be replaced by selective introduction of the better varieties which can give the best return out of the nutrition in the water. (Para 3.8)

26. For a two crop routine which is more profitable method, fry of the right type has to be available at the right time. It should be possible generally by collecting the fry from the area where it is available to send it to the grower in the season when he wants it. The problem here is the transport of fry. While scientists should find out the best method to reduce transport mortality, obviously steps have to be taken to produce uniform batches of fry so that transport losses can be minimised. (Paras 3.11 and 3.12)

27. The Committee would recommend that the Ministry of agriculture, taking into consideration the various experiments that have been done and innovations introduced, should prepare a model for a production centre for prawn fry. The cost-benefit of the production and the price at which the fry has to be sold will also have to be established. The coastal States should have at least one pilot centre close to an area where culture prawn fisheries are now under development. (Para 3.13)

28. The development of paddy-cum-prawn culture can probably be introduced quickly all over the coastal states provided areas are identified, extension work is done and necessary arrangements made for fry supply on demand. The Committee recommends that each coastal state should now do the basic investigations as has been done by West Bengal for Sundarban and identify suitable areas for development and lay on the expertise and extension and provide the necessary infrastructure including arrangements for fry supply. (Para 3.14)

29. Culture prawn fisheries is a capital intensive industry. Whilst the fishermen class should be given every facility to enter into this new line and given reasonable help by way of loans, grants, etc., the Committee feels that there is a limit beyond which the fishermen class

as individuals will not be able to avail of this programme. A corporation idea on the lines of the Assam Plantation Corporation Act may be helpful. Various conditions will have to be imposed on the lease holder so that the programme is operated as a whole and individual vagaries do not spoil it. It may be worthwhile for the Ministry of Agriculture to set up a Working Group to study this problem and suggest a model project. (Para 3.17)

30. It will be much easier to introduce controller culture in small farmer's holdings under brackish water with holdings between 2—5 hectares. In effect, this will be small industry. The Committee recommends that these enterprises should be treated on the same footing as small industries and all the benefits given to the small industries should be made available to such entrepreneurs in addition to such benefits as are given to small farmers. (Para 3.18)

31. The Committee recommends that a few areas of 100 to 200 hectares may be given out to large entrepreneurs under very strict conditions including utilisation of local labour. One condition should be that they would put up a fry production centre and supply fry, on fair price, to the small farmed entrepreneurs round about. The Working Group dealing with the fishermen's programme can also look into the development of a model contract form for lease of these areas with large entrepreneurs. (Para 3.19)

32. One of the major constraints to the development of aquaculture has been the paucity of trained personnel at various levels. Training of fishermen and others offering supporting services has to be carried out on a very large scale by each of the coastal states. (Para 3.20)

Marine Fisheries

33. Any development of the coastal saline areas must stabilise the traditional economy of the non-mechanised boat sector who almost had monopoly in fishing in the coastal areas which are the most remunerative areas for fishing in the sea. At the same time, we have to support mechanised craft which can go far beyond the depths and distances which the traditional craft can handle and can exploit that vast fishery resources of the economic zone of the country. Where there is pressure and conflict between the mechanised and traditional crafts in certain highly fished areas, there are many areas along the coast where not much fishing is taking place because of lack of basic

facilities like communications, fresh water and easy access to a fresh fish market. (Para 4.13)

34. Where there are large concentrations of catemarans and dinghis it can be examined by pilot schemes whether a mechanised boat can be engaged to pull them out to the fishing areas in numbers. The Committee would suggest that pilot schemes of this nature should be started and the cost benefit worked out and demonstrated so that a methodology can be developed applicable to the various coastal states. (Para 4.16)

35. It is possible to introduce labour intensive mother vessel fishing to enable traditional fishermen to go out far into the sea. (Para 4.17)

36. The most important diversification that can be done with the present technological knowledge is introduction of purse-seining for catching pelagic fish in the coast. (Para 4.20)

37. The Committee would seriously recommend that the ground level statistics of rempaniusers and mechanised boat users in all those areas where conflict has arisen should be done and, if possible, an introduction of the joint interest method followed in Karnataka may be a solution. (Para 4.21)

38. The allegation that the purse-seiners are interfering with the coastal movement of the pelagic fish in season may not at all be scientifically tenable. It is desirable that the fishery research and oceanic research look into this problem so that unnecessary conflict by lack of proper knowledge may not continue. (Para 4.22)

39. Now that a reasonable amount of survey of fishery resources mainly polagic has been done on both the coasts, areas where long lines and pole and line fishing by improved means can be introduced should be demarcated. (Para 4.23)

40. Mechanised boats require jettis for landing. A programme for construction of fishing jettis round the coasts at such locations where jettis can be constructed and where the available potential is not being exploited close to the coast by traditional fishermen and in the distance by mechanised boats can be identified and jettis constructed. This will help in diversifying mechanised boats from highly fished areas to the new areas. This planned deployment should be attempted. (Para 4.24)

41. The question of subsidising the price of diesel for mechanised boats or reducing the excise is a problem continuously under examination. Some concrete steps in this direction would greatly improve the economics of mechanised boat fishing. (Para 4.25)

42. There is over exploitation of juveniles of prawns in certain back waters of the country. In the interest of both the traditional fishermen and the mechanised boats, regulations to conserve the juveniles and allow for the breeding cycle to go through without serious interference is an immediate necessity. (Para 4.26)

43. Much of the cat fish caught are the incubating males. Hence operation of high efficiency gear has to be regulated in terms of number, area of operation, period of operation, mesh size, etc., as unbridled introduction of modern craft and gear can have a devasting influence on the fishery. (Para 4.27)

44. Deep sea fishing will not greatly add to direct employment opportunities for the fishermen class in the coastal areas. At the same time, without deep sea fishing the country will not be able to exploit the vast potential within the economic zone which at present is being peached upon by fishing crafts of various countries. The Committee has not been able to examine the problems of deep sea fishing in any great depth and, therefore, can only say that in the interest of all concerned, it is desirable to increase the fishing vessels force for deep sea fishing and also attend to the infrastructure to make the fishing economics. (Para 4.30)

45. The Committee would seriously recommend that the Ministry of Agriculture must take up a comprehensive marketing programme for fish by supporting pilot projects of innovating marketing. Linkages will have to be established between the coastal States and interior States who can be the consumers. The Committee would recommend that the Ministry of Agriculture should carry out a survey all along the coast finding out the seasons when there are large catches in particular pockets of the cost leading to a sharp fall in prices and, at the same time, identify markets in the country where such fish can be sold at economic prices allowing for the transport charges. (Paras 4.33 and 4.34)

Crop Planning and Allied Programmes

46. Soil and water salinity and the lack of irrigation are the principal constraints affecting crop planning in saline coastal areas. (Para 5.1)

47. If efforts are made to evolve and introduce a scientific crop planning in the coastal saline areas, it should be possible to increase crop productivity substantially. For this purpose, it is necessary to

make more intensive efforts for evolving suitable crop patterns for different salinity conditions and soil characteristics. The long duration nature of kharif crop is recognised as a constraint for increasing the land use intensity in such areas. Therefore, measures have to be considered how far long duration kharif paddy can be replaced by short duration paddy and suitable rabi crop, viz.; barely, sugarbeet, sunflower, cotton, etc., which can be grown after harvesting of the kharif crop. (Para 5.7)

48. Cropping intensity in coastal saline areas provides tremendous scope for improvement. This can mainly be done by providing irrigation facilities and also introducing dry farming techniques in these areas. All the sweet water reserves, surface as well as underground, need to be exploited and put to more judicious use for improving productivity. As much of fresh water as possible needs to be conserved for raising rabi and summer crops. As irrigation water is likely to be scarce, advantage of the moisture present in the soil at the time of kharif harvest would have to be taken for raising early short duration and rabi crops. (Para 5.9)

49. The Central Soil and Salinity Research Institute at its Canning and Research Station has succeeded in identifying a few useful rice varieties and other salt tolerant crops. Development of period bound varieties is desirable so that harvest can be controlled. The newly developed varieties should be tried on the cultivators field before introducing on a large scale. (Paras 5.10 and 5.11)

50. Due to high saline soil and poor water quality, no crop other than kharif rice is generally possible under commercial cultivation. It is essential to introduce a suitable second crop (rabi) which can tolerate salinity effectively and can grow better than others in moisture stress conditions. (Para 5.13)

51. Possibilities of introducing inter-cropping should be fully explored. For instance, possibility of prawn culture along with coconut, development has been proved. Similar experimentation are desired for making optimum use of natural resources. (Para 5.17)

52. Trial-cum-demonstration farms need to be established in affected areas which should operate under the guidance of technical hands. The introduction of new rabi crops, e.g., vegetables will require the establishment of new marketing input supply and credit arrangements. Hence measures to introduce new rabi crops in the area must be accompanied by steps to establish an appropriate credit, input supply and marketing infrastructure in these crops. Sundarban has

established that, given the necessary support, vegetables can be an important crop in some of these areas. (Para 5.18)

53. Canning experimentation is an heavy black soil. In other areas the situation is different. As such location specific research would be desirable. (Para 5.19)

54. There is plenty of scope to develop horticulture in coastal saline areas by introducing technology capable of giving good monetary returns to the growers. The obvious strategy would, therefore, be to select and propagate right type of fruit crops suited to local topographic and salinity conditions. Further, improved varieties of fruits with a view to raising their yields and resistivity to salinity and water logging conditions which are common in these areas, would have to be evolved through field research conducted at different centres set up for the purpose. (Para 5.21)

55. The most successful horticulture plant is coconut which has immense potential for plantation in coastal areas. Coconut plantations with suitable inter-cropping can be an important employment and income generation measure in these areas. The gross return per free is quite profitable. Moreover, there could be substantial opportunities for non-agricultural employment in processing units, e.g., coir. (Paras 5.22 and 5.23)

56. Cashew can be cultivated quite successfully in sand dunes which at present are unutilised and often encroach on adjoining farm lands year after year. Cashew trees once stablished stabilise the soil. An integrated pattern of coastal horticulture involving coconut, cashew and causarina holds great promise. (Para 5.24)

57. Amongst fruit trees Sapota and Guava have potential for development in all areas. In many areas having temporary water stagnation, Jamun could be planted. If salinity is brought down through reclamation measures, many other fruit crops can also be grown. (Para 5.25)

58. Area-wise approach has to be made for selecting suitable fruit crops for different ecological conditions and research support would be necessary to develop special species of different fruits so that good crop yields are achieved and horticulture becomes more remunerative to the people. The essential requirements for these purposes are (a) the availability of suitable planting material, (b) enough sweet water to sustain the plant in the early stages of growth, (c) arrangements for credit during the long gestation period; and (d) arrangements for marketing. (Para 5.27)

59. Multipurpose afforestation of coastal areas is the need of the hour. On the eastern coast, shelter belt plantation requires to be taken up along the entire coast. This could be achieved only if the participating farmers are ensured of economic returns from such plantations and also their requirements of fuel and timber are met from such farm forestry. There is very good scope for forestry development on west coast also. Salinity resistant trees for meeting the local requirement of fuel and wood may be raised all along the coast which would also check the menace of felling of trees in the adjoining forest areas. (Paras 5.29, 5.30 and 5.35)

60. For any meaningful enhancement of livestock production work in the coastal saline areas, the main problems are provision of drinking water, feed and fodder, marketing facilities and legistics. In addition, there is at present dearth of infrastructure for supply of foundation and production stock of cattle, pigs and poultry including ducks. (Para 5.40)

61. As a basic approach, a balance between cows and buffaloes and other animals on the basis of ecological conditions in different regions has to be struck and seasonal adjustment made. (Para 5.41)

62. For improving different breeds of animals, artificial insemination programme would have to be extended to these areas in a phased manner. Breed improvement programme should have the dual purpose of increasing the livestock products as well as the drought quality of farm animals, Veterinary Dispensaries and Live Stock Aid Centres need to be set up at convenient places to cover such areas. Mobile veterinary dispensaries may have to be organised for meeting the requirements of difficult areas. (Para 5.41)

63. Supply of drinking water for animals may be made from tanks and ponds which have embankment protection from ingress of saline water. Small tanks protected by ring bunds can also store fresh water for use of animals. In some regions, drinking water supply to the animals may be made by sinking of shallow/deep tubewells depending upon the ground water aquifers of the area. (Para 5.42)

64. As the biggest single constraint in the livestock farming relates to the proper nutrition of the animals, improved fodder cultivation is of urgent necessity. Suitable varieties of fodder, fodder trees and shrubs should be propagated in these areas. It would be advisable to establish experimental fodder farms for trail of various types of salinity resistance fodder plants. Fodder seeds and cuttings of successful varieties should be distributed to the farmers under a fodder

development programme. Arrangements for supply of feeds in promising areas may also be taken up by these farms. (Para 5.43)

65. Duck farming should be encouraged in coastal saline areas on an intensive scale provided it does not, in any way hamper with the progress of brackish water fishery development in these areas. (Para 5.44)

66. Poultry development also needs to be intensified for supplementing the incomes of the people in these areas. Economical poultry rearing in Kerala is done due to the large availability of cheap protein from fish waste and other sea products. Thus must be studied so that similar system can be developed elsewhere. (Para 5.45)

Irrigation, Drainage and Salinity Control

67. Persistence of high water table with poor quality of ground water calls for a good sub-surface drainage system in coastal saline areas. Due to marine origin and the impeded surface and sub-surface drainage the soils have become highly saline and present unfavourable characteristics for crop growth. So far not much work has been done on the sub-surface drainage of these soils. (Para 6.22)

68. The age old method for controlling the salinity in coastal areas has been the construction of embankments as a protective measure to stop ingress of sea water to these lands. There is also need to protect rest of the areas by constructing saline embankments along the sea coast in between the area demarcated by creeks and streams. (Para 6.25)

69. A suitable shelter with trees or grasses has to be developed around bunds, so as to check the wave action. Provision of shelter belts will protect drifting of saline sands into the inland areas thereby protecting the land from salinity. (Para 6.26)

70. The dykes/embankments have to be provided with one way sluice gates so that the ingress of sea water into the land is prevented during high tides and the inland excess water is drained out to the sea during the low tides. (Para 6.27)

71. In some areas, flushing the saline fields with sweet water followed by fresh water irrigation to leach the salts down the soil profile is a practical method adopted by the farmer. (Para 6.28)

72. One of the curative measures which has been found useful in improving the saline soils is the use of chemical amendments such as gypsum, sulphur, iron sulphates, etc. But they are costly and their use

require close technical supervision for deciding the dose and the particular kind of chemical to be used. (Para 6.29)

73. Various studies carried out at canning indicated that:-

(i) Surface soil mulching with rice husk helps in improving the soil physical conditions;
(ii) Mixing rice husk with surface soil by ploughing during fallow winter period after the harvest of kharif rice significantly increases the rice yield during following monsoon; and
(iii) Manipulation of the surface 15 cm. of moderately heavy textured soil either through addition of sand or rice husk improves the leachability of the soil. (Para 6.30)

74. Where there is inundation of sea water, stagnant surface water ditches turn saline. Treatment of the water with powdered charcoal reduces salinity to some extent. (Para 6.32)

75. While natural depressions, creeks, channels, etc., having saline water may gainfully be utilised through development of brackish water fishery, sweet water resources have to be protected from the ingress of saline waters and utilised for irrigation and drinking purposes. Surface water flow during the rainy season has to be regulated through a well planned system of drainage works for controlling the salinity in the top soil. Embankments and bunds are to be erected for protecting sweet water from the ingress of sea water and other saline waters. (Para 6.33)

76. The present groundwater development in coastal tract is very limited but when the groundwater withdrawals are to be increased, the existing saline and fresh water disposition may be disturbed and the process of ingress of saline water may be accelerated. Hence scientific management at the vital groundwater resource will require critical evaluation of the changes, brought about consequent to withdrawals and must so regulate the draft as to prevent the ingress of saline water in fresh water bodies. (Para 6.46)

77. Due to the peculiar and complex hydrogeologic set up in the coastal belt be set with salinity hazards, the following precautions are required to be taken for proper development and management of groundwater:

(i) Geophysical investigation must precede tubewell designs so that the strainers are located against fresh water aquifers;

(ii) The shrounding materials between the fresh water aquifers and saline water aquifer are required to be sealed by a quick setting cement to avoid contamination;

(iii) Gravel shround materials should be carefully selected to avoid sand fillings in tubewells;

(iv) Indiscriminate pumping from tubewells should be discouraged;

(v) In the coastal areas of Gujarat there is said to be salinity ingress from the sea. In such areas exploitation should be controlled and induced recharge of fresh water coming from the upper hinterland should be prevented escaping straight into the sea by means of small dams, etc., so that percolation of fresh water underground might increase. (Para 6.59)

78. The Committee would like to emphasise that there is considerable scope for exploitation of ground water in the coastal areas and would, therefore, recommend:

(a) In the alluvial plains deep tubewells for irrigation are now taken up as a stage programme in aquifers as deep as 400 ft. Keeping to the cost benefit acceptable generally such wells should be taken up in the coastal areas, even if they are deeper;

(b) In particularly difficult areas where both top and sub-soil water is saline and salinity persists to great depths, if alternative sources of fresh water for better agriculture is lacking, it may be necessary to stretch a point and allow for deep tubewells for irrigation even if it is a little more costlier than levels so far accepted; and

(c) Even if the economics of deep tubewell water is generally adverse for agriculture, as a drinking water amenity and for industrial purposes like cleaning and processing of fish, it is necessary to provide deep tubewell systems wherever possible. This is a basic amenity which the Committee will recommend as necessary. (Para 6.60)

79. For good agriculture, the first essential is to ensure that saline intrusion is reduced as much as possible and whatever saline intrusion does take place, it is leached out by suitable introduction of fresh water during the rainy season wherever possible. (Para 6.61)

80. Where saline intrusion in summer is now taking place, the

areas should be investigated on a watershed basis and low ridges provided on the ridges of the watershed. The investment in these structures will not be very much and the Committee would recommend that priority selection of such areas and urgent steps to see that this is done may be taken up. (Para 6.62)

81. The fresh water drainage from the hinter land will have to be suitably guided and directed towards the watersheds where the salinity has to be leached. At the same time, steps should be taken to see that such introduction does not lead to heavy water logging in the lower reaches of the watershed as has happened in the Sundarban. (Para 6.63)

82. In many of the delta areas of the country, there are irrigation systems which extend towards deltas. These irrigation systems are themselves the cause of heavy water logging in the coastal areas which together with admixture of saline water makes these areas unfit for agriculture. The normal irrigation practice is to leave tail ends of the canals open. In these areas where water logging is a serious problem, canal control is essential. If canals have to be drained, there should be definite drainage structures leading them away from the low lands. Further, the fresh-water available in such canals can also be utilised in the off-season for flushing out the salinity in the coastal agricultural areas. This planned development of the lower reaches of irrigation system must be done in each state on a priority basis. (Para 6.65)

Development of Saurashtra and Kutch Areas of Gujarat

83. While recognising the sea ingress problem to be the prime problem of the Saurashtra area, the National Committee would like to stress that the control measures would have to find the most economic engineering solution. It feels that tidal regulators may be a high cost technology and would sound a note of warning towards its adoption without judiciously weighing the *pros and cons*. The Committee feels that recharge technique would be much more economic and reasonable for adoption. The Committee has observed effective use of one way regulation, in mini creeks and run-off in the Sundarban region of West Bengal and would recommend for its adoption after careful detailed study. The Committee has also noticed difficulties in controlling large creeks and here again would recommend the adoption of techniques tried successfully in Sundarban. (Para 7.8)

84. The suggested device of a static barrier or impermeable cut-off wall for the salinity control measure, beside being quite costly,

cannot prevent upward movement of salt water which already underlies the overdrawn extraction area. The Committee would recommend an earnest-pilot research to establish whether in methods could alleviate the problem. (Para 7.9)

85. At present, hardly any measures for checking of surface flow are there and as such a large portion of the monsoon precipitation goes over to sea. One way of tackling that would be through control of river flows in the upper reaches and measures to induce water retention in upper reaches. Further, down the course of rivers, check dams, percolation tanks and recharge wells in hard area locations are the possibilities open for adoption. The possibilities can be studied through a detailed investigation of the area on a comprehensive watershed approach, be adopted. (Para 7.18)

86. A single line of gates can regulate the manageable parts of any flood throughout the monsoon season. The Committee would urge the adoption and optimum utilisation of such measure and introduction of any design modifications, if called for. (Para 7.19)

87. On the problem of afforestation, the Committee would like to reiterate the suggestion that the tree selection should be the one which benefits the water balance and not prove counter productive in terms of recharge. (Para 7.21)

88. The broad conclusion of earlier Commissions, etc., had been that the Kutch area can be agriculturally improved if part of the Narmada flows could be diverted to this area. Such a measure would not only substantially mitigate the acute problem of drinking water but also create conditions for reclaiming substantial area of the Rann for agricultural purposes. In this context the feasibility of bringing water to the Little Rann to control salinity for brackish water fish culture could also be considered. (Para 7.27)

89. The developmental efforts in the Kutch areas have obviously to be directed toward aquaculture development. (Para 7.28)

90. The Committee feels that in the Rann of Kutch very large areas are suitable for development of brackish water fisheries. The Committee would urge that the proper assessment of these areas should be done through a detailed survey with basic parameters. The two vital aspects needing special attention are checking of tidal ingress and the supply of fry. Measure for tidal ingress have already been dealt with at length. With regard to the supply of fry, the Committee visualise two practical ways, to catch the fry where it is and put the same in these areas, or to bread the fry elsewhere and then bring to these areas. The

Committee is confident with effective tackling of the problems and with suitable provisions for nutrition in the water and design development, brackish water fish culture can become a major base for the economics of Saurashtra and Kutch area of Gujarat. (Para 7.37)

91. The pattern of water use in Kutch areas is likely to undergo a change after the completion of and the operation of the Sardar Sarovar Dam. In such a situation brackish water fisheries may not provide the answer for optimum utilisation of the resources of the area. For that purpose a fresh look at the problems would be desirable to evolve suitable development strategies for the areas with a balance between fresh brackish water culture. Pilot schemes and sufficient research effort should be carried out to take full advantage of the changed conditions when they occur. (Para 7.38)

Development of Sunderban Area in West Bengal

92. Considering the physical and other characteristics of the Sundarban area and keeping in view the constraints pointed out above, the strategy for development in this area has necessarily to be as follows:

(i) Extending irrigation by utilisation of excess rain water, construction of sluices and network of drainage, channels to remove drainage congestion;

(ii) Once irrigation becomes available, an attempt should be made to convert the present non-cropped area into two-cropped area to the maximum extent possible. Whatever little has so far been attempted has clearly established that given the irrigation, the yield in rabi can be very much higher and the crop production can also be diversified;

(iii) Land-use should be made more intensive in order to raise production status, particularly, of small and marginal farmers;

(iv) There is a lot of potential for the development of fisheries and there is already a ready market in the Calcutta city. Next to agriculture, fisheries would appear to be the most important programme of development in this area;

(v) There is also good scope for taking up horticulture, animal husbandry, fishery, poultry, piggery, dairy, etc., which would create new avenues of productive employment;

(vi) Natural resources and local skills must be utilised for development of cottage and small industries;

(vii) Infrastructural facilities including extension support, input supply credit facilities, marketing/processing arrangements, communication, etc., would have to be provided; and

(viii) The last but the most important point is that the organisation structure would have to be so streamlined that not only there is adequate delegation of financial and administrative powers to the development authority, but it has the necessary powers to coordinate, supervise and monitor the execution of programmes. (Para 8.29)

93. The Committee found that the works in the Growth Centres on the Sunderban area being excuted by the board and that there is no support at all to the programme from the Agricultural or Animal Husbandry Departments. The Committee feels that this sort of truncated approach will not do. If these Growth Centres have to succeed, the sub-plan strategy of Tribal Welfare Programme would appear to be extremely relevant. (Para 8.37)

94. The Committee would like to stress the development of a comprehensive plan of irrigation through drainage and optimum utilisation of tank development. The economics of tank development are favourable and hence need to be encouraged. If energetic steps are taken for appropriate development of tanks to store rain water, there are immense possibilities of increasing the second crop acreage and also raising the yields of the crops grown therein. (Paras 8.43 and 8.45)

95. Coconut cultivation can go up substantially and the field enquiries show an awareness. But there is no arrangement to supply good quality seedlings either for 'Dab' or 'Hardnut'. The Sundarban Development Board should consider temporary hiring of services of out side expertise on development of high-yielding varieties of coconuts. (Paras 8.47 and 8.48)

96. Bee keeping is one of the fields which holds bright prospects for enhancing the production of honey in the area. (Para 8.52)

97. Inland water transport being the main mode of transport, the development of boats is the natural solution. The Committee would suggest that either loans should be advanced to individuals who want to adopt plying of boats on Commercial basis or to Cooperative Societies for owning and renting the services of the boats. (Para 8.53)

98. The Committee would strongly urge that the concept of delegation of powers, both financial and administrative, as

recommended by it in its report on "Organisation of Administrative and Financial Structures for Backward Areas Development" should be fully implemented if the organisation has to be effective. Also, it would be necessary that proper linkages are established with the State level Technical Departments so that expert advice and technical guidance at a higher level is available to the personnel working in the Sundarban organisation. (Para 8.56)

99. It is essential that as many of the project personnel as possible stay in the project areas and do not have the tendency to stay in nearby Greater Metropolitan Calcutta and come for work to the project. (Para 8.57)